GUIDE TO NONTRADITIONAL CAREERS IN SCIENCE

GUIDE TO NONTRADITIONAL CAREERS IN SCIENCE

by

Karen Young Kreeger

 Endorsed by American Institute of Biological Sciences

USA	Publishing Office:	TAYLOR & FRANCIS 325 Chestnut Street Philadelphia, PA 19106 Tel: (215) 625-8900 Fax: (215) 625-2940
	Distribution Center:	TAYLOR & FRANCIS 47 Runway Road, Suite G Levittown, PA 19057-4700 Tel: (215) 269-0400 Fax: (215) 269-0363
UK		TAYLOR & FRANCIS 1 Gunpowder Square London EC4A 3DE Tel: +44 171 583 0490 Fax: +44 171 583 0581

GUIDE TO NONTRADITIONAL CAREERS IN SCIENCE

1 2 3 4 5 6 7 8 9 0

Printed by George H. Buchanan Co., Philadelphia, PA, 1998.

A CIP catalog record for this book is available from the British Library.
⊗ The paper in this publication meets the requirements of the ANSI Standard Z39.48-1984 (Permanence of Paper)

Library of Congress Cataloging-in-Publication Data

Kreeger, Karen Young.
    Guide to nontraditional careers in science / Karen Young Kreeger.
        p.   cm.
    Includes index.

    1. Science—Vocational guidance.   I. Title.
    Q147.K73   1998
    502.3—dc21   98-41616
                                                                          CIP

ISBN 1-56032-670-0 (pbk.)

CONTENTS

FOREWORD

So you are a scientist or considering training to be one. Have you ever wondered what it would be like to:

- apply for a patent,
- pursue environmental law,
- teach high school,
- describe research to a senator,
- take a laboratory product to market,
- sell scientific equipment,
- draw the human body,
- write a newspaper article,
- develop a computer-based expert system, or
- start a company?

If you have, Karen Young Kreeger's *Guide to Nontraditional Careers in Science* is about to tell you what it is like and what it takes to pursue any of these lines of work, based on concise stories and advice from dozens of scientists. Karen has assembled practical guidance about the homework necessary to embark on science careers in business, education, law, media, public policy, informatics, and other professions.

You may have been confused by what is meant by "alternative" or "nontraditional" careers. Such careers have been suggested more frequently as faculty positions and research funding have become more difficult to obtain. (See, e.g., *Rethinking Science as a Career*, referenced in Appendix 1.) Karen clarifies these terms by relaying to us what it really takes to pursue employment in nontraditional settings.

You may already have read Dr. Cynthia Robbins-Roth's recent, edited book, *Alternative Careers in Science: Leaving the Ivory Tower* (see Appendix 1 for more information), in which Robbins-Roth has compiled her story and first-person accounts from 23 other scientists about their alternative career paths. *Guide to Nontraditional Careers in Science* is complementary and provides another source of stories and options, in this case organized by profession, as well as comprehensive lists of resources—people, professional societies, Web sites, training programs, for example—to guide your exploration and potential access to a nontraditional path.

The *Guide* provides advice on the competition in these professions from different practitioners and insiders' views of what it takes to get the necessary qualifications and your foot in the door. We are reminded that even if we are equipped with a Ph.D., freshly minted or otherwise, and are quick learners, we will still likely have to start a new path with humility at a rung somewhere near the bottom of the professional ladder.

In addition to providing examples of Ph.D. holders pursuing diverse career paths, the *Guide* includes stories about those with baccalaureates, masters, J.D.s, and M.D.s. This inclusiveness reminds us that there are relatively few jobs that legally require a Ph.D. For many employers, experience on the job counts as much or more than an advanced degree.

If you are exhausted at the thought of needing to get a J.D., M.B.A., or M.D. on top of an M.S. or Ph.D., take note of the stories about scientists working with others who possess J.D.s, M.B.A.s, and M.D.s. For some jobs and people, additional qualifications will be a benefit or necessity. But you do not necessarily have to spend another two or more years in school, since many other jobs require working with other experts, rather than trying to do it all yourself.

Some scientists have always pursued career paths outside academia or an industrial research lab, either for all or the latter portion of their careers. What is new today is the number of scientists in nontraditional settings and the appearance of books that capture their career paths.

Perhaps the prevalence of so many scientists doing such diverse activities outside the lab will finally put to rest the misconception held by some that there is a small number of appropriate job positions for scientists. Science is accomplished in the many different ways exemplified in the *Guide*. I remember a science meeting early in my "third career," when someone referred to those working outside academic research as "leakage" (as in from the pipeline). In contrast, the examples in the *Guide* conjure up images of healthy flows through diverse lines. Also as exemplified, scientists come with diverse aptitudes and interests, despite the stereotypes.

So who should read this book? Obviously, if you have not yet pursued a nontraditional career path, this is a great place to start. If you are a faculty advisor and some of your students or graduates are heading off for internships or employment in nontraditional settings, the *Guide* provides vignettes of these different worlds and resources to pass along to them. If you have already pursued a nontraditional career in science, you will enjoy reading the *Guide* and saying to yourself, "So I am not the only one who:

- thought I was leaving my field and could never go back;
- felt out of his or her element at first;

- felt fulfilled in a line of work outside the lab;
- believes scientists can contribute in many roles to society and science;
- might try yet another nontraditional profession."

I have worked primarily in nontraditional settings, having trained as a research psychologist, worked for a dozen years in nuclear power plants and on Navy projects, and now direct a nonprofit. As such, I found I had a lot in common with those who have been pulled or pushed to go into ventures they did not expect. How was I to imagine that the Three Mile Island incident would be the impetus for my first job analyzing operator performance data? Many other scientists in the pages of the *Guide* share similar stories.

The *Guide* reminds us that you often do not know the background of those with whom you work and interact, until you ask. There are scientists in places you may never have expected. Thanks for the enlightenment, Karen.

Catherine D. Gaddy, Ph.D.
Executive Director
Commission on Professionals in Science and Technology
Washington, DC
May 1998

PREFACE

I guess it's only fair that I answer the same questions that my interviewees for this book so generously did, and give you some insight as to how a budding fisheries scientist ended up becoming a science writer and now a first-time book author and editor.

In the couple of talks that I have given at career workshops in the last two years, panelists have usually been asked to talk about their backgrounds and career-decision processes. For me, it's easier to talk about each together since they're intertwined, as they are for most people. I started working on a Ph.D. in fisheries biology at Oregon State University (OSU) in 1987. I came in with an M.S. from the University of Delaware in marine studies. In the Ph.D. program, I went through classes, started research, and took my written qualifiers. Even before this, I started to feel hemmed in, unsure that this was the direction in which I wanted to head for the rest of my life.

But, what I was sure of was that I wanted to stay connected to science, in some way. I thought that I wanted to work more with people. Moving into education or policy crossed my mind. I worked in education for a while, even before the feelings of uneasiness with my future really surfaced. I volunteered for the Boston Museum of Science's Science-By-Mail program, taught at nature centers, and gave dockside lectures for tourist whale-sighting ventures. But this avenue didn't gel for me.

Meanwhile I pursued my research in juvenile chinook salmon biology. A major part of my applied project was tied to a salmon aquaculture facility whose future was tenuous. It eventually went belly up.

Because of this and other factors, I had to refocus my research a few times, eventually changing one part of it to a more basic question on salmon biology. (I eventually published this as a sole author.)

When I was about three years into my Ph.D., I spent several months soul-searching—mainly talking with friends and family—looking for ways to redesign my graduate school experience. As part of this, I looked through the OSU course catalogue for programs in which my class credits would apply and that would rekindle my interest.

I read a description for a new program for an M.S. in scientific and technical communication (STC). I met with the director, explaining that I thought this area was a viable option for me. At that first meeting, he suggested that I was just suffering from Ph.D. burnout. But in the end, he saw I was serious about giving this direction a try and recommended that I take some of the program's core classes. I took two that winter quarter.

I ended up doing very well, and more importantly, I actually looked forward to my academic future for the first time in a long time. I still worked on finishing up my salmon experiments because of personal goals and grant obligations. So, for almost two years I had one foot in each area while I was making the transition. I've heard many people say that this was the case for them as well. I think that, for the most part, a dual life is unavoidable for an interim period.

An equally important aspect to my initial positive experience with the communications courses was that I met other people with similar backgrounds and experiences—other people dabbling in career switching. I learned just as much from our informal talks over coffee or a beer as I did from formal classwork.

I finished the STC program in a year and a half, trying to time my graduation date to within several months of my husband's, who is also a marine scientist.

During that time I tried to build up my portfolio, an essential ingredient in looking for a job in writing. I blended my interests and expertise in marine and environmental biology by writing educational and planning materials for aquariums in Oregon and a monthly newsletter for scientists at the U.S. Forest Service working in the Pacific Northwest. After I graduated, I freelanced for a year in the United Kingdom as a writer and editor for science news magazines, textbook publishers, and the Plymouth Marine Laboratory. At that point in my writing career, I basically didn't say no to any project that crossed my path.

But, why writing and why not education or policy, as I thought before? I've always enjoyed the communication aspect of science, especially writing. (I had to push myself to do the public speaking aspect, but got to enjoy it and gained confidence with time.) In my tenure as a grad student, I received a lot of positive reinforcement for my writing and editing ability. Up until the communications courses, I looked at science writing and editing as an integral skill within the process of science—which it is—not the primary focus of a career.

After coming back to the United States in 1993, I worked at *The Scientist*, a trade newspaper for life scientists, as a staff writer for almost four years. There I worked primarily on the section that covers hard science, although I contributed to all departments of the paper. I covered all sorts of beats, from environmental science to biomedical science to career issues, ethics, and policy. Since the summer of 1997, I've been a science writer at the University of Pennsylvania Medical Center writing about and handling media queries for information on basic biomedical discoveries.

The variety of what I write about in both settings is what I was looking for and didn't get from research science. Those feelings of being hemmed in are gone, and I haven't looked back since I went into writing full time seven years ago.

A few pieces of general advice:

For me, the strongest motivation to change careers was to find a vocation that made me happy. In my case I slowly realized I wanted to be a generalist rather than a specialist in science. Writing fulfills that for me. It lets me dabble, albeit on a schedule of deadlines.

There are no magic bullets, no one-size-fits-all advice for career switching. Everyone's path is unique, given different personal situations: significant others, kids, families, interests, personalities.

Transition is gradual: you phase in one career and phase out the other. I was extremely busy for two years; despite this, I really enjoyed my new track, so I knew I was on to something. The risk of the change was simultaneously exciting and scary.

To get experience or to investigate a new tack, volunteer at professional societies, museums, educational groups, environmental groups, charities, and graduate student groups; organize business roundtables. In my case this was to get clips for my portfolio. By all means try a new area out first. Learning what you're not interested in is just as important as learning what you are interested in.

Many people, both in and out of science, have helped to bring this book to light and have unselfishly given me their emotional and professional support. First, I thank all of the scientists and engineers who left the bench or field to pursue different careers and shared their stories with me. Their willingness to talk about some very personal decisions and their generosity of time and advice is the heart and soul of this book.

I also send my thanks to the many reviewers of all or part of this book and those who have given me helpful advice: Russ Altman, Kevin Aylesworth, Maria Betty, Ann Caudle, Debra Clapp, Doug Curran-Everett, Don Doering, Mary Heiberger, Frank Hoke, Lynne Friedmann, Dan Kreeger, Ursula Maul, Seth Nehrbass, Jimmy Reddoch, David Sander, Neeraja Sankaran, Barbara Spector, Linda Temple, Julie Vick, Ora Weisz, Teri Willey, and many, many others.

In addition, I thank Frank Hoke for bringing this project to my attention in the first place. Many thanks also go to Richard O'Grady, my former editor at Taylor & Francis, Michael Brown, my current editor, and Laura Haefner, Beth Gallagher, and Elizabeth Cohen, for making the manuscript tighter and more readable, and their patient guidance through the book-publishing process.

My express appreciation also goes to my parents, Joyce and Bill Young, for being truly supportive of every career decision I have made.

Above all, my special thanks go to my husband, Daniel Kreeger, for his love, encouragement, editorial and content suggestions, pride, and patience over the last two-plus years of weekends and evenings devoted to putting this project together.

Karen Young Kreeger
June 1998

"The Myth" and Beyond

☐ Setting the Stage

For the past several years, the scientific press has blared with headlines of overproduction of Ph.D.s and a growing unemployment and under-employment of researchers. Universities in the United States awarded a record 27,230 Ph.D. degrees in science and engineering (S&E) in 1996 —nearly a 3 percent increase from 1995—according to the National Science Foundation (NSF). By comparison, 19,894 S&E doctorates were awarded in 1987, a 27 percent change over the 10-year period. This ex-pansion is far more than anyone ever projected and is in part due to a sharp increase in the number of students—both U.S. citizens and for-eign students—who have been entering graduate school since the late 1980s. At the same time, because of a complex set of economic, demo-graphic, and societal factors, the number of permanent research posi-tions in academia, industry, and government has dwindled since the early 1980s.

As a result, the world of science is filling up with more and more young investigators who are highly qualified and trained, yet are struggling to find permanent positions. The 1995 unemployment figure for recent Ph.D.s, defined as one to three years since graduation, was 1.9 percent, according to an NSF data brief (http://www.nsf.gov/sbe/srs/pubdata. htm). The foundation also reports that 4.3 percent of recent Ph.D.s were working involuntarily outside of their fields because a full-time job was not available in their field. But, of the recent Ph.D.s awarded between 1993 and 1995, half of those who were unemployed

1

or involuntarily working outside their field in 1993 found jobs in their field by 1995. There were differences in this figure, however, by discipline: 6.3 percent for physical science Ph.D.s; whereas the proportion of life scientists working outside their field was only 3.4 percent.

Although S&E unemployment figures are well below the 1995 national unemployment figure of 5.7 percent for all U.S. workers, more and more recent Ph.D.s are having to do multiple postdocs, with concomitant long hours and low pay, making the balance with other parts of life more difficult.

But there's much more that the raw numbers don't and can't measure, such as attrition from graduate programs. How many people enter graduate school and end up leaving with no degree or one different from what they set out to get? The numbers also don't show the degree to which researchers are satisfied with their "traditional" careers in academia. Of those recent graduates that do land tenure-track positions, how well are their job expectations being met?

In 1997, the Commission on Professionals in Science and Technology, a nonprofit organization concerned with advancing public understanding of scientific and technical professions, completed one of the first studies, *Postdocs and Career Prospects: A Status Report* (Commission on Professionals in Science and Technology, Washington, DC, 1997; http://www.cpst.org), that tracks the fate of postdocs in today's job market. Some of the report's highlights:

- There were 26,000 postdocs in doctorate-granting institutions in science and engineering in 1995. More than half of these were in the biological sciences; 22 percent in physical sciences. The 1995 figures represent a 32 percent increase from 1988.
- Of the biological science postdocs, 39 percent were still in postdocs three to four years after obtaining their degree. And, 18 percent were still in postdoc positions five to six years after getting their degree.
- Overall, of those in first postdocs in 1993, 13 percent were in tenure-track positions two years later; for those in their second or third postdocs in 1993, 16 percent were in tenure-track positions by 1995.

Many of these budding researchers are having to recast their career plans in ways they never imagined and were never trained to handle. A 1995 National Academy of Sciences (NAS) report, entitled *Reshaping the Graduate Education of Scientists and Engineers* (National Academy Press, Washington, DC, 1995), found that more than half of new graduates with Ph.D.s now find jobs in nonacademic settings. In some disciplines, such as chemistry and engineering, the figure is greater than that. The report also found that the number of science and engineering Ph.D.s employed in academia fell from 51 percent in 1977 to 43 percent in 1991. *Reshaping,* usually called the COSEPUP report after the Committee on Science, Engineering, and Public Policy that authored it, calls for graduate education to better serve "the need of those whose careers will not center on research" (p. 3).

The discouraging figures outlined in these and other reports render the old bromide, "Work hard and you'll land a plum tenure-track position," obsolete. Today, this situation only holds true for a small proportion of new science Ph.D.s. For example, in 1997, Douglas Boyd, chairman of the department of tumor biology at the M. D. Anderson Cancer Center in Houston, conducted a survey (http://gsbs.gs.uth.tmc.edu/alumni/87survey/87survey.html) to determine the professional fate of 1987 Ph.D. graduates from his department. Of the 23 doctoral students who finished that year, 16 had permanent jobs in a variety of settings, with 10 of these in research positions in an academic or industrial setting. Only five of the 23 ended up with traditional posts, which Boyd defined as tenure-track teaching and research positions at a university. After 10 years, 7 of the 23 are still in postdoctoral positions.

Many organizations have also begun to survey the attitudes of graduate students and postdocs regarding career prospects and job availability. Because of a changing employment vista, graduate students and postdocs are starting to look beyond the typical job postings to fulfill their professional needs. In December 1996, a study sponsored by the BioMedical Association of Stanford Students, entitled *At the Edge of a New Frontier: A Profile of the Stanford University Biomedical Ph.D. Class of 1996 and Recommendations for the Future,* surveyed recent graduates about their career prospects. It had this to say about alternative careers:

- Over 70 percent of the respondents stated that their career goals changed or broadened while in graduate school, specifically noting a shift away from academic career plans.
- Respondents pursuing research careers perceived themselves to have been better prepared for their future careers by their Ph.D. education than those pursuing nonresearch careers.
- Respondents pursuing alternative careers were the most optimistic that they would achieve their career goals.

☐ Where This Book Fits In

The purpose of this book is to show you, the person contemplating a career switch, that you *do* have choices. There are many fields in which you can use your scientific training to nurture a satisfying professional life and make important contributions to the process of science. I hope that the dozens of examples—in many fields, using personal stories of career switchers—in this book will demonstrate the many doors open to scientists like you.

I do not presume that the options presented within this book are a panacea for the very real career and personal-life predicaments with which you may be faced. I aim to provide you with examples of options that might not be obvious and to illustrate how and why some scientists who first embarked on a traditional career path have made the choices they have made.

Within the eight career chapters (Chapters 3–10) are one-on-one interviews with close to 100 people at different stages of their careers who have made a switch from a research-oriented track to a related field. These mini-profiles include many recent Ph.D. recipients, some midcareer professionals, some who never set out to obtain a Ph.D., and some who switched in the midst of doctoral studies.

They talk openly and honestly in their own words about their experiences, the pluses and minuses of their decisions; and what strategies worked and didn't work for them when they were in the midst of their career moves. In addition, in each career-specific chapter, I provide resource information for relevant professional societies, education and training programs, and jobhunting and networking outlets. Chapter 2 synthesizes the common advice and concerns raised by these career switchers and others. See the sidebar "How to Use This Book" for some pointers as to how to use these various types of information.

When first envisioning how this book would take shape, I tried to cast a broad mental net in defining the potential audience. I anticipate that the primary readership will undoubtedly be graduate students and postdocs who started school thinking research in academia was their only career path, but now need or want to make a change. I assume that you want to stay tied to science in some capacity; it's just the size of the step, jump, or leap away from a traditional path that's in question.

I also hope this book will provide some insights for the people and organizations with whom you interact in your graduate training: thesis advisers, thesis committee members, administrators looking for career information, academic career centers, job recruiters, policymakers, professional societies, and your friends and families.

This book is not intended to be an exhaustive essay on what's wrong with graduate-level training in the United States. Others have covered this extensively: for example, *Reshaping the Graduate Education of Scientists and Engineers* (Committee on Science, Engineering, and Public Policy, National Academy Press, Washington, DC, 1995), *Rethinking Science as a*

(text continues on p. 7)

HOW TO USE THIS BOOK

Career change is a process of self-discovery. The issue is to find the best fit between your personality and career path. You need to remind yourself that it's okay to build on your scientific training and experiences to find a position that is more fitting and that will make you happy. You've focused on your scientific training; now you want to focus on the next step. Start asking yourself: "What are the active steps I need to make in order to change?"

I asked a diverse range of people both within and among the chapters the same two questions. Their answers obviously varied quite a bit depending on background, age, experience, gender, discipline, and interests—as will the advice you'll get from others you'll encounter. There are many interviews to go through, but I did this on purpose. I wanted you to see the diversity of jobs—and the similarities —in which people with scientific training are happily employed. Take it all, or part of it, in. Then tailor the information to your own needs.

At first, all of these interviews (close to 100) may seem overwhelming, but here are a few suggestions on how to use this book as an efficient source.

- Read the main introductions and the introductions to the subchapters for a big-picture view: where people are employed, and the special skills and attributes required for a certain line of work, for example.
- Peruse the introductions to the individual mini-Q&As to find people similar to or different from yourself who are working in the area in which you're interested.
- Read the individual answers to the questions for their tailored advice. There are many similarities, yet many differences, among the experiences reported, both within and among chapters.
- Go to specific chapters, for example, "Education" if you're interested in working with children.
- Once you've gained a better idea of an area in which you're interested, take a look at the resource section of each chapter or subchapter and the two appendices for relevant professional society contact information, continuing educational or volunteer opportunities, and jobhunting and networking outlets.

This book contains many different resources that are meant to demonstrate and gather the wealth of resources already available on alternative careers in one place: professional societies, Web sites, and chat groups. But, these change over time. The ones listed here were current as of the time of publication. Take a look at them, but as with the interviews, personalize them to see what is appropriate for you.

Common Strategies For Making a Switch

These are some of the common approaches and attitudes that inter-viewees say worked for them:

- Talk with people. Conduct informational interviews with people already in the field in which you're interested. Ask them about what to expect on the job, salary ranges, entry requirements, op-portunities for advancement, and the milieu for scientists, for example.
- Research the profession in which you're interested on the Inter-net, in books, at career centers, and with relevant professional societies.
- Work on your writing and oral skills. Remember that these must be tailored to your area of interest. Writing an article for the gen-eral public as a science journalist is very different from writing a brief on science funding for a congressperson as a science policy fellow.
- Read broadly and get a well-rounded education. Audit classes outside your field, if possible.
- Take relevant courses in the field in which you're interested; for example, in technology transfer, take classes in licensing, negotiat-ing, and business.
- Get an additional relevant degree, for example, an M.B.A. for ca-reers in business or technology transfer. In some professions it will eventually be necessary to get an additional degree or certifica-tion, for example, a law degree to become a practicing attorney or a certificate to teach in most classrooms.
- Attend professional society workshops and meetings to make con-tacts; learn the lingo of a new field; take continuing education classes; conduct informational interviews; and simply immerse your-self in a new area.
- Read outside of your "old" field. Read the trade magazines, news-papers, journals, and society newsletters of the profession into which you're interested in switching.
- Test your interest in and aptitude for a new area—and gain ap-propriate experience—through internships, fellowships, volun-teering, and consulting.
- Know the difference between an academic CV and a resume. Organize your resume by skills learned via scientific training, not by scientific achievements. Seek help from career centers for this.
- Present yourself as someone willing and able to learn and as open-minded.

- Pursue what you're interested in, not the field du jour. Critically assess what you like and dislike about your experience with a scientific career and education thus far.
- Demonstrate your credibility to potential employers in your "old" career, as well as your interest in and sincerity regarding switching to a new area. Establish that you're not just switching because you're floundering in your present situation.
- In fields where it's appropriate, such as writing and illustration, building up a portfolio is key. Tailor what you show to each client.
- In fields where it's appropriate, such as education and policy, get involved in community outreach at universities, work, schools, museums, professional societies, church groups, and political parties.
- Find scientist-mentors who are understanding of your desire to do something "different."
- Maintain an open mind regarding the definition of a career in science.

Career: Perceptions and Realities in the Physical Sciences (Sheila Tobias, Daryl Chubin, Kevin Aylesworth, Research Corp., Tucson, AZ, 1995), and the October 27, 1995 issue of *Science* magazine, which was devoted to the current state of scientific careers.

This book is also not a guide for how to handle yourself in an interview or how to prepare a resume or cover letter, although many career switchers featured in the personal vignettes address that topic specifically with examples from their own experiences. Several other publications have handled these and other topics in a general way for scientists: for example, *Outside The Ivory Tower: A Guide for Academics Considering Alternative Careers* (Margaret Newhouse, Office of Career Services, Harvard University, Cambridge, MA, 1993), *A Ph.D. Is Not Enough: A Guide to Survival in Science* (Peter J. Feibelman, Addison-Wesley, New York, 1993), *To Boldly Go: A Practical Career Guide for Scientists* (Peter S. Fiske, American Geophysical Union, Washington, DC, 1996), NextWave's "Tooling Up" (a series of articles on-line at http://www.nextwave.org), and *The 1998 What Color Is Your Parachute?* (Richard Nelson Bolles, Ten Speed Press, Berkeley, CA, 1998).

Appendix 1 lists these and other resources for further reading. Appendix 2 lists Web sites dedicated to career information and job information, with a subset devoted exclusively to jobhunting in the sciences and engineering. Many specific career-oriented and professional society Web sites are also listed throughout the eight career chapters.

☐ What "The Myth" Hath Wrought

Many trace the need for a book such as this and others to "the myth," a once widely held misconception that there would be a shortage of scientists for a flood of available positions coming open in the 1990s. Observers point to a few studies from the late 1980s as the source for this thinking. One report was *The State of Academic Science and Engineering* (National Academy of Sciences, U.S. Government Printing Office, Washington, DC, 1990). This report and others suggested that there would be a shortfall of academic scientists based on the number of academicians who would be retiring in the 1990s and a simultaneous increase in college enrollment from the children of the baby boomers. At the same time, however, the number of Ph.D.s graduating in the United States has increased sharply, so much so that it is surpassing the demand for the available jobs in all sectors.

A 1996 NSF-funded study by Mary Frank Fox, a sociologist at the Georgia Institute of Technology, touches on some of the reasons for the disconnect between the supply and demand of jobs for Ph.D. researchers. The study analyzed the fields of chemistry, computer science, electrical engineering, microbiology, and physics regarding students' perceptions of career prospects. In the study, Fox stated that in 1992, of those university professors who retired, only one in three was replaced. According to Fox, three economic and demographic changes over the last several years contribute to the imbalance in the number of Ph.D.s produced and academic research positions available, and hence students' career prospects:

- ever-increasing federal and state budget deficits and their effect on research funding and hiring;
- the end of the Cold War and a shift in emphasis away from defense-related research;
- the lifting of the mandatory age of retirement and the related lack of openings of tenure-track spots at academic research institutions.

Other observers cite three additional factors: an increased number of foreign students, many of whom stay on to seek employment in North America; a shift in private firms' focus and resources from centralized corporate research labs to more opportunities in marketing and manufacturing; and a shift in academia from full-time tenured positions to more part-time, nontenured posts.

☐ Changing Attitudes

Addressing employment issues for science graduates at all levels, especially Ph.D. recipients, is gaining more attention from national organizations. In June 1996, NAS's COSEPUP brought together 340 graduate students, faculty, university administrators, industry leaders, government officials, granting organizations, and others to discuss what doctoral science and education should be like in the future. A report on the meeting entitled *A National Conversation on Doctoral Education: An Emerging Consensus* (June 15, 1996, National Academy of Science Committee on Science, Engineering, and Public Policy, Washington, DC) can be found on the Web at: http://www2.nas.edu/convo/. Many of the presenters agreed that in the future more and more scientists would likely change careers.

"A lot of what was discussed at the meeting suggested that the difficulties for people choosing to leave scientific research to pursue an alternative career involve both awareness and attitude issues on the part of the thesis advisor," recalls Michal Freedhoff, a science policy advisor for the House of Representatives Science Committee (Democratic staff). She led discussions in a breakout session entitled "Illuminating Different Career Paths" at the meeting.

"Many supportive advisors have no idea how to direct their students in careers very different than their own, and many others think of any alternative to academia as less prestigious and take such a choice as a personal affront to their own career decisions," notes Freedhoff.

Some attendees reported a "culture gap" between students and advisors, saying few faculty are in tune with what their students need. Many faculty assume that students aspire to land a position like their own. A related problem is that students are often reluctant or unable to turn to their advisors, even when their worries or questions interfere with work or personal lives. Some of the concerns listed in the report include doubts about scientific abilities, self-image, networking, professional contacts, career opportunities, letters of recommendations, and family obligations.

Other participants stressed that the student–advisor relationship is not a one-way street: students must take an active role in letting their advisors know what they need and expect. They also said that students should assume that a single advisor or thesis committee cannot give them all they need to know to succeed in today's job climate. Sharon Hays, a then-Ph.D. candidate in biochemistry at Stanford University who attended the meeting, reported that the most successful students took a proactive approach to their careers, with many arranging their own experience in allied areas like teaching, writing, and policy. Hays is now a Congressional science fellow in the office of Representative Vernon J. Ehlers (R-MI).

"I believe that some of the negative attitudes towards taking a non-research position are slowly changing, but what I heard at the meeting was that faculty who do not encourage their students to pursue their interests was a major barrier," says Freedhoff. As such, her working group developed some suggestions for faculty and departments to help them open up options for students while not compromising the students' research:

- Departments should place an emphasis on a faculty member's record as a mentor and career counselor as part of the tenure process.
- Departments should think about running seminar series that bring in speakers who have Ph.D.s but have pursued other career options.
- Students who wish to audit courses outside science, such as those in political science, business, and journalism, should be allowed to do so within reasonable limits.
- Summer internships with industry or other organizations should be encouraged, when practical.
- Advisors should try to encourage students to pursue careers that emphasize their interests and aptitudes.
- Alumni directories should be kept up to date to give students a ready network for informational interviews, role models, and examples of where people from their program are employed.
- Departments should take a look at where their grad students end up, and contact those companies and organizations to find out how to better prepare their students.
- Departments should solicit position-wanted ads from alumni to circulate to departmental graduate students.
- Departments should provide more general career information to higher levels of administration in academia, for example, councils of department chairs, deans of colleges, and presidents of universities.
- Universities should establish more career offices for graduate students.

☐ Grassroots Efforts

Some professional societies, graduate-student groups, academic departments, career centers, and others are already doing what Freedhoff's group suggested. To fill students' need for more information, these organizations are holding courses, seminars, and roundtables to discuss career survival skills and potential routes of employment, many of which address nontraditional paths as a possible choice. The sidebar

(text continues on p. 13)

EXAMPLES OF GRASSROOTS EFFORTS

In June of 1996, NAS's Committee on Science, Engineering, and Public Policy brought together 340 graduate students, faculty, university administrators, industry leaders, government officials, granting organizations, and others to discuss what doctoral science and education should be like in the future. A report on the meeting, entitled *A National Conversation on Doctoral Education: An Emerging Consensus* (June 15, 1996. National Academy of Science Committee on Science, Engineering, and Public Policy, Washington, DC; http://www2.nas.edu/ convo/), followed. Posters describing programs in science careers, some of which included information on allied career paths, were also a part of the meeting. Contact information and a detailed description of each one can be found at: http://www2.nas.edu/convo/212a.html. The following are some examples of programs primarily started at the grassroots level. These were found through the NAS, Internet listservs, and word of mouth.

Professional Societies

American Society for Cell Biology (http://www.ascb.org/ascb). ASCB sponsors Career Discussion Luncheons at their annual meetings. These feature roundtable talks about nontraditional career options for scientists, among other topics.

Women in Neuroscience (http://www.beemnet.com/win/index.htm). WIN, in conjunction with the 1997 Society for Neuroscience annual meeting, held a symposium entitled "Career Options in the New and Changing World of Science." Invited speakers were all trained as bench scientists but are now using their training in seeking funding for, writing about, observing, managing, or marketing science.

Academic Departments and Graduate Student Groups

BIO-Opportunities (BIO-Ops), Northwestern University (http://nuinfo.nwu.edu/neurobiology/bioopp.html). BIO-Ops is a question-and-answer format seminar series that attempts to raise the awareness of science graduate students and postdocs to a variety of career possibilities. The aim is to encourage students to explore career options that will use their scientific training and maximize their personal strengths and talents. In 1997 the program covered science journalism, patent law, and law enforcement. Whenever possible, panelists are Northwestern alumni, so attendees see tangible examples of what may be accomplished with a degree from that university. The program is sponsored by Northwestern's three life sciences graduate programs.

Yale University (http://penguin.csb.yale.edu/acb/). In 1995, a group of graduate students in cellular and molecular biology at Yale University started a seminar series to bring in speakers who are now working in nontraditional careers. The 1997 seminar series included a patent lawyer, a biotech entrepreneur, and a National Research Council staffperson who spoke on summer internships. The group's Web site also has links to other career resources on the Internet.

University of Alabama at Birmingham Industry Roundtable (http://www.uab.edu/graduate). The Industry Roundtable is a student-initiated and -run group sponsored by the UAB Graduate School. It provides a forum for networking with representatives from industry and fosters awareness of career opportunities outside academia. The 1996–1997 guests included scientists who spoke on intellectual property law, technology transfer, and biotech entrepreneurship.

Survival Skills and Ethics Program, University of Pittsburgh (http://www.pitt.edu/~survival/homepg.html). For the last few years, Michael Zigmond, a professor of neuroscience, and his colleagues have been conducting courses in career survival skills for faculty, graduate students, and postdocs. The courses include units on nontraditional job markets, transferable skills, and new ways of looking at doctoral education.

Case Western Reserve University School of Medicine. In 1996, Case Western's schools of medicine and graduate studies sponsored a one-day symposium called "Science in a New World: Biomedical Curricula and Careers." It examined career issues both inside and outside academia, with one speaker talking about making the transition from research to science journalism.

City University of New York (schwartz@aps.org). CUNY offers a jobhunting skills course for physical scientists and engineers, which is led by Brian Schwartz from the Graduate Center at the City University of New York. It includes information on the business world and nontraditional careers.

University of Alaska, Fairbanks. Graduate students at the University of Alaska, Fairbanks can participate in a program called Innovative Chemical Education, where chemistry and biochemistry students go into the community to work with elementary school teachers in the classroom, special science-oriented assemblies, and science fairs. The students get experience teaching and learn educational techniques from the teachers, as well as general skills in communicating science.

University Career Services Centers (for links to many, see http://www.rpi.edu/dept/cdc/carserv). Many universities have active career services offices for graduate students—some well-established, some newer. Some of these include Duke University, Harvard University, MIT, University of Chicago, University of Michigan, and University of Pennsylvania. Many of these services include seminars on non-traditional careers, career survival skills, and other resources for scientists exploring possibilities beyond the bench. Consult the career center at your university to see what services and activities they provide to graduate students.

Other Organizations

National Institutes of Health Office of Education (http://www.training.nih.gov). In 1996 and 1997, the NIH Office of Education offered a six-part seminar series about science careers, including information about careers other than the traditional academic path at a large university. The speakers included Ph.D.s or M.D.s working at the U.S. Patent & Trademark Office, in technology transfer, in biotech venture capital, high school science, science journalism, and grants management. This office has also held courses in career survival skills.

Howard Hughes Medical Institution (http://www.hhmi.org). In September 1997, HHMI held a meeting entitled "Science Careers: Future Trends and Current Realities," in conjunction with their annual Program Directors Meeting. Nontraditional careers was a major topic of discussion at the meeting. Proceedings of the meeting will be on the HHMI Web site in late 1998. The institute's staff also say that they have more science-career meetings planned for the future. In the meantime, HHMI donated $825,000 in late 1997 to AAAS's NextWave to create a one-stop shopping site for information on fellowships, graduate programs, job openings, and other opportunities.

"Examples of Grassroots Efforts" describes some of the efforts that groups have come up with to introduce and prepare graduate students for the job hunt.

An example of one such endeavor is the University of Alabama at Birmingham Industry Roundtable, which was set up in 1996 by then-life-science graduate student James Reddoch, who is now an analyst for Gerard Klauer Mattison, an investment banking firm in New York. As a doctoral student in biochemistry and molecular genetics, Reddoch established the seminar program to bring together graduate students and scientists who work outside academia.

He cites three things that led to the formation of the Roundtable. First, he recalls that when he was interviewing for graduate school in the early 1990s, some of the prospective advisors he spoke with "had a theory there was a huge contingent of older researchers out there about to retire and that a surplus of jobs would become available." But, he says, that contrasted with what he read in articles about the COSEPUP report, which stated that almost half of recent Ph.D.s find employment in nonacademic settings. "That meant that half of my cohort who entered grad school in 1992 expecting to end up in a faculty position had the wrong expectations," notes Reddoch.

Another eye-opener, he adds, was that the COSEPUP study and *Rethinking Science as a Career: Perceptions and Realities in the Physical Sciences* (S. Tobias, D. E. Chubin, K. Aylesworth, Research Corp., Tucson, AZ, 1995) were encouraging a broader, rather than a more narrow, approach to graduate training. *Rethinking Science* focuses on the experiences of recent Ph.D.s in chemistry, physics, and mathematics who are looking for their first permanent position. One of the book's take-home messages is that, in light of the current dismal job market, students must expand their sights to embrace the possibility of nonresearch careers.

A third point he found revealing was that both reports suggested that grad students need earlier access to career data. "By the time I had been in grad school for four years, I had never once seen an advertisement for a job fair or a career day for science graduate students." This, he suggests, stands in stark contrast with the professional schools, particularly business and law, which are very active in affording students opportunities to interact with prospective employers.

Reddoch and others say that conducting extracurricular activities like career workshops can be a touchy subject in research-oriented graduate programs. This is because, in the estimation of some mentors, it

---

TIPS FOR ORGANIZING YOUR OWN
NONTRADITIONAL CAREER WORKSHOP

- Seek advice from people who've set up workshops before. See the sidebar "Examples of Grassroots Efforts" for suggestions.
- Work with career services centers, alumni offices, professional societies, and corporate human resources and recruiting offices for help locating speakers, scheduling, and advertising.
- Seek help from academic departments for funding, advice, and lending a cosponsorship to establish university support, both financially and philosophically.
- Keep the agenda simple, with plenty of time for questions at the end.
- Don't forget career services professionals as potential speakers.
- Consider a virtual chat room format for an on-line discussion if you're strapped for time and money.

takes the focus off the research, so, by and large, grad students have had to be proactive and organize such activities themselves. "Thus, the Industry Roundtable was formed," explains Reddoch. See the sidebar "Tips for Organizing" for advice on putting together a nontraditional science career seminar.

The Roundtable is not alone in its efforts. The American Association for the Advancement of Science (AAAS) has been the most visible innovator in this area. For the past five or more years, AAAS has sponsored a seminar series at its annual meetings on alternative career paths, making a transition to new career areas, and other career-development topics. And, in 1995, AAAS's *Science* magazine launched NextWave, a Web-based forum (http://www.nextwave.org) for career information "for the next generation of scientists."

Collectively, these efforts are starting to make science policy administrators take notice of students' needs and desire for such information. In a January 5, 1998 commentary in *The Scientist*, Richard Zare, chairman of the National Science Board and a professor of chemistry at Stanford University, wrote:

> I applaud efforts on the part of universities and NSF to prepare new Ph.D.s for a changing job market and for encouraging fundamental change in the way they perceive job prospects. There will continue to be a need and a place to pursue research and teaching in the U.S. There will also be a need for Ph.D.s in many places besides labs and classrooms. With proper education and training, a Ph.D. holder has an immense advantage in the marketplace. The skills acquired while earning a Ph.D. are easily applicable to many professions. . . . Reshaping the Ph.D. degree to take into account that most such degree holders will not be pursuing careers in research universities makes sense. To that end, it is important that we build breadth and flexibility into Ph.D. preparation. (p. 10)

Definitions, Themes, and Advice

☐ Alternative or Nontraditional Careers?

Before I launch into a synthesis of what career switchers suggest, I think it's first important to define what I mean by an alternative or nontraditional career. For the purposes of this book, I mean a nonresearch position, but one in which a scientifically trained person still uses the skills, knowledge, and expertise learned in graduate school.

To some, using the words "alternative" and "career" in the same breath imparts a negative quality to an individual's career decision, and implies that somehow there is one desirable direction (that is, university-based research scientist) and that all other choices are second rate. Obviously, that's not true, but many career switchers mention that they did experience some questioning of their decision by thesis advisers and colleagues. So, I will try to use the term "nontraditional career" when referring to positions people now hold in such related science fields as policy and writing.

Catherine Gaddy, the executive director of the Commission on Professionals in Science and Technology, a nonprofit organization concerned with advancing public understanding of scientific and technical professions, describes a gradation of emerging opportunities for scientifically trained people. "Some are new extensions of traditional research and development, for example, chemists working on designer fuels," she remarks. "Other opportunities, particularly for fields that have been harder hit in terms of reduced employment opportunities for recent graduates, are in applications seemingly outside the field of graduate degree, such as physicists working in computer science. Another area is scientists working in a multifield or -disciplinary context, such as a biochemist working in pharmacoeconomics. Yet another category are those people working outside the standard definition of science and engineering altogether, such as in business management or journalism." This book really concentrates on Gaddy's last category, and to some extent the penultimate group.

This book highlights eight nontraditional career options in separate chapters:

- science education;
- scientific and medical illustration and imaging;
- science and technical writing, editing, publishing;
- informatics;
- technology transfer;
- business;
- law;
- science policy, advocacy, and regulation.

These eight broad areas are the most commonly suggested alternatives in books, seminars, and Web sites, but in researching examples, I've run across people happily working and applying what they learned in graduate school in many additional categories that are difficult to pigeonhole:

- environmental health and safety;
- quality control and technical services (http://www.nextwave.org/pastnich/pastnich.htm);
- manufacturing (http://www.nextwave.org/pastnich/pastnich.htm);
- environmental analysis for insurance companies;
- software design and computer programming;
- managing the grant peer-review process for government agencies;
- grant writer and administrator;
- fund-raiser;
- translator for biomedical companies;
- biological database management.

☐ Common Advice

Although I interviewed nearly 100 scientists and engineers now working in seemingly disparate science and technology careers, many had very similar advice to impart to someone thinking about leaving research. Some of the common themes they mentioned follow.

Do what makes you happy. A career change is really a process of self-analysis to find a good fit

As your own situation allows, follow your heart and do what makes you happy. Unfortunately, determining what makes oneself happy often takes time and sometimes uncomfortable soul-searching. But, recognizing the qualities about a particular line of work that attract—or repel—you can eventually make a difference in your professional success and personal happiness. The sidebar "Questions to Ask Yourself" lists questions that will help you to pinpoint important career attributes that might work for you. "My advice for career changers is this: Make sure you know why you're doing what you're doing," says Victoria McGovern, a biochemist now working as a grants coordinator at the Burroughs Wellcome Fund. "That the job market in science is scary isn't a reason to become a lawyer or a management consultant. If you're leaving science, it ought to be because science isn't a good fit for you. And why move from one poor fit to another? Do something that gets you out of bed in the morning, not something you read was a hot field for the '90s. I think people who want to change careers really need to go sit on a rock and do some difficult and honest self-analysis. Ask yourself: 'What has kept me from getting ahead in science?' If you have been doing well in science but aren't happy: 'What could my next life have to give that science hasn't?'"

You should also start thinking about careers sooner, suggest many observers. "Generally the feeling is that you should get the degree over with and *then* start worrying about what to do next," says Michal Freedhoff, a science policy advisor for the House of Representatives Science Committee (Democratic staff). "Students should be assessing their interests constantly, networking at conferences and within their university, and seeking information long before they are set to graduate."

Identify and acknowledge the element of risk associated with any career change

"There are many concerns, angst, and conflicts in people going through this kind of change," remarks Don Doering, a senior fellow in the Wharton School of Business at the University of Pennsylvania. "Choosing to change careers takes initiative or need, and at the same time you have to accept the risk inherent in this decision. Anything other than science seems scary. The commitment to a career in science involves a series of very-long-term commitments toward one far-off eventual goal. Grad school, for example, is typically four to eight years, more for some. However, in most professional fields it is quite customary today

QUESTIONS TO ASK YOURSELF ABOUT A CAREER:
WHAT MAKES ME HAPPY? UNHAPPY?

One of the common pieces of advice that career switchers give is that you must, as your own situation allows, follow your heart and do what makes you happy. Determining that takes time and sometimes uncomfortable soul-searching. But recognizing the qualities about a particular line of work that appeal to you, and perhaps more importantly, don't appeal to you, can make a difference in your happiness. By asking yourself some of these questions, you may be able to pinpoint what attributes click with you. The following list is adapted, with her permission, from a presentation given by Linda Pullan at a University of Pennsylvania graduate career seminar in March 1997. Pullan is the collaborations manager in the Technology Access Group at Zeneca Pharmaceuticals.

Do I think like a generalist or a specialist? For example, am I better suited for the focused work of a research scientist or for applying the broad aspects of my scientific knowledge to multiple tasks and subjects, as one does in, say, science policy or science and technical writing?

Am I excited about the quantitative or qualitative aspects of scientific research? Do I want to be close to the data? Am I numbers- and statistics-oriented? Or, do I want to be more involved in a big-picture view of my discipline?

Am I a concepts-oriented person or do I get more enjoyment out of executing the details of a project?

How do I get satisfaction on the job; am I self-motivated, or do I need external recognition? Do I need frequent feedback from my peers and other colleagues, such as one gets from making presentations and interacting with clients about ongoing projects? Or, do I derive satisfaction from projects with a longer time horizon for completion that entail less interplay with outside sources? Is most of the satisfaction from my own assessment of a job well done or from the sense of being useful to others?

Do I need to see the immediate relevance of what I am doing? Am I more motivated by the practical application of a project or by the intrinsic beauty of creating knowledge and understanding of biological and physical phenomena?

What aspects of pay, benefits, hours, need to travel, and work environment are important to me?

Do I enjoy communicating my scientific findings? Do I like to write and speak about science to a general audience?

Do I like a dynamic job environment that will continually provide new challenges, perhaps even risk, where I'll have to always be learning new skills, or one that provides more stability and security? For example, does the often risky, ever-changing world of biotech entrepreneurship appeal to me or the more predictable, orderly world of quality assurance and regulatory affairs?

Do I enjoy managing many projects at the same time or do I need a position that allows me to focus on a few projects more in depth?

Would I like the responsibility and control of managing projects and staff, or do I want a lower-stress position that may require less accountability for other peoples' actions?

Is it important for me to interact with a diverse set of people on a day-to-day basis, or am I more comfortable with independent, solitary pursuits?

to change jobs every two to three years. I believe scientists have a fear of career change because they feel they are signing up for another four- to eight-year commitment."

Some of the advice given by career changers might not be realistic for everyone. Such personal commitments as caring for children and older parents or debt from mortgages and school loans may preclude following some of the advice given by the people featured in this book. In the final analysis, your personal and professional situation is obviously unique and you must determine your optimal career path, considering fully all the inherent risks and benefits.

Don't go it alone. Networking is often key to professional success and personal support

Talk with everyone. You never know where you will get job leads, inspiration, positive feedback, and moral support. Career centers based at universities are good places to start to get individualized advice. These centers often have searchable directories of alumni and well-stocked libraries. In addition, most technical societies have public outreach, education, and science-policy divisions. Society staff are there to give members advice and recommend other people to contact.

"When I was going through my career change, no one ever turned down my requests for help or advice," says Freedhoff. She received her Ph.D. in physical chemistry from the University of Rochester in 1995 and immediately began working in outreach, education, and policy at the American Institute of Physics. "For areas such as law and finance, a technical society membership division might be able to direct students to another member who has chosen that route."

In graduate school, attend diverse seminars, classes, and events. "If your department won't invite a speaker that you really want to hear, organize a group of students and invite them yourself, or organize panel discussions on alternative careers," suggests Freedhoff. "Be proactive."

Talk with as many people as possible, says Doug Curran-Everett, a physiologist at the University of Colorado Health Sciences Center department of pediatrics who spends 70 percent of his time conducting basic research and the remainder working on ninth-grade science curriculum. "Ask people you know for the names of other people you can talk with; usually the first people you talk with will not be the 'paydirt' you're after, but eventually you will hit that paydirt by virtue of one of their suggested contacts. Believe that anything is possible, and persist until that 'anything' happens. But, this takes energy, so find people to support you so you can maintain your energy and enthusiasm. Get inspiration or encouragement from any source you can. Get it as often as you feel you need it. It is much easier to persevere when you have people supporting you."

Try out a new area first

How to go about getting experience for a nontraditional science career is certainly one area where many research-trained scientists feel quite lost, notes Janet Joy, a neuroscientist who now works as a study director at the Institute of Medicine.

Many career switchers get experience by volunteering. In some areas like education, policy, and writing, volunteering can provide you with concrete nonscientific work to show to potential employers, to help you make new professional and personal connections, to help you gain broadened perspectives, and to demonstrate your commitment to a new field. However, in such areas as business and intellectual property law, where proprietary knowledge is central to the profession, volunteering may be infeasible.

"I found that volunteer work done before the actual switch involved maximal gain for minimal effort," recalls Joy. "It's incredibly hard to imagine a life you've never seen—much less think it would make you happy—without trying it on for size." Joy recommends going to public libraries for information on foundations and professional societies. She sent resumes to these places and volunteered for them, in particular the Commission on Professionals in Science and Technology.

"Somehow get experience," stresses Finley Austin, a human geneticist who is now administrative director of the Merck Genome Research Institute. "If you don't have any experience in a new area it's doubtful anyone will take you seriously, and you'll probably be competing against someone with experience."

Start defining yourself by your skills rather than your field

This involves a change in thinking about your career self. For example, if you're a meteorologist who uses computer modeling, start selling yourself as a computer modeler who applies that skill to meteorology rather than strictly as a meteorologist. In graduate school, students can develop a myriad of transferable skills, gain general experiences applicable to many fields, and hone attributes that pay off in all aspects of life. The sidebar "Transferable Skills, Attributes, and Experiences" lists some of the skills and attributes for which many employers are looking.

"The barrier for many students is not having any idea how to present themselves to future employers in areas other than academia or industrial research," says Freedhoff. "The identifying phrases one uses to describe oneself within the academic sphere are entirely different than anywhere else. Students need to recognize that by earning [an advanced degree] they have learned how to think critically, ask questions, solve problems, work independently and in a group, and do research in any field. Students have to market themselves as having a set of skills, not as scientists. A breakdown of their specific technical areas of expertise into skills that are transportable to other careers is necessary. The Ph.D. *process* becomes the job qualification, not the Ph.D. itself."

☐ Is the Grass Always Greener? A Realistic View of Allied Fields

Jobseekers in many of the nontraditional fields say they experience just as much competition as those vying for research jobs at universities, in industry, and in government. They also emphasize that their nontraditional careers are not a panacea for the employment troubles faced by many science Ph.D.s today, but offer their stories as examples of the many things you can successfully and happily do with your degree.

(*text continues on p. 26*)

TRANSFERABLE SKILLS, ATTRIBUTES, AND EXPERIENCES DEVELOPED AND HONED IN GRADUATE SCHOOL

These lists were developed by Stanford University's Career Planning and Placement Center and excerpted from "The Skills Employers Really Want," by Peter Fiske on NextWave (http://www.nextwave.org/tool9. htm), with the permission of the AAAS (copyright 1997) and the Stanford University Career Planning and Placement Center.

Marketable On-the-Job Skills

- adaptability; ability to function in a variety of environments and roles
- teaching, conceptualizing, explaining
- counseling, interviewing
- public speaking
- computer skills, information management
- debating; ability to support a position or viewpoint with argumentation and logic
- conception and design of complex studies and projects
- project management, completion of projects, meeting deadlines, following through
- knowledge of the scientific method to organize and test ideas
- data organization and analysis, interpretation, and synthesis
- combining and integrating information from disparate sources
- critical evaluation of a given situation
- investigation of a problem, using many different research methodologies
- ability to work with the committee process
- advocacy work
- open-mindedness
- ability to suspend judgment, to work with ambiguity
- ability to make the best use of "informed hunches"

Personal Attributes

- ability to learn quickly
- ability to make good decisions quickly
- being analytical, inquisitive, and logical
- ability to work well under pressure and the willingness to work hard
- competitiveness and enjoying a challenge
- ability to apply oneself to a variety of tasks simultaneously
- thoroughness, organization, and efficiency
- good time-management skills

- resourcefulness, determination, and persistence
- imagination and creativity
- cooperativeness and helpfulness
- being objective and flexible
- good listening skills
- sensitivity to different perspectives
- ability to make other people "feel interesting"

What Skills Nontraditional Career Employers Will Be Looking At

- negotiating skills
- communication skills
- teamwork skills
- judgment
- business acumen
- honesty
- work ethic
- adaptability
- reliability

Five Most Valuable Skills in the Outside World That Are Learned in Graduate School

In 1996, Peter Fiske polled 22 scientists at various stages of their careers and asked the following question: "Of the many skills that people develop while in graduate school, which ones are the most valuable in the outside world? The top five answers were:

- ability to work productively with difficult people,
- ability to work in a high-stress environment,
- persistence,
- willingness to circumvent the rules,
- ability and courage to start something even if you don't know how yet.

Steps to Identify Your Own Set of Transferable Skills

- Make a list of all the tasks that you do during a typical day, month, or year as a scientist, be it teaching, ordering supplies, creating an experiment, giving a seminar to a lay audience, organizing a journal club, advising undergraduate students, or your involvement in a professional society.
- If appropriate, make another list of what you do outside of science, be it volunteering with a kid's soccer league, teaching

Sunday School, volunteering for your political party or a favorite nonprofit organization, or writing articles for a club newsletter.

- Match these activities with the lists of transferable skills. Assign skills you think you learned in each activity to your lists. Now you have a personalized, matched list of skills with examples from your own experiences, both in and out of science, which is important to recognize in many of the nontraditional paths.

- Look at the wording in your lists. Are the identifying phrases you have used "too academic?" Familiarize yourself with the wording of the job advertisements in the field in which you're interested. Use those same words in cover letters, resumes, and interviews. As James Reddoch says in his Q&A on p. 176 of Chapter 8, if the duties stated in an ad include "data collection, analysis of biotechnology and pharmaceutical industry trends, and competitive analysis of companies and technologies," think about it this way: "If there's anything a scientist has been built to do, it's collect data and analyze trends. But rather than protein levels following varying doses of an inhibitor, it's cash flow, for example, that you've got to be talking about."

- Ask yourself: What skills are on the list that you would like to have? How can I go about attaining them? Volunteering? Internships? Auditing classes? Taking on a special project like a seminar series?

- Start thinking about how you could rearrange your CV to market yourself as having a set of skills, not as a scientist per se. Contact your career center for help with this.

Alternative careers shouldn't be touted as a cure-all, thereby becoming the "new myth," adds Austin. "It's understandable that people are reluctant to leave their postdocs. This is familiar, and research is something they know they can do and want to do."

Is the world outside of academia (other than industry) really clamoring for science Ph.D.s? "This is a very difficult question to answer, as it is terribly person-dependent," says Sara Beckman, former codirector of the Management of Technology program at the University of California, Berkeley. "We have had students in our M.B.A. program who have Ph.D.s, and have a terrible time getting a job when they leave. Prospective employers seeking candidates with more typical M.B.A. profiles are unsure what to do with them. In some of these cases it is difficult to separate age problems from degree problems. Other students come into the M.B.A. program with Ph.D.s and have no problem at all. I think it depends to some extent how much 'common sense' they have, their ability to communicate and interact with others, and their interest in learning about business. Difficult 'placement' of these M.B.A. students is no different than placements of academic faculty from any field in nonacademic jobs—they come across as 'too academic!'"

Not many employers are really clamoring for science Ph.D.s, says McGovern. "But what they do want are people who can think and communicate and solve problems, which are often things Ph.D.s are good at. In my experience, in the real world you actually have to convince people you're not like their impression of scientists—that you're not tied to an ivory tower, not so stuck on minutia that you can't finish a job. Scientists who hope to use their research experience in a job change can't be so focused that they never think about the real world problems underlying their work."

☐ Upsides/Downsides

What are the advantages and disadvantages of having a science background and/or a Ph.D. for work in an allied science area? Might a Ph.D. be considered overqualified for some of the jobs in some of the areas? And how might this affect a job-search strategy?

"When I worked at Hewlett Packard I was frequently called an 'academic,'" recalls Beckman. She received her Ph.D. in industrial engineering from Stanford University in 1987, worked at Hewlett Packard from 1985 to 1993, and has taught at Berkeley since 1987. "At Berkeley, with my industry experience, I am frequently referred to as not a 'true academic.' Nevertheless, both places hired and promoted me. So, I think that some companies are more open than others, due to their culture, to considering Ph.D.s for various jobs." According to Beckman, business cultures that are open to hiring Ph.D.s include ones that embrace workers who question the status quo and appreciate very bright employees.

"Ph.D.s are likely overqualified in the academic sense for many industry jobs," notes Beckman. "It is up to the Ph.D. to decide whether or not all of their 'qualifications' will be brought to bear on the job."

One of the biggest risks in switching careers is that once you leave any field it is very difficult to return to that field. Reentry into academia is difficult, if not impossible, say many observers.

☐ A Question of Commitment

One of the deterrents to making a career switch that many postdocs and senior graduate students cite is having to overcome colleagues questioning their commitment to science. It's traumatic enough to realize that you're not happy doing something you spent years developing—and maybe tens of thousands of dollars—not to mention the things you put off, like personal relationships, having children, vacations, or cultivating hobbies and sports. For some, it's like pouring salt into an open wound to have people even hint at your decision to leave research as a sign of failure or some inadequacy.

"There are two ways to look at this," says Julie Rehm, associate department manager at Battelle Memorial Institute, in Cleveland, OH. Rehm received her Ph.D. in chemistry in 1996. "One has to do with your ability to convince people you are qualified to do something other than the traditional research jobs and that is why it is critically important that you market yourself effectively. The second has to do with other scientists looking at you and questioning your commitment and, quite frankly, in some cases, your intelligence and ability. They're both difficult to address. Number one is easier: you need to spend some serious time developing your resume and cover letter with someone who can give suggestions and make corrections. Number two gets easier with time. After you spend time figuring out what you want to do, then it is easier to explain to someone who asks. For me, it was simple; anyone who knows me knows I would not be happy spending my career in a lab because I have a very outgoing personality.

"Remember your decision is not cast in stone! You can alter your career path as needed to accommodate your changing lifestyle, interests, and circumstances. Too many of us start out on a charted course and refuse to deviate from 'The Grand Plan' for fear of disappointing ourselves or colleagues or family. This will inevitably lead to unhappiness and grief. Be flexible and relax."

Gayatri Saberwal, who received her life science Ph.D. in 1992 from the Jawaharlal Nehru University in New Delhi, India, tells a similar story. "For several years during my doctoral studies, I battled the question: 'Do I really want to do research?,'" she recalls. "It's not that I was bad at research. I'm sure I could have carried on if I'd wished, and probably done moderately well. But somehow I was dissatisfied."

She went on to do a postdoc in physiology and biophysics at the Cornell University Medical Center. "All I knew at the end of my postdoctoral work was that I didn't want to do research, without really knowing what I wanted to do. I think it takes a bit of courage to make a career switch, especially if it's on the blind. One is racked with questions: 'Does a switch mean failure?,' 'Will I never be satisfied, and therefore keep switching?,' 'Will everyone else think I've flunked out?'"

In retrospect, she says she feels that although such questions are

(*text continues on p. 30*)

SOME MORE ADVICE

Daniel M. Kammen, assistant professor of public and international affairs at the Woodrow Wilson School of Public and International Affairs and chair of the Science, Technology, and Environmental Policy (STEP) Program at Princeton University, has put together a Web site with career information in the environmental and energy policy field (http://www.wws.princeton.edu:80/~kammen/energy-jobs.html). The following observations, excerpted from the Web site with Dr. Kammen's permission, were originally intended for people interested in environmental and energy policy careers, but the general sentiment of each piece of advice is applicable to many allied careers in science.

Start Talking to People

There is no clear "path," no university, agency, or society, that consistently trains people in environmental or energy policy. Similarly, jobs in this area often arise in unexpected environments. The more diverse contacts you have, the more likely you are to identify interesting opportunities.

Develop a Thick Skin

Rejection and skepticism are rampant in this field, where projects are chronically underfunded and understaffed. Be prepared to justify your interest and explain your credentials, and to persevere.

Contact People, Not Programs

Address your inquiries to individuals. Take the time to research who is engaged in what project. Read their papers. Always mention your contacts: if Dr. Doe recommended that you call Dr. Smith, say so (and indicate this in your cover letters, too).

Specify Your References

Do not list "references provided upon request" on your resume. Let people know who you would ask for a recommendation. If possible, tailor the list to the organization you are approaching. You may not have taken a course in energy policy (few have!), but if you volunteered at a relevant organization, list it and your reference there up front. Similarly, many technical skills are transferable. If you are applying to, or contacting, a group modeling climate change and you have taken a course in fluid dynamics, inorganic chemistry, or classical mechanics, make that explicit.

reasonable, at some level one has to understood one's own needs and act on them. "In the final analysis one has to live with oneself and try and create the happiest life one can," she concludes. At the end of her postdoc in 1996, she returned to India. Since then Saberwal has found satisfaction in science communication and fund-raising. She's written children's stories on medicinal plants, coordinated a documentation project involving the Human Genome Project, organized an international meeting, collated and edited an annual report for the National Center for Biological Sciences, Bangalore, and is now involved in raising funds for that center.

☐ Take-Home Messages

Time and again, the career switchers I talked with told me that the most important element in their experience doesn't really center on jobseeking. It's about personal fulfillment and being true to yourself. "In the long run, personal fulfillment will lead to success in your chosen profession," says Mark Frisse, Associate Professor of Medicine, Medical Informatics, and Computer Science at Washington University. "Most scientists know their world—clinical or scientific—is changing. They have the feeling they don't have the complete skill sets. You can adopt core values and a set of core skills—I think both are essential—but ultimately it is your spirit of inquiry and optimism that will make or break you. I think every individual has to make their own path, define their own career. No two are alike."

Scientists need to know that things are changing, says Austin. "For me, the job and lifestyle I set out to get when I was an undergrad as an academician no longer really existed by the time I was a postdoc. Part of the solution for dealing with change is self-exploration. Students and postdocs have to have a change in attitude and realize that life is part opportunity, part persistence, and part desire. Most important, though, even though the road may be difficult: strive to be happy and never waste time being bitter."

CHAPTER

Science Education

Many scientists have a desire to work with children and young adults and have sought to do this through teaching. They are primarily employed at one of two places: informal science education (ISE) centers such as science-and-technology centers, natural history museums, aquariums, and zoos; or in a middle or high school classroom setting.

According to educators who have worked in both arenas, teaching in classrooms is much different from that in museums. Jobs in informal science education are less structured than they are in public or private schools. In a museum, you see different students each day, whereas public or private school classroom teachers see the same 20 to 30 students (times four to five classes) develop over the entire year. For some science educators this longer time to impact a child's science education has different professional rewards than the somewhat transient nature of science-museum education. The real plus, they say, is that you get to witness the child's growth and maturation over the entire year.

To start out in this career, observers suggest that you get involved in community outreach activities at your university, in your community, or where you work, or that you organize your own. Volunteer at local science museums or in elementary, middle, or high schools. Many public schools lack the resources or background to present science in an updated way and might appreciate a guest lecturer or field trip for their class, or help in designing and implementing activities that model scientific inquiry.

CHARACTERISTICS OF A SWITCH
TO A CAREER IN EDUCATION

These attributes may not strike every reader the same way. Depending on your background and interests, you may view some of these as either attractive or unappealing.

- You'll need a passion for and an ability to educate others, a desire to work with children and young adults, and an interest in how people learn.
- You'll need to be able to communicate science to the broadest possible audience.
- The competition for jobs, especially in the museum field, can be stiff, and the pay may sometimes be low.
- You could work in a variety of settings and capacities, and with people from diverse professions and backgrounds.
- It's a one-way switch.
- A Ph.D. is not absolutely required in most cases.
- You could make a tangible, social contribution in sharing with others your love and understanding of science and the natural and physical world.
- Classroom teaching requires a special type of patience and eventually a teaching certificate for those who go this route.
- You get to work with the broad aspects of science.

☐ Informal Science Education

According to the Association of Science-Technology Centers (ASTC), science museums employ many people with scientific training, especially those who are interested in the popularization of science. They help develop exhibition concepts, work with youth programs, offer teacher education programs, run hands-on science activity centers in the museum or at outreach sites, and direct science centers.

Competition, however, for any position at science museums is high. Established institutions rarely have vacancies. But some established centers are engaged in major expansions, for example, the Orlando Science Center, the California Science Center, and the Science Museum of Minnesota. And new centers are being created, such as the Kansas City Museum's "Science City" in Missouri. In 1997, close to 250 institutions were members of ASTC, and nearly 50 developing museums and centers were preparing to open their doors within a few years.

"When there are openings, for either existing or new positions, there is a shortage of experienced candidates, but no shortage of unexperienced ones," notes Alan Friedman, director of the New York Hall of Science. Friedman says it is relatively easy for a scientist or engineer with prior museum experience to be hired right away, but much harder for someone who has never worked in informal education before, making it important to get related experience in any way possible.

"It's not the sort of job that a new Ph.D. could get," says Thomas Humphrey of his position as senior scientist at the Exploratorium in San Francisco. "You have to grow into it." He did graduate work for CalTech at the Fermilab in elementary particle physics during the early 1970s. Humphrey is responsible for the physics content of exhibits at the Exploratorium and works with a lot of people in developing this exhibit material. His duties include strategic planning, writing grants, teaching staff and visitors, developing individual exhibits, writing articles for the museum magazine, consulting on book and graphics projects, and lecturing outside the Exploratorium at various physics, art, museum, and education conferences, seminars, and symposiums.

"I think that there are real possibilities in the field of informal science education and these positions are already attracting the attention of scientists in more traditional roles," he states. Humphrey says that a number of tenured university professors have approached him on the topic of a career change.

"My own biography, and that of the leaders of most of the hundreds of science-and-technology centers around the world, proves that there are choices for scientists who are interested in nontraditional roles for their skills and interests," remarks Friedman. "Flexibility and confidence in your own ability to learn and adapt are essential. It is not for everybody, and cannot accommodate everybody. But a lot of us are happy we made the leap."

Read on for some of the personal stories and practical advice of a few scientists who have made that jump.

One-on-One with Science Museum Educators

Alan J. Friedman, Director of the New York Hall of Science in Flushing Meadows Corona Park, NY

Friedman, who was given the 1996 American Association for the Advancement of Science Award for his contributions to the Public Understanding of Science and Technology, has always been interested in science. He traces this back to his childhood love of science fiction. Friedman obtained his Ph.D. in low-temperature physics in 1970 from

Florida State University. Later, while on sabbatical at the University of California, Berkeley, he interacted with people from the university's Lawrence Hall of Science. A year later he became the Hall's director of astronomy and physics. Friedman moved to the New York Hall and has been there since 1984.

What general advice would you give a person thinking about embarking on a career in informal science education?

Retooling and getting experience in informal science education depends so much on the particular institution and the jobs they have open. In general, any experience working in a similar institution would be invaluable. Volunteering would be an excellent way to get that experience. If I need an exhibit developer, for example, a candidate who has actually developed an exhibit or two, tried them out on the public, and made them work, has a vastly better shot at the job compared to someone who has no experience in making exhibits, no matter how bright and well versed they are on subject matter.

There are some workshops at the Association of Science-Technology Centers annual meetings, for example, that are very helpful. There are few formal courses. Museum studies at most universities is strictly art and history, with little or no "hands-on" science museum content.

General skills of great value are the ability to effectively manage a project, its staff, and its funds; excellent writing and oral communications skills, especially in explaining science to nonscientists; grantsmanship; and experience teaching nonscientists at various levels, from kindergarten to adult.

There are some trade-offs with working at a science museum versus a career in research. Negatives: Tenure is not an option at most places. There are many more deadlines to meet than in science. Multiple tasks every day (even every hour) do not allow for more single-minded pursuits, which characterize much of the life of an academic scientist. And you must meet and work with a vastly broader variety of people than in academe.

Positives: There are no agonizing, gut-wrenching tenure fights to go through, as either candidate or judge. You use a greater range of your abilities as a human being and interact with a greater variety of people. Because the science museum field is much smaller and younger than formal education and than academic science, you may have a greater chance to make contributions to your community, institution, and the world.

What practical advice would you give on how to prepare and market oneself for a career in informal science education?

Jobs in informal science education are less uniform than they are in regular science or classroom science education. For example, "exhibits director" in a science center can mean lots of different things, from a manager of multi-million-dollar contracts for exhibit design and construction to a hands-on builder of mechanical or electronic exhibit units. So it is essential to know the particular institution and the job you are interested in obtaining. You can try to learn as much as possible from correspondence, and might get an interview that way, but I'd strongly recommend a visit first. What do they actually want? Can you provide that?

The letter, resume, and interview should all flow from an accurate knowledge of the institution and its needs. Sometimes a long list of scientific publications will be helpful. Other times, it may convince the institution that you really want to do serious research, an opportunity the museum is not likely to offer. So tailor your approach to their needs.

Particularly for large institutions, a Ph.D. is considered highly desirable for the most senior positions, such as director, exhibits director, or education director, but is not absolutely required. This is because the Ph.D. gives credibility, especially to outside funders. However, the degree of specialized knowledge that comes with a Ph.D. is rarely, if ever, needed.

Paul Doherty, Director of the Teacher Institute at the Exploratorium in San Francisco

Doherty received his Ph.D. in solid state physics from the Massachusetts Institute of Technology in 1974. Doherty was a tenured physics professor at Oakland University, where he conducted research and taught. In 1986 he came to the Exploratorium Teacher Institute and became its codirector in 1989.

What general advice would you give a person thinking about embarking on a career in informal science education?
Breadth of science knowledge is very important. Unlike a university atmosphere, where there are experts on many topics next door, at a science museum there will be few if any scientists, so the ones that they do have must cover a lot of ground. It also helps to be skilled in answering questions framed in nonscientific language.

One good thing about working in a museum is that there are often so few scientists that a scientist employee can be called upon to do a wide variety of things. Daily activities seldom behave according to plan. This makes life exciting. For example, in the summer of 1996 after the "Life on Mars" news was released, I got a call from a local TV station and had to spend a fair amount of time answering questions about that subject.

What practical advice would you give on how to prepare and market oneself for a career in informal science education?

I suggest a one-page cover letter giving your academic background and your experience dealing with the public or with teachers. We look for people who have strong academic backgrounds and for people who are excellent teachers. We hope to find people who are both. In a resume I am looking for past jobs or volunteer work that show teaching ability in a wide variety of venues. Volunteer and do whatever is necessary to get experience presenting science to the public or working with local teachers and schools. We interview people by having them teach a class on a topic of their choice to a group of 12 science teachers from middle and high schools.

Kathy Krafft, Exhibits Coordinator at the Sciencenter in Ithaca, NY

In 1982, Krafft received her Ph.D. in low-temperature experimental physics from Cornell University, where she stayed on for a two-year postdoc. After Krafft and her husband, a computer scientist, had the first of their three daughters, she decided to stay home with her children. Krafft, along with her family, joined the Sciencenter in 1987. Her volunteer work designing and building exhibits for the museum started in 1991 and turned into a three-quarter-time position in early 1996.

What general advice would you give a person thinking about embarking on a career in informal science education?

I find that my experience in experimental physics is invaluable in problem-solving for exhibit design. It gives me the confidence that I will come up with a solution to a design problem, although it may take trying out several different ideas. I do not directly use much of the graduate-level course work—that is far beyond the interest level of museum visitors. But a graduate education does increase your understanding of the fundamentals of how nature operates. A graduate education in experimental science particularly yields a lot of experience in problem solving, trouble shooting, and thinking creatively, as well as knowledge of materials and fabrication skills—all important for this type of career. There is a lot of similarity between getting an experiment to work and creating an exhibit that is interactive, safe, attractive, and effective.

I do use my research skills as I develop an exhibit or write interpretive signs. I also use my organizational skills a great deal to keep track of ideas and exhibits that need work. I find my interest in all areas of science to be valuable because I also work on exhibits that have nothing to do with physics.

A major disadvantage is pay level: working for nonprofits is never going to be lucrative. The work environment is sometimes chaotic: getting a new program up and running, or getting a group of exhibits on the floor, for example. A major advantage for me is flexibility. Aside from a few meetings or appointments with volunteers, in a typical work week I usually don't have to be anywhere at a particular time. I can do work at home in my own shop or office.

A real plus for me is that I really feel I am making a difference, not just to this museum but to the whole field: encouraging the sharing of ideas, designing exhibits that are really better than any done before on certain topics, and making lots of interactive, hands-on exhibits. There's a real opportunity in this field to take a leadership role. I greatly enjoy working with other staff who are also passionately committed to science education. We all feel that we are making a significant contribution to society via our work.

Another personal plus for me is the positive feedback we get in our comments book or from museum staff and guides. Working outside and listening to kids squeal in excitement as they walk across your arch bridge, or swing on your coupled swings, or lift up their parents using your 24-foot-long overhead lever, is *very* rewarding. Knowing that kids and adults are getting turned on to science and exploration is really satisfying.

What practical advice would you give on how to prepare and market oneself for a career in informal science education?

I don't have a real answer for resume and cover letter style, interview skills, and so forth, since I basically skipped all that as my career evolved from volunteering to building an exhibit or two into the position I now hold. However, if I were to receive a request from a jobseeker interested in working in the museum field, I would surely want to see someone who has displayed an interest in science education. If they were interested in exhibits, I'd expect to see photos and descriptions of displays they have built in the course of their graduate education, or better yet, things they have built for lecture demonstrations, or best of all for a local science museum typically as a volunteer or summer intern. Positive visitor comments regarding what they've built for a museum would be a plus.

If they are more interested in education and outreach, I'd want to know what kinds of programs they have done with youth groups such as the Girl Scouts, their teaching background, and their ideas for new programs.

In either case, a love of basic science and an interest in conveying the real guts of the science is essential for working in science museums—visitors will not be interested in the fancy calculations and equations typical of graduate-level science. Conveying your passion for the subject and the process of discovery with an open-ended exhibit that allows the visitor to explore the phenomena *will* excite and stimulate visitors.

I'd also expect people to have visited a number of scientific museums and be able to comment on what they saw in the museum that they liked, what they thought was poorly done, and what they observed, for example, how visitors interact with exhibits. For building exhibits, I'd suggest acquiring practical experience with tools and materials. Work with carpenters and people who work with plastics, sign writers, and painters. There is probably much opportunity for that in a university setting, if you look around.

Barry Aprison, Director of Science and Education, Chicago Museum of Science and Industry

Aprison received his Ph.D. in biology from Brandeis University in 1984, after which he spent three years on a National Institutes of Health (NIH) postdoctoral fellowship at Indiana University studying fruitfly genetics.

"Towards the end of my project at Indiana, I wasn't getting the professional satisfaction I was looking for," recalls Aprison. "I was exercising my creativity, yes, but not in terms of education, which was and is, of course, important to me. Teaching biology in big lecture halls wasn't gratifying to me. In addition, I've always been interested in how people learn and remember concepts. I started thinking that perhaps I could apply my experiences, training, and interests toward a career in science museums."

When he had the chance, Aprison visited museums all over the country to study how exhibits were designed and concepts presented. In 1987, he put together a cover letter, resume, and ideas for exhibits and sent it to the president of the Chicago Museum of Science and Industry. The president called him and invited him for an interview, although Aprison was clearly not responding to an advertised position. He was soon offered a position with the museum as a senior scientist and has been there ever since. One of Aprison's achievements is the first major permanent exhibit explaining the science of AIDS, which has been in place since 1995.

What general advice would you give a person thinking about embarking on a career in informal science education?

First, if you decide to go this route or any other nontraditional path, you can't go back, although I never wanted to. Obviously your decision will profoundly affect the direction of your career. You need to imagine yourself away from research. If you can imagine yourself happily doing this, then that's half the battle.

What practical advice would you give on how to prepare and market oneself for a career in science education?

Do your homework. Even before I sent my package to the president of the museum, I talked to museum folks about what their jobs were like. I visited science museums and took photos of exhibits to compare and contrast how they presented subject matter. I read articles on museum design and how people learn. This helped me put together a well-crafted letter and articulate several viable ideas for exhibits. It also demonstrated my enthusiasm for the field and how serious I was about working in science education within museums.

To get experience, some people volunteer their time and expertise for science museums; others find soft-money opportunities as part-time consultants on short-term projects at museums or for creative design firms. Other people gain experience through internships at science centers.

Roberta Cooks, Senior Scientist and Senior Exhibit Developer at the Franklin Institute in Philadelphia

Cooks received her M.D. from the New York University Medical School in 1984, after which she did a residency at the Hahnemann University in Philadelphia. In the late 1980s, she took a leave of absence to spend more time with her young child. "My career change wasn't exactly planned, although I contemplated whether I should stay in medicine," she says. In addition to her M.D., Cooks has a Masters of Fine Arts in Creative Writing, and has always been interested in incorporating writing and working with children into her career. In fact, while still in medical school she wrote a childrens' fiction book. "At that time I wondered: 'How could I combine all of these interests?,'" she recalls.

"I wrote to the Franklin Institute and asked if there were any openings for someone with my background," she remarks. After about six months, she started work at the science museum as a part-time consultant for the scientific content of an exhibit on bioscience and the heart. "This gelled for me and eventually my job became a full-time position." She has been at the Franklin Institute for 10 years.

Cooks says that her medical training is invaluable to her work at a museum. "I wrote a National Science Foundation grant to do an exhibit on the brain, and I couldn't have done that without my background in medicine. I started out on biomedical exhibits only, but now I'm involved with all sorts of exhibitions." Last year she developed one on the

Internet, another on China, and most recently one called "The Powers of Nature" that explains the forces behind such natural phenomena as volcanoes and hurricanes. Her position entails writing text, developing an exhibit's design and story line, and developing interactive elements, as well as some grant writing and interfacing with exhibit-assembly teams, artists, and other scientist-experts in various fields.

What general advice would you give a person thinking about embarking on a career in informal science education?

You have to ask yourself: "What do I love doing?" In my case it was a combination of medicine and science, writing, and working with children. Many people ask me: "Don't you think all of your training has gone to waste?" They're wrong. Here, I'm using all of my training. It's amazing how much I use the breadth of knowledge that my medical education gave me.

What practical advice would you give on how to prepare and market oneself for a career in informal science education?

First, find out if you're cut out for this type of work or not. There is a large learning curve, and you have to be comfortable not starting at the top. You need to learn how to simplify scientific concepts for a broader audience, which takes a specialized kind of writing.

For example, one person who was volunteering with me was thinking of leaving research. Ultimately he went back to research. It might've been money, or not being able to use his knowledge in the way in which he wanted. He liked probing the depth of a scientific question better than taking a broader approach to a problem, which is required in communicating scientific concepts at a museum.

So, if you're thinking of changing your career, trying it out first by volunteering is very important. Many scientists have come and asked to work with me. Volunteering doesn't have to be a tremendous commitment of time—perhaps a few hours a week. You don't get paid, but can learn an invaluable lesson of what a given field is really like.

Scott M. Lanyon, Director of the James Ford Bell Museum of Natural History, and an Associate Professor in the Department of Ecology, Evolution, and Behavior, both at the University of Minnesota, Minneapolis, MN

Lanyon received his Ph.D. from Louisiana State University in 1985, where he studied ornithology. "I started my professional career as a research curator at the Field Museum of Natural History in Chicago, where I was eventually elected chair of the Department of Zoology and appointed Deputy Vice President for Academic Affairs," he says. "Although I had a very successful research career, I felt very strongly about the importance of museums in society, and thought that I could perhaps do more as a director of a museum than as a researcher. This was my reasoning when I applied for and accepted the offer of director of the Bell Museum." He has been there since 1995.

As director of a university natural history museum, he oversees public outreach, collections management, and research activities. The primary skills required, he says, include the ability to make decisions, manage conflict, raise funds, establish a work environment that maximizes the productivity of employees, forge a team from disparate types of people, be a good listener, and perhaps most important, assess institutional strengths, weaknesses, opportunities, and constraints and from that assessment chart the most promising course of action for the institution. "The fact that I have strong research credentials and the fact that I have public outreach experience provides me with credibility across the institution," he concludes. "Without these credentials I could not lead such a diverse organization."

What general advice would you give a person thinking about embarking on a career in informal science education?

Understanding how to conduct a scientific study to answer a question is an incredibly valuable tool that one gains from scientific training. There are many careers in which the interpretation of impressions, opinions, and empirical observations are thoroughly mixed together, and communicating science to a broad audience is no exception. An ability to determine which of these "facts" are based on good science and which are not can be critically important. An ability to determine how to go about conducting research to replace opinions and impressions with scientific observations and conclusions is also important in all kinds of allied science careers.

What practical advice would you give on how to prepare and market oneself for a career in informal science education?

Obviously, the appropriate way of retooling and getting experience in a new area is heavily dependent on the new area into which you are headed and the "old" area you are leaving behind. However, I think that it is always a good idea to contact someone who has the kind of position you want and talk with them. Upon closer inspection you may well decide that this is not where you want to be. Alternatively, this conversation should provide a much clearer understanding of the steps you need to take to land a position in the "new" area.

I generally advise students to take advantage of as many seemingly disparate opportunities in graduate school as possible—lab work, field work, outreach, public speaking, and popular writing, for example—and to keep an open mind about career opportunities. The more doors you leave open, the more likely it is that at least one will reveal a great job opportunity. The most dissatisfied Ph.D.s I know are those that had extremely narrow definitions of what would constitute a good job and were unsuccessful in their attempts to land such a position.

John Falk, Director, Institute for Learning Innovation, Annapolis, MD

John Falk received a joint Ph.D. in ecology and science education from the University of California, Berkeley in 1974. From there he went to the Smithsonian Institution's Chesapeake Bay Center for Environmental Studies, where he was the associate director for education. "This position allowed me to pursue both educational learning research and ecological research," explains Falk. "It was an opportunity to realize a dream I had to create a research and development group committed to understanding learning as it happens outside of schools."

Eventually his research group was "institutionalized" to become the Smithsonian Office of Education Research, which he directed. But in the late 1980s the emphasis on nonclassroom learning research at the Smithsonian was discontinued under a new administration. "So I left the Smithsonian and created a nonprofit learning research and development organization called Science Learning Inc., and 11 years later I'm still at it," says Falk. "We focus on how learning occurs outside of school. We work with such museums and community-based organizations as the Smithsonian Institution, California Science Center, Pacific Science Center, Orlando Science Center, Museum of Science and Industry in Chicago, Girl Scouts of America, YWCA, and the Astronomical Society of America."

Falk and colleague Lynn Dierking, Associate Director of the Institute for Learning Innovation, are working on a book entitled *How People Learn When They Don't Have To*. It's about free-choice learning, which attempts to synthesize information from the neural, cognitive, anthropological, and social sciences, and is due out in late 1998.

What general advice would you give a person thinking about embarking on a career in informal science education?
There's a bias in the world of science education—even in informal science education—that the science component is more important than the education component. So for a scientifically

trained person, the good news is that if someone starts with a science background, it will be a benefit to them. Frankly, in my experience, having a Ph.D. in a science and working exclusively in the education realm has been a real plus.

The advice I would give to someone is to enjoy the credibility that an advanced degree gives you. But, for many with a strong background in science, there's a sort of missionary zeal to turn students into budding scientists. However, the truth is there are very few people out there who have the desire or need to be a scientist.

So, enjoy the benefit that you will reap from your educational background, and if you're serious about pursuing a career in science education, get on with the serious business of what it means to be an educator, that is, learning how to teach and not trying to recreate students in your own image.

What practical advice would you give on how to prepare and market oneself for a career in informal science education?

Volunteering at science museums in all sorts of situations is invaluable in terms of seeing real people interacting with exhibits, responding to hands-on lessons, and so forth. I believe there are some profound changes going on in terms of how we are coming to understand the way in which people think and learn. It is unlikely that someone who has gone down a science track will be aware of these developments, so I think it's important for someone interested in informal science education to also do some background reading on how people learn. I would recommend newer psychology books. If you go to any large book store, go into the psychology section; there are tons of books out there on the brain and learning, and I think there would be lots of fodder there.

Resources

Professional Societies

Association of Science-Technology Centers (ASTC). ASTC represents close to 500 individuals and institutions, including science and technology centers, nature centers, planetariums, aquariums, zoos, natural history museums, and children's museums, as well as science professional societies and exhibit design firms, all engaged in science education. Contact:

Association of Science-Technology Centers
1025 Vermont Ave., NW, Suite 500
Washington, DC 20005-3516

202-783-7200
Fax: 202-783-7207
http://www.astc.org

American Zoo and Aquarium Association (AZAA). AZAA represents professionals in zoos, aquariums, wildlife parks, and oceanariums in North America, most of whom are engaged in science education, especially wildlife conservation. Contact:

American Zoo and Aquarium Association
7979-D Old Georgetown Rd.
Bethesda, MD 20814
301-907-7777
Fax: 301-907-2980
http://www.aza.org

American Association of Museums (AAM). AAM represents the professional interests of museums of all types, from art to history to science centers. Contact:

American Association of Museums
1575 I St., NW, Suite 400
Washington, DC 20005
202-289-1818
Fax: 202-289-6578
http://www.aam-us.org/aam

Education and Training

For an account of the recent state of training and education programs for science museums, read "Creating an Academic Home for Informal Science Education," by Alan Friedman (*Curator,* 38/4:214–220, 1995).

According to staff at the ASTC, one of the best ways to get experience in the science center field is to contact a local museum, find out what projects they are planning that might benefit from a scientist, and offer to volunteer. Many opportunities may exist: working on the exhibit floor with the public, speaking at a career day, serving on an advisory committee for an exhibit or education project, helping to develop a public demonstration or planetarium show, or writing a grant proposal that's on the museum's priority list. By doing this you can get acquainted with the possibilities, and the museum gets to know you. If a paid opportunity comes up or is created, you may be the first in line.

Sometimes the best opportunities occur in museums that are planning a major expansion or new science centers that have raised major support and need content people to help with exhibits. The ASTC Web site includes a "Science Center Travel Guide," which links to many science-technology centers all over the world. This could be useful in getting up-to-date information on a museum's status.

The ASTC Web site also lists seminars and workshops and academic degrees or certificate programs of special interest to science center and other science-related museum employees; however, these listings do not distinguish those specifically geared to the sciences.

The Smithsonian's Museum Reference Center maintains a bibliography on careers and training in museum studies in all areas, including science and technology. The Center also holds museum training workshops. Although they are not specifically geared towards scientists, many people with science training do attend, say center employees. Contact:

Smithsonian Institution Libraries
Museum Reference Center
Arts & Industries Building
Room 2235, MRC 427
900 Jefferson Drive, SW
Washington, DC 20560
202-786-2271
Fax: 202-357-3346
http://www.si.edu/newstart.htm

Jobhunting and Networking

The ASTC Web site has a Career Corner with job listings as well as such general career information as links to newspaper employment ads and other Internet job listings, jobhunting manuals, and outdoor and seasonal employment. Job listings for the field also appear in ASTC's bimonthly newsletter. At the national level, the largest forum for networking with science center folks is the annual ASTC conference.

The AAM lists jobs for all types of museums—art, history, and science—in their monthly job newspaper, *Adviso*. Send a $4.00 check to AAM to receive a copy of the most recent issue.

Top-level positions may be listed in the *Chronicle of Higher Education*, and on the *Chronicle*'s on-line version called "Academe Today" at http://merit.chronicle.com.

☐ Classroom Teaching

Researchers from all disciplines and from all educational backgrounds—from people with B.S. degrees who have worked in a research setting to Ph.D.s in tenure-track positions—have opted for classroom teaching. What they all seem to have in common is a passion for education and an innate desire and enthusiasm to work with children and teenagers. In fact, many say that they were already volunteering with youth groups or somehow involved informally with education long before they made a conscious decision to switch careers.

"I had always had a desire to teach and in fact had served as a mentor to several local high school students," says Bill Eyl, now a senior high school teacher at Longmont High School in Longmont, Colorado. Eyl was an analytical chemist and spectroscopist with a B.S. degree in geochemistry before moving into teaching.

Despite dedication to their new careers, scientists-turned-teachers all warn that teaching is not for everyone. Classroom teaching requires a unique brand of patience. Research, they say, requires a patience that involves waiting for results and understanding that it may be years before the outcome of one's work is fully realized, while working as a teacher requires a more immediate type of patience to deal with the day-to-day needs of adolescents.

"I personally feel that my experiences prior to teaching have made me very versatile," says Eyl. "The number one benefit is working with intelligent young people. But, the job is very demanding: Consider developing and setting up a lab activity for 60 to 90 students at a time and grading all of those reports." His advice to people thinking about a career in classroom teaching: "If you think teaching is a stress-free profession, think again. How patient are you? There is always the class or student who is willing to test it."

To test your metal, educators suggest getting involved with a local teacher by becoming a mentor or classroom assistant. One thing is clear: schools are always looking for volunteers. "Before working with teachers, grad students, postdocs, and researchers need to appreciate that teachers are experts about education," remarks Doug Curran-Everett, a physiologist at the University of Colorado Health Sciences Center Department of Pediatrics who spends 70 percent of his time doing basic research and the other 30 percent working on ninth-grade science curriculum. "Few people that go through the process of graduate training or teach at an institution of higher education learn what education and learning truly involve. When you work with a teacher, realize that your partnership must be an equal one. Many outstanding teachers of science are those teachers who have little, if any, formal training in science. They model enthusiasm about learning, and they model the ability to say to their students: 'I don't know, but how can we find out?,' and they model curiosity. In essence, they model the process of scientific inquiry."

Read on for the experience and advice of scientists-turned-teachers.

One-on-One with Classroom Teachers

James W. Laughner, Physics Instructor at the Maine School of Science and Mathematics in Limestone, ME

Laughner received his Ph.D. in solid state science from Pennsylvania State University in 1982. In his career as a research scientist, he worked as an engineer for Corning Glass and Owens-Brockway Container, and taught physics at Alfred College. He now teaches physics and science ethics at the Maine School of Science and Mathematics in Limestone, a residential public magnet school for advanced 11th and 12th graders. Throughout his entire research career, working with children has been extremely important to Laughner: he has volunteered with 4-H clubs, Scout troops, and church youth groups.

> *What general advice would you give a person thinking about embarking on a career in science teaching?*
>
> Get a teaching certificate. It's a pain in the butt, but it shows you are serious and you will learn something. But also go beyond the texts and the classroom and look for the research into science teaching that has the potential to revolutionize your classroom.
>
> But, many of the "emergency certificates" are not helpful. In some states the opportunity to compete for an opening is available only if *no* applicant with a certificate has applied for the job. This means at the very least you will be waiting until August for all the certified candidates to withdraw their applications, and then taking a really poor job.
>
> Starting in a private school is a good idea *if* you have solid Ph.D. experience and extensive evidence of youth work. $30,000 is possible at excellent private schools, so salary is not a stopper.
>
> A person who is contemplating moving from research to teaching should not do it to be less busy, especially for the first year or two. Remember also that summers are *not* free; you must take courses to maintain certification. Of course, if you really like teaching these courses can be excellent. I learned a lot about geology, for example, while rafting the Grand Canyon at a savings through a teacher association trip.

What practical advice would you give on how to prepare and market oneself for a career in science teaching?

To market yourself, prepare yourself on paper and in your life. Get involved with students *now*. Tutor. Take education courses. Lead a youth group. In fact, if you are not already doing these things, reconsider teaching. Certainly don't make the move without a few years trying these approximations to full-time teaching.

Never soft-pedal your research experience when interviewing. The school should *want* your experience. If interviewing at private schools, this will be obvious since they use your degree and experience to sell the program's excellence to the parents. Public schools should (and in my experience many will) be just as thrilled to interview someone who actually does science and did it for a living.

Make sure you tell your story about why you want to teach and back it up. In my case I had all my evidence from over a decade of youth work and then the gap when I was a professor to show why I wanted to move to high school and combine my vocation with my avocation.

Dina Bizzaro, Middle School Life Science Teacher at Roseville Area Middle School, Roseville, MN

Dina Bizzaro, who has a B.S. in political science and chemistry, worked in research for several years on a wide variety of projects, including investigations on diabetes and acid rain, as well as preparing samples for electron microscopy. While making the transition from researcher to educator in the early 1990s, she simultaneously worked toward her M.S. in science education at the University of Minnesota and as a research scientist on amino acid content in animal feed. She received her masters degree in 1996. Now she is a seventh-grade life science teacher.

What general advice would you give a person thinking about embarking on a career in science teaching?

I took a postbaccalaureate program in education prior to earning my master's in education. This program allowed me to acquire the necessary credentials to teach. I think one needs the help that you get in education courses to learn classroom and curriculum management. Volunteering is definitely the way to go to start getting experience. For example, my husband, an engineer, volunteers a lot. He works for Honeywell and they have the INVEST program, which allows engineers and scientists to go into classrooms and do demonstrations. He also works with my science club.

What practical advice would you give on how to prepare and market oneself for a career in science teaching?

I think that before they enter the classroom, they should do some of the actual things they are going to teach the students. Bring some examples of work to the interview; talk about how to incorporate this into the curriculum. Demonstrate a particular lab activity for students. Resumes should include some experience with children. Without this I wouldn't bother applying for the job. Teaching children can be extremely challenging, in many ways. Find a school that provides a one-year mentor program, but research the background of the mentor first.

Having a Ph.D. may hinder some cash-poor districts from hiring you. It is difficult even with a masters degree. Having a science background is extremely beneficial for the students, especially when trying to make the curriculum more relevant. A disadvantage is that other staff members may be intimidated by your background. Not having an educational background and being female was disadvantageous for me initially, but not for long.

John Davis, Math Teacher at West Baltimore Middle School, Baltimore, MD

Davis received his B.S. in engineering in 1989 at Ohio State University, after which he worked as a Manufacturing Engineer at Textron Lycoming in Stratford, CN for three years. "During those years, I was an assistant high school basketball coach and thoroughly enjoying my time with student athletes," recalls Davis. "Because of that experience, I decided to look into teaching full time. When I heard about Teach for America [see p. 54], I applied and was accepted. Basically, engineering wasn't enough for me. I wanted to work with people, and teaching definitely filled that desire."

This is Davis's sixth year of teaching. During his first two years, he took outside classes to earn his standard professional teaching certificate. Teach for America helped Davis land his teaching position.

As a middle school math teacher, he plans and implements lessons to prepare students for high school. He's also involved with many school activities including the School Improvement Team and Mathcounts, an after-school activity devoted to difficult math problems.

> *What general advice would you give a person thinking about embarking on a career in science teaching?*
>
> Hone your ability to analyze a situation objectively, draw conclusions, and implement action. In any work situation, honestly reflect upon the work completed, how it could have been done better, and think of it as you begin something new. For example, when you finish a project, take a few critical components and analyze your performance. Could your communication have been

better? Did you manage your time effectively? Was the final result effective? After you answer these questions, make sure your next project incorporates these new-found ideas.

A teacher, especially in the first few years, learns more than the students. A teacher must be able to constantly, honestly, and objectively criticize one's teaching. It is difficult to fully take this responsibility on, but an honest critique helps. Unfortunately, you cannot really get experience unless you start teaching. That is why constant learning on the job is such a big deal. A teacher must be continually planning, implementing, reflecting, and then begin planning again.

What practical advice would you give on how to prepare and market oneself for a career in science teaching?
The skills needed to teach are varied and difficult. It is not just standing up there and talking about what you know. To prepare for teaching, you should talk in depth with some excellent teachers to begin to understand the strategies and methods that help students learn. An open, flexible attitude also helps.

Antonio Monterrosa, Science Teacher at Manual High School, Denver, CO

Monterrosa received his Ph.D. in August 1997 from the Department of Molecular, Cellular, and Developmental Biology at the University of Colorado at Boulder. "I was lured into biology by exciting, dynamic junior and senior high school teachers in Anchorage, Alaska who made science classes so much more fun than other classes," he recalls. "After working as a commercial fisherman and for the Department of Fish and Game in Alaska, I thought that I would become an ecologist. However, I was attracted to molecular biology by a very nurturing college professor who spent plenty of time making sure that I appreciated and understood genetics and molecular biology. I also (mistakenly) thought that there would be more job opportunities in molecular biology than in ecology.

"During graduate school, however, I never felt very comfortable or happy with either myself or the environment, although I had the world's greatest advisor, wonderful coworkers, and a seemingly straightforward thesis project. It seemed like there was no way for me to fail. But, I struggled to flourish primarily due to so many failures in my laboratory experiments. I also struggled to fit in with the graduate school environment, partially because I felt there were so few people that I could relate to—folks whose families weren't all college-educated, or ethnic minorities—and partially because I couldn't believe that there was a culture that actually frowned upon taking vacations or spending your weekends outside of the lab." Despite some of these intrinsic misgivings and problematic experiments, Monterrosa persevered and finished his degree.

He points to one shining aspect of his graduate education. "Ever since I finished high school, I had always wanted to go back to a very ethnically and socioeconomically diverse high school and teach science. I had the opportunity at Colorado to work with the Howard Hughes Medical Institution Science Squad, a group of graduate students that traveled to Denver Public Schools and presented lab activities to students for an entire academic year. It was the best experience, because I was able to do any science project I wanted to, *not* just my frustrating thesis project. The Science Squad experience verified what I had suspected all the time: that I belonged with teenagers, doing my best to educate, entertain, and help them on the difficult road that is their lives."

Right after finishing graduate school, Monterrosa was hired by the Denver Public School District. He started as a full-time classroom teacher in the fall of 1997. "Now that the year has started, I find myself working incredibly hard and always falling behind, but absolutely loving almost every moment that I spend with the kids."

During grad school, says Monterrosa, the feeling that he wasn't doing anything with his life to help other people gnawed at him. "That feeling has now dissolved," he remarks.

> *What general advice would you give a person thinking about embarking on a career in science teaching?*
>
> My most important piece of advice: Do whatever makes you happy. If it happens to be research science, then do it well and make sure you're happy and having fun. If lab work is not making you happy, then there are a million other things you can do with your life that will pay the bills. If you opt for classroom teaching, always remember the experiments and activities that you've experienced that made you excited, and then pass these on to a new generation of kids thirsting for scientific interest. Practice your smiling and social skills, because life outside the lab involves people who have so much more to worry about than just thesis projects and experiments.
>
> Teaching requires patience, creativity, very good social skills, lots of understanding, and a willingness to adjust and be flexible. Teaching science also requires a solid fundamental knowledge of every facet of chemistry, physics, and biology. That's what I like so much. In graduate school, I spent six years focused and fixated upon a single tiny gene. Now, I can talk about everything that science has to offer, and kids are great because they ask so many questions and make the subject pretty entertaining.

My present job is challenging because my high school, Manual High, is very poor. An estimated 92 percent of the students are at or below the poverty line, and it is 52 percent Hispanic, which can lead to language barriers. It is also challenging because it is my first year, and I'm teaching six completely different subjects, which requires a lot of planning time. I often find myself failing to meet up to my standards for "the perfect day, every day, full of labs and exciting demonstrations." However, I just have to accept the fact that there is a limit to the amount that I can expect of myself during this first year. I look forward to having more experience and a bigger "bag of tricks" to draw from.

What practical advice would you give a person on how to market him- or herself for a career in science teaching?

Volunteer your time in a classroom and help teach a teacher a new experiment while you get kids excited about a subject that is so often perceived as being impossibly difficult. You may find yourself having fun and wanting to pursue a career in educating youngsters. If you decide that teaching is the profession for you, then find a school that you want to teach at, speak to the principal or the science department chairperson, and find out if you have the skills they're looking for.

I never attended any accreditation program. I was an emergency hire. The reality in many urban school districts in the 1990s is that they are in dire need of two types of teachers: science and bilingual, that is, Spanish-speaking. So, if a putative teacher with no credentials exhibits a proficiency in these skills, then that student may stand a strong chance of attaining gainful employment in a high-school setting. I plan to get accredited as I teach; that way, I can get paid from the moment I start.

Resources

Professional Societies

National Science Teachers Association (NSTA). NSTA is the largest international professional society dedicated to science education and educators. In 1997, they had more than 53,000 members, representing science teachers, school-district science supervisors, administrators, scientists, and businesspeople, among others. Contact:

National Science Teachers Association
1840 Wilson Blvd.
Arlington, VA 22201-3000

703-243-7100
publicinfo@nsta.org
http:\\www.nsta.org

National Association of Biology Teachers (NABT). NABT represents biology and life science instructors, from elementary through college-level educators. In 1997, the organization was almost 8,000 members strong. Contact:

National Association of Biology Teachers
11250 Roger Bacon Drive #19
Reston, VA 20190-5202
703-471-1134
800-406-0775
Fax: 703-435-5582
NABTer@aol.com
http://www.nabt.org

American Chemical Society (ACS) Education Division. This section of the largest chemistry professional society helps high-school chemistry teachers by providing curriculum and classroom materials, teacher training, grants, and career fairs and workshops. ACS also provides many other resources for those interested in science education at all levels. Contact:

American Chemical Society
1155 16th St., NW
Washington, DC 20036
202-872-4600
http://www.chemcenter.org/education.html

American Association of Physics Teachers (AAPT). AAPT is the main professional society for physics educators at all levels. Its Web site contains resources for those interested in physics education. Contact:

American Association of Physics Teachers
One Physics Ellipse
College Park, MD 20740
301-209-3300
Fax: 301-209-0845
aapt-exec@aapt.org
http://www.aapt.org

Education and Training

According to NSTA, each state has its own certification requirements, although some states recognize the certificates of others through reciprocal agreements. Almost all states offer some type of alternative certification program, but programs vary by state. If a state offers such a program, it is important to investigate how many people are hired through that route versus the traditional route of obtaining a degree in education.

Alternative certification is designed for individuals who have a bachelor's degree or higher and want to teach but have not taken the required education courses. Individuals are allowed to teach while they complete these education course requirements. But, the question must be asked: How often are they hired through such a route? Also, such individuals can often teach in private and parochial schools without being certified. NSTA recommends that interested individuals contact the department of education in the state in which they want to teach for more information.

Another way to identify teaching positions is through Teach for America, part of the AmeriCorps Program. It aims to attract students to teaching careers, especially in underserved rural and urban districts. In exchange for a two-year commitment, graduates, including math, science, and engineering majors, can gain a fast-track certificate and experience in classroom teaching. So-called corps members participate in a five-week, intensive training program. During their teaching commitment, math, science, and engineering participants are paired with scientists and engineers in academia, government, and business to enhance their students' education. Contact:

Teach for America
Math & Science Initiative
20 Exchange Place, 8th Floor
New York, NY 10005
212-425-9039
http://www.teachforamerica.org

NSTA staff members do not know of any specialized certification programs especially designed for scientists. The quickest way to become certified (not an alternative certification, but a regular certification) is to get an M.S. in education or an M.A. in teaching to teach high school science in the subject in which you are experienced. These are accelerated programs consisting of course work in education theory and teaching methods, plus a semester of student teaching that runs about a year and a summer. Some states have programs for people from industry who want to teach. Also, many newer charter schools do not require formal certification to teach.

Science magnet schools, where programs emphasize math, science, and technology, are specialized public or private schools. Some are residential academies, while others are part- or full-day programs. Since the emphasis is on science in these settings, teachers with superior scientific credentials are sought. Two organizations, Magnet Schools of America and the National Consortium for Specialized Secondary Schools of Mathematics, Science, and Technology, represent the hundreds of magnet schools in the United States. Contact:

Magnet Schools of America
Donald R. Waldrip, Executive Director
PO Box 8152
The Woodlands, TX 77387
281-296-9813
Fax: 281-298-6822
director@magnet.edu
http://www.magnet.edu

National Consortium for Specialized Secondary
   Schools of Mathematics, Science, and Technology
Cheryl Lindemann
Central Virginia Governor's School for Science and Technology
3020 Wards Ferry Rd.
Lynchburg, VA 24502
804-582-1104
Fax: 804-239-4140
http://www.ncsssmst.org

Jobhunting and Networking

According to NSTA, job postings for classroom teachers are advertised in newspapers and such specialized journals as *Education Week* and *Teacher Magazine,* among other places. Interested candidates should also contact the local school districts and private and parochial schools in their area. NSTA posts some positions in their newspaper, *NSTA Reports,* in a column called "Professional Opportunities." The society also sponsors a job fair at their annual convention, as do the other professional teachers societies. Interviews are conducted on site with various institutions. Many also recommend simply looking in the local library in the town where you want to teach to find schools and their locations, and then contacting the personnel office of those school districts.

For teaching in private schools, Laughner suggests trying a placement agency like Carney Sandoe & Associates. This agency recruits teachers and administrators for positions in private, independent schools in the United States and abroad. Schools pay for the services, not candidates. Contact:

Carney & Sandoe Associates
136 Boylston St.
Boston, MA 02116
800-225-7986
Fax: 617-542-9400
recruitment@carneysandoe.com
http://www.carneysandoe.com

Staff at NSTA recommend visiting several Web sites that may list science teaching positions:

- NationJob Network (http://www.nationjob.com/education)
- *The Chronicle of Higher Education* (http://chronicle.merit.edu/.ads/.links.html)
- Educational Placement Service (http://www.educatorjobs.com/)
- National Educators Employment Review (http://www.teacherjobs.com)
- Academic Employment Network (http://www.academploy.com/)

Regarding networking, NSTA runs four conventions each year where teachers can attend workshops and learn from one another as well as interact informally. State teacher organizations and other science teacher societies also provide forums and conventions for networking. NSTA also has a chat room on their Web site where teachers interact, and that might be a good place to ask specific questions about entering into science teaching or about jobhunting strategies.

Scientific and Medical Illustration and Imaging

For people who want to combine their loves of science and art, a career in science, natural history, or medical illustration and imaging may be a good way in which to blend interests and talent. Practitioners in this field mix their artistic talents with a keen understanding of and appreciation for technical accuracy and precision.

Illustrators primarily work in two fields: science illustration and medical illustration. In natural science illustration, the principal task is to prepare accurate drawings from scientific specimens. Computer imaging is becoming more and more important in the field of scientific illustration. In addition to the precise depiction of a subject, an understanding of the science behind the subject matter is also necessary.

Scientific and natural history illustrators work in museums, with newspapers and magazines, and in publishing houses, among other places. Many illustrators are self-employed, performing freelance work for a wide variety of clients: natural history museums, zoos, aquariums, advertising agencies, astronomical observatories, healthcare organizations, greeting card companies, and various publishing outlets. Many illustrators also teach. Still others work producing computer-generated graphics for various outlets.

The difference between medical illustration and natural history, scientific, or biological illustration is the subject matter. For medical illustrators, it's primarily the human body. For other types of illustration the subject matter could literally range from astronomical phenomena to zebras. Increasingly, say illustrators, they are called upon to illustrate concepts and less tangible subjects like theories about astronomy and physics, as well as reconstructions of dinosaurs and their habitats. In this respect, science illustrators must often be storytellers, but without words, so design skills and a great visual imagination are important.

According to the Association of Medical Illustrators, medical illustration is "art as applied to medicine," and medical illustrators are "artists who chose medicine as their subject." Medical illustrations are used in all sorts of outlets: advertising, textbooks and journal articles, instructional materials, and television programs, among others. Recently there has been an increasing demand for these types of drawings for educating patients and juries in medically related trials.

Biomedical photography and imaging is also an area that attracts people with an interest and training in science. All scientifically oriented specialties within illustration and imaging tend to attract people who have had a lifelong interest in art, in one medium or another.

Science illustrators' backgrounds are quite varied, with some having advanced degrees in science or art, but very few with Ph.D.s in science. For many illustrators with scientific training, their avocation has evolved into their occupation.

☐ Natural History Illustration

According to some illustrators, people are attracted to natural science illustration for two primary reasons. For some, it's an interest in sci-

---

**CHARACTERISTICS OF A SWITCH TO A CAREER
IN ILLUSTRATION AND IMAGING**

These attributes may not strike every reader the same way. Depending on your background and interests, you may view some of these as either attractive or unappealing.

- The field provides a way to combine your love of science and the natural world with your artistic skills.
- The field is not for everyone; you need an innate artistic skill.
- Most scientific artists have had a lifelong interest in drawing, photography, and other media.
- Many in the field are self-employed, with its concomitant ups and downs.
- The job market is highly competitive.

ence and scientific communication; they see their skills as an artist as a way to contribute to, and remain active within, the realm of scientific studies. For others, it's an interest in representational art; they love the precision celebrated and required in biological and natural history illustration.

Scientific illustrators list a wide range of jobs within the field, including freelance artist, art director, museum staff illustrator, field artist (especially in archeology and paleontology), museum exhibit designer and illustrator, and science photographer, among others.

Interviews with the following natural history illustrators highlight the similarities and differences in their educational and experiential paths, as well as offer practical advice on how to pursue a career in this area.

One-on-One with Science Illustrators

Jen Christiansen, Editorial Staff—Art, National Geographic Society, Washington, DC

Christiansen double majored in geology and studio art at Smith College in Northampton, MA. The fall after graduating from Smith, she enrolled in the University of California, Santa Cruz (UCSC) Graduate Program in Science Illustration. After graduating from UCSC's program in 1996, she became assistant art director at *Scientific American*. In April 1998, she became a member of the art department at the National Geographic Society. Her responsibilities include researching and directing the illustrations used in the society's magazine.

"I have always been passionate about art and the natural sciences," says Christiansen. "But as a college student I was suddenly faced with a decision that involved focusing on one area at the expense of the other. I was frustrated with the narrowing scope and made the decision to double major and spend equal time in the geology lab and art studio." Her job at *Scientific American* stemmed from an unpaid summer internship as an illustrator for the magazine. Both this job and her current position arose from a portfolio review and conversations with art directors who were invited guests of the UCSC program.

> *What general advice would you give a person thinking about embarking on a career in science illustration?*
> If time and money allow, volunteer work early in the game can prove beneficial, although I know several people that argue that this practice compromises the field with regard to pricing expectations, among other issues. I started by volunteering at the Natural

Illustration by Jennifer Christiansen

History Museum of Los Angeles County for several summers in the early 1990s and not only ended up with several published pieces for my portfolio, but gained experience with such equipment as the camera lucida.

Class assignments often require you to work on a project that you might not otherwise have explored, which serves to broaden your portfolio. Also, class assignments really help to set aside time to work on projects, and typically provide a group of people who will give feedback while the project is in progress.

As an undergraduate, I incorporated images and diagrams into science papers, projects, labs, and exams. It's a great way to bolster personal understanding of the subject, develop interpretation and visualization skills, and have your work be seen. An added bonus is that several professors followed up with paying jobs.

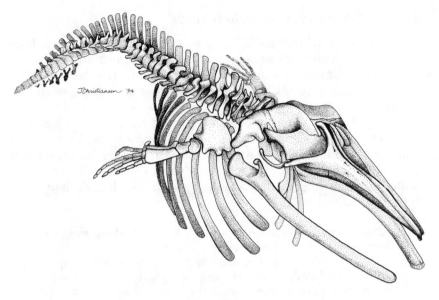

Illustration by Jennifer Christiansen

What practical advice would you give on how to prepare and market oneself for a career in science illustration?

The portfolio is *key*. Clients don't want to take a gamble. Research the client and include illustrations that are directly related to their needs. (Personally, I like to tuck in a few slightly tangential pieces as well to demonstrate flexibility in skill and approach, but don't lose sight of the client or potential employer's needs.)

As far as resumes are concerned, if I'm sending a portfolio to a potential client, I'll include a resume, but I make sure that the major points are included in the cover letter. Very few potential clients have ever asked to see my resume. The bottom line is that the illustrations need to speak for themselves, and reflect the experiences outlined in the resume, especially regarding freelance jobs.

With respect to interviewing and portfolio reviews with potential clients: maintain your confidence. Art can be highly objective, albeit a bit less so in the exact art of scientific representation. If the artist falters, or begins to question or defend her or his own artwork in an in-person portfolio review, the integrity of the portfolio is undermined. I recommend reading the *Graphic Art Guild's Guidelines for Ethical Pricing* [contact the Graphic Artists Guild, Paul Baptista, Executive Director, 11 W. 20th St., New York, NY 10011; 800-878-2753; paulatgag@aol.com for more information] as a good source for the business end of things.

Rachel Taylor, Freelance Illustrator

Taylor graduated from the UCSC Graduate Program in Science Illustration in 1995, after which she completed an internship with the Arizona Sonora Desert Museum. She is now working as a freelance illustrator for magazines, textbook companies, museums, and government organizations.

"I've always had a love for both animals and art, but grew up headed toward veterinary medicine," says Taylor. "I went to the University of California at Davis, where I received a B.S. in zoology, and wanted to be a wildlife vet. During my sophomore year, while working at a rehab center for birds of prey, I did some pen-and-ink identification drawings. That started me off."

> *What general advice would you give a person thinking about embarking on a career in science illustration?*
>
> If you're interested in science illustration, get as much experience in school as possible. My science background is invaluable. Scientists I have worked with respect my opinion and know I require accuracy and detail in my work. As an undergraduate, I worked with many different professors to figure out what field I enjoyed most. I highly recommend doing this, but be wary of people wanting work for free. Take your work seriously, and you will be taken seriously.
>
> You will definitely need computer skills to survive. I recommend computer classes as well as any art classes you can take. Also, if you're planning on freelancing, be prepared for a lot of business and paperwork. Learn about tax laws and copyright laws.
>
> *What practical advice would you give on how to prepare and market oneself for a career in science illustration?*
>
> To market yourself, you have to know what type of work you want to pursue. Research that field and make sure your portfolio has only your best work pertaining to that field. You need to be confident, but you also need to be ready for rejection. Be persistent. I like calling the people I'll be sending examples to first, so they'll be expecting them. Whenever meeting with people, be very professional and confident. Listen very closely; job opportunities may come up in your everyday conversations.

Portia Rollings, Scientific Assistant, American Museum of Natural History, New York

Rollings is a 1995 graduate from the UCSC program. "I seem to have come into scientific illustration from left field," jokes Rollings. "As an undergraduate, I majored in English and psychology. I did start out in pre-med and did a fair amount of artwork on my own. After school, I was the manager for a home for women with Alzheimer's, then a veterinary technician. Both satisfied my interest in medicine, the latter in particular."

Eventually Rollings realized that she wanted to pursue her interests in illustration. "Later I found I was attracted to paleo-illustration—reconstruction in particular," she recalls. "I guess that is because I can use all of my experiences to help tell the story of an animal that had once existed, thus simultaneously satisfying my artistic side, my English-major-storytelling side, and my scientific side."

> *What practical advice would you give on how to prepare and market oneself for a career in science illustration?*
>
> I can only give advice for getting a staff position since freelancing is not my primary source of income at the moment. It seems to me that the order of importance is one, your portfolio; two, your interview; and three, your resume. I would say to be sure to include in your portfolio exactly what you want to do; then you are sure to end up with the job you want.
>
> In your interview do not point out your weaknesses. Instead try to come up with answers like: "Since I have knowledge of so many techniques, I can trouble-shoot new problems that may come my way." I also suggest that you look at work that was previously done for that client and try to do something similar, perhaps with an improvement. Your resume helps you get your foot in the door—don't be shy. There are many, many resumes that employers have to sift through.

Richard L. Jones, Freelance Illustrator

Jones studied art in college; in 1985, after graduating from Washington State University with a B.A. in Fine Arts in drawing and painting, he sailed for five years on an oceanographic vessel out of Woods Hole, MA. "This is really where my deep interest in science began," says Jones. "My previous art skills became a way for me to explore the wide variety of things I was learning about the world while at sea."

Jones graduated from the UCSC program in 1996 and completed an internship at National Geographic Magazine in late 1996. After this he started work as an illustrator for West Office Exhibit Design, which is contracted to design exhibits for the California Museum of Science and Industry in Los Angeles. He also co-illustrated a book on native Californians for Heydey Books in Berkeley, CA. Since then, he has continued as a freelancer, seeking and attaining work from a wide variety

Illustration by Richard Jones

of sources, including *Scientific American*, local graduate students, and the California Academy of Sciences.

> *What general advice would you give a person thinking about embarking on a career in science illustration?*
>
> If someone is considering a career in science illustration, I would advise them to quit everything and commit to it full time. Taking classes or workshops is a good idea. Not many periodicals or museums are hiring staff illustrators now, so it really is a freelance

market, which means 40 to 50 percent of an artist's time could be taken up with business dealings. You have to really *want* to do it.

What practical advice would you give on how to market and prepare oneself for a career in science illustration?

There are as many ways to present yourself as there are artists in the marketplace. Presenting your best work, in an attractive, compelling fashion is a start. Interviewing and negotiating skills are the hardest to master. Be honest, and ask a lot of questions about what the client is looking for.

Resources

Professional Society

Guild of Natural Science Illustrators (GNSI). The guild, an international organization of over 1,100 members, started a little over 25 years ago when illustrators scattered throughout the Smithsonian Institution became aware of each other and started to hold meetings. Regional chapters have formed in several areas across the United States. Contact:

Guild of Natural Science Illustrators
PO Box 652
Ben Franklin Station
Washington, DC 20044
Phone and fax: 301-309-1514
gnsihome@his.com

Education and Training

GNSI offers a comprehensive list of scientific illustration courses and books for $7.00 to nonmembers. It lists graduate and undergraduate degree programs, single courses offered during the academic school year, summer-break workshops, and internships, as well as courses in Europe and Canada.

Jobhunting and Networking

For networking, illustrators universally point to GNSI. Most cities have their own artist guilds, and GNSI can help in getting in touch with those. Illustrators find that being in contact with other artists is helpful emotionally as well as practically. The Guild has recently set up a listserv for illustrators to discuss their profession. Email gnsihome@his.com for sign-up instructions.

As far as jobhunting goes, illustrators suggest a mix of informal and formal avenues. Universities have job postings; others get jobs or freelance assignments by meeting with art directors of various organizations, sending out examples, and networking with other illustrators and family and friends. The GNSI newsletter also lists internships, chapter news, and upcoming conferences and workshops.

Some illustrators recommend maintaining contact with research scientists with whom you can discuss projects and network. Still others have found that Web searches are great for stimulating ideas for future projects and for locating contacts.

☐ Medical Illustration

Though closely allied to natural science and biological illustration, medical illustration and imaging concentrates primarily on human biology, and to a lesser extent, veterinary medicine. According to the Association of Medical Illustrators (AMI), "a strong foundation in the basic sciences is necessary to enable the illustrator to understand and conceptualize, for example, complex neurochemical and neuroanatomical relationships." The association also emphasizes strong organizational and computer skills, an ability to visualize relationships in three dimensions, and an aptitude for research and writing.

The most common outlets that employ medical illustrators as staff are medical centers and universities. There are also large medical practice groups, such as those in orthopedics or neurosurgery, that hire medical illustrators, if they do a lot of publishing and teaching. Currently, however, about 60 percent of the medical illustrators in the United States work as freelancers. Their clients are usually book publishers, journal publishers, pharmaceutical companies, and medical professionals.

Many medical illustrators are also employed in dental schools and veterinary medical schools. Others work for medical publishers, pharmaceutical companies, advertising agencies, physicians, or attorneys. Some illustrators specialize in three-dimensional media, creating anatomical models and designing prostheses.

For many people in this field the terminal degree is an M.S. in illustration, although there are a few Ph.D.-level scientists working in the field. Read on for the advice and experience of a medical illustrator and biomedical photographer, both of whom first started their careers studying science.

One-on-One with Medical Illustrators

Martha "Kit" Hefner, Medical Illustrator at the State University of New York Health Science Center, Syracuse

"I have always been interested in art," remarks Hefner. "As a child I drew and painted, and loved to color. In high school I had hoped to go to an art school, but my parents had other ideas. I was to get a 'career' first, then I could do anything I wanted because I would always have something to fall back on." She entered college to study for a nursing degree, taking an avid interest in histology. "We had to keep an illustrated lab book of the various slides we had studied, which I had much fun doing." She eventually got a certificate from University Hospital, Ann Arbor, MI in cytotechnology, or cell biology.

After working for four years in this field and now "having a career to fall back on," as she puts it, Hefner returned to undergraduate school at the University of Michigan to study fine art. Four years later Hefner entered the master's program in medical and biological illustration at Michigan.

"Since I really enjoyed working in a hospital environment and loved the science courses, I thought this would be the perfect career to mesh my two interests," she notes. Hefner completed the two-and-a-half-year program in December 1981. "The rest is history. I took a job here in Syracuse right out of school and I've been here since January 1982." She now manages the department, as well as prepares medical illustrations for faculty and staff.

What general advice would you give a person thinking about starting a career in scientific and medical illustration?

Someone about to begin a career in this field needs to have a solid background in biology and anatomy—at an undergraduate level—and very good illustration skills. I'm going from the premise that a person pursuing this career path will do so by attending an accredited graduate program. I think this is a much better educational path to follow, as when graduates interview, employers are often looking for candidates from the accredited schools. This gives the graduate an advantage, to say nothing of the fact that the accredited programs themselves will be better structured and have a lower student:teacher ratio.

In undergraduate studies, concentrate on fine art and the sciences. Drawing and painting courses are important, and photography and design are also recommended. One way of determining if this is truly the career for you would be to attend a workshop in scientific illustration that will touch on the various techniques and methods used by medical illustrators. These are offered through the Guild of Natural Science Illustrators, or various universities may offer a class. Volunteering in a medical-illustration department is also a good way to get a feel for the profession.

What practical advice would you give on how to prepare and market oneself for a career in medical and scientific illustration?

I would highly recommend that one gain experience by pursuing a graduate degree in a medical illustration program. There are five accredited schools in the U.S. The intense study involved, the amount of information acquired, techniques learned, and medical knowledge gained through graduate study make this a very good professional investment. I personally feel that because of the intense medical knowledge needed and illustration techniques peculiar to medical illustration taught in these programs, this is the best route to take. This has become a rather competitive field and going through a graduate program definitely gives a person an edge when seeking a job.

A person also has to have a well-designed resume and a very good portfolio. The portfolio needs to demonstrate excellent illustration skills as well as anatomical accuracy. This is what separates a medical illustrator from an illustrator: their vast medical knowledge of anatomy and the ability to represent this in their illustrations.

James E. Hayden, RBP, Biomedical and Scientific Photographer, President and Owner of Bio-Graphics, Lansdowne, PA

Hayden received his B.S. in biology and biophotography in 1983 from Quinnipiac College in Hamden, CT. "My motivation for creating my undergraduate double major stems from applying my early interest in photography to my life-long fascination with biology," notes Hayden.

After graduation and a short stint at Chesebrough-Pond Inc. in Trumbull, CT, as a photographic analyst, he took a permanent position as an electron-microscopy technician at the University of Pennsylvania School of Veterinary Medicine in 1984. After a few years he was promoted to research specialist. He held that position until 1995, when he became a full-time biophotographic consultant, devoting all of his time to Bio-Graphics, his then-eight-year-old independent business.

"Throughout my education and career, I've always described myself as a generalist, although I work in a specialized field of photography," says Hayden. "It is the variety of the subject matter, clients, and photographic techniques, as well as being able to market and run my own business that I find stimulating." Hayden concentrates on scientific photog-

Comparison of blue light sensitivity in *Arabidopsis thaliana*, proving the existence of a blue-light photoreceptor in plants. Photograph by James Hayden/Bio-Graphics.

raphy, graphics, and imaging for publication and presentations, along with image analysis, forensic documentation, and legal photography. He is also extremely active in the Biological Communications Association (BCA), the main professional society for scientific photographers.

What general advice would you give a person thinking about embarking on a career in medical and scientific imaging and illustration?
Personally I think that coming at this field with a science back-

ground is a better way to go than from a strictly fine-arts training. My scientific training helps me to understand what my technically sophisticated audiences need. I understand the subject matter and can bring marketing and imaging skills to a project. I try to combine the aesthetic and the scientific in a way that is both appealing to the eye and technically accurate.

But, actual jobs in this area are few and far between. When there are cuts in budgets at healthcare organizations, the biomedical photography departments are usually the first to go, but medical photography isn't the only area in which photographers and illustrators can work and use their skills. Many of the people in the field work only with the clinical aspects and do not see the need in the research fields, especially in other natural science areas such as botany. They tend to think in terms of medical photography and not biological imaging, which covers a broader field of subject matter and allows for a wider interpretation of imaging techniques that include computer-based capture and manipulation. The majority of scientific papers written are from basic researchers, not clinicians, and they need the graphic support we can provide.

Hospitals are not the only place where scientific photography is used. Research universities and pharmaceutical and biotech firms also need these types of images. Also, stock photo houses need work and the legal field can be interesting. Forensic techniques apply to materials and crime scenes, not just bodies.

Many people in this field start out as freelancers, so a flexible, nonconventional attitude towards the craft as well as potential clients from the outset also helps.

What practical advice would you give on how to prepare and market oneself for a career in medical and scientific imaging and illustration?

First, start amassing your portfolio. Start it on your own time. This way you can gradually make the transition into a full-time position, or at least become more competitive for one. Keep multiple copies and records of your work. Remember to include examples from work and hobbies to show your range.

Join the BCA certification program. It can take up to five years, but you can go at your own pace. It helps you amass items for your portfolio and forces you to network to get access to subject matter and special equipment. Some of this might end up in freelance work for you. The program also offers training seminars at BCA annual meetings, another venue to learn new skills and network. The certification program forces you to learn a wide variety of new techniques, and to perform them at a professional level. A side effect of accomplishing this is that you must network with your professional peers to gain access to the needed materials. A second

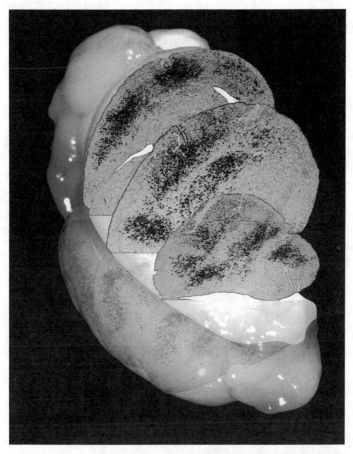

Digital composite of a mouse brain illustrating the distribution of corrected neurons after gene therapy to treat a genetically inherited cell-storage disease. Photograph by James Hayden/Bio-Graphics.

side effect is that you wind up with a nice portfolio to help in your future efforts.

Resources

Professional Societies

Association of Medical Illustrators (AMI). AMI formed in 1945 to promote excellence within the field of medical illustration. In conjunction with the Health Sciences Communications Association and the Association of

Biomedical Communications Directors, AMI publishes the academic journal *The Journal of Biocommunications* four times a year. Contact:

Association of Medical Illustrators
1819 Peachtree St. N.E., Suite 620
Atlanta, GA 30309
404-350-7900
Fax: 404-351-3348
aasnhq@atl.mindspring.com
http://Medical-Illustrators.org

Biological Communications Association (BCA). Mainly photographers with a fine-arts background belong to this over-65-year-old society, with 80 percent working in hospital and medical-center departments of biomedical communications. BCA publishes the *Journal of Biological Photography* and *BPA News.* Contact:

Biological Communications Association
1819 Peachtree St., Suite 620
Atlanta, GA 30309
404-351-6300
Fax: 404-351-3348
assnhq@mindspring.com
http://www.thebpa.org

Health Sciences Communication Association (HSCA). HSCA is the professional society for those communicating health-sciences information to a variety of audiences. Contact:

Health Sciences Communication Association
One Wedgewood Drive, Suite 28
Jewett City, CT 06351
860-376-5915
Fax: 860-376-6621
hescaone@aol.com

Education and Training

According to AMI, most medical illustrators in the United States and Canada have a master's degree from one of six accredited programs. They are located at: the Medical College of Georgia, University of Illinois at Chicago, the Johns Hopkins School of Medicine, University of

Michigan, University of Texas Southwestern Medical Center at Dallas, and the University of Toronto. These programs generally accept from 3 to 12 students each year. Requirements vary but all students have some training in both art and science. Contact AMI directly or visit its Web site for more information on the programs. In addition, the association also offers summer internships, scholarships, and continuing education workshops.

BCA sponsors a certification program in biological imaging and photography, as well as runs workshops and seminars at its annual meeting. BCA members also open up their facilities to budding biophotographers for internships and midcareer exchanges. The society maintains a list of volunteer counselors who are available to answer questions about the profession. Contact BCA directly or visit its Web site for more information on these programs.

HSCA sponsors workshops and seminars at its annual meetings.

The Rochester Institute of Technology (RIT) sponsors a B.S. degree in biophotography, one of the few dedicated programs of its type in the United States. RIT and BCA also hold an intensive, week-long workshop each summer for those just entering the field as well as for midcareer continuing education. For more information on RIT contact:

Michael Peres
Rochester Institute of Photography
70 Lomb Memorial Drive
Rochester, NY 14623
716-475-2775
Fax: 716-475-5804
mrppph@rit.edu

Jobhunting and Networking

According to AMI, because the number of medical illustrators who graduate each year is low and because medical research is growing by leaps and bounds, the employment outlook is generally good. AMI regularly sends job notices to all members, as well as offers a job placement and resume service at their annual meeting and throughout the year. Every two years, the association publishes the AMI Sourcebook, a full-color book featuring examples from over 150 freelance medical and scientific illustrators and photographers. AMI's Web site also includes links to members' home pages.

BCA maintains a 24-hour job hotline to help members locate jobs. Call 770-717-4968. Hayden mentions that at BCA annual meetings, there is a bulletin board where resumes and job announcements are posted, but that "word-of-mouth activity at the meeting is mostly responsible for getting the word out about jobs." Occasionally jobs are listed in BCA publications, but there is a problem with time lag. He notes that more and more career information is being posted to the BCA Web site all the time. Hayden adds that there is little assistance for freelance activities, and that he is one of the few BCA members completely on his own.

Science and Technical Writing, Editing, and Publishing

Science communication is an area that has become more attractive as a career for science-trained individuals. "I teach a science writing course nearly every semester, and science students weighing a career change sometimes make up half the class," notes Sharon Dunwoody, a professor of journalism at the University of Wisconsin, Madison. "I even get the occasional scientist, who usually participates in a nondegree capacity."

There's an incredible diversity of career paths for scientists who have a way with words and an eye for detail. It's hard to draw clear distinctions between some areas of science writing and editing, especially over the course of an entire career. Most of those scientists and engineers now employed in writing, editing, and/or publishing, work or have worked in these areas:

- science writing and journalism,
- public affairs and information,
- journal and magazine editing and publishing,
- book editing and publishing,
- other areas, including technical writing and editing, marketing communications, and grant writing.

People making midcareer changes can be found in all kinds of university courses and programs these days, Dunwoody and others note. A Ph.D. in science is useful, although not essential, for a career in science writing or editing, they say. "In my [previous] job at the journal *The*

**CHARACTERISTICS OF A SWITCH TO A CAREER
IN WRITING, EDITING, AND PUBLISHING**

These attributes may not strike every reader the same way. Depending on your background and interests, you may view some of these as either attractive or unappealing.

- You could work in a variety of settings and capacities, and with people from diverse professions and backgrounds.
- You must be comfortable communicating about science broadly rather than in depth.
- It's a one-way move.
- Many in the field are self-employed, with its concomitant ups and downs.
- There's a competitive job market in most areas.
- You must be a quick study.
- Most scientist-writers, -editors, and -publishers have had a life-long interest in writing, books, words, and language.
- A background in science is not essential, but helpful in many instances.
- Many in the field say one major satisfaction is the tangible final product, whether it's a book, article, or issue of a publication.

Plant Cell, my scientific background was absolutely essential for asking the kinds of questions that would result in a story of interest to a scientifically sophisticated audience," says Rebecca Chasan, editor of the journal *BioScience.* "And it is essential now in giving me a sense of how to edit articles for the *BioScience* audience."

Many scientists probably never look back on their science writing or publishing career choice with regret, but there are trade-offs. One obvious one, notes Chasan and others, is that for most people, a career in science writing or editing effectively cuts off a career in research. "But this is not necessarily a bad thing," she adds. "Someone who really wanted to pursue a single research area in depth probably wouldn't want to specialize in the communication of a broad array of scientific findings. But science writers and editors clearly do stay connected to research by virtue of what their jobs entail, although their connection is broad rather than deep."

☐ Science Writing and Journalism

Increasingly, people with scientific training are entering the field of science reporting and writing. They work for a variety of outlets and in many different capacities, including television and radio broadcasting, daily newspapers, magazines, trade journals and magazines, news sections of scientific journals, Web sites, corporate publications, government agencies, and university publications. Many are freelancers, while a majority hold salaried positions.

"Of those scientists or science students interested in science writing whom I encounter, some come for entire degrees, others for a course or two," notes Dunwoody. "A few others get into the field through a more experiential door—American Association for the Advancement of Science [AAAS] internships, for instance. Science writing programs increasingly cater to science-educated individuals. Some, in fact, limit their applications to science majors (the University of California, Santa Cruz, for instance). But others, like the one at Wisconsin, accepts potential science writing professionals from any type of background."

Advice for beginning science writers can be found on the National Association of Science Writers (NASW) listserv (http://www.nasw.org/advice/htm). It contains frank advice and examines how to break into the field of science writing; training programs and philosophies; making the transition from scientist to science writer; and the perceived difference between science journalism and science writing. For first-hand accounts of scientists who became science journalists, read AAAS's NextWave (http://www.nextwave.org).

One-on-One with Science Writers

Laura Lane, Reporter at the Arlington Morning News, *Arlington, TX*

Lane received her M.S. in biology from Stanford University in 1997. "I had always had an interest in journalism but either never made time or never had time to try it," she recalls. "When I arrived at Stanford, I decided to try writing a few articles for the *Stanford Daily*'s science section. I found that I really enjoyed it and it was very gratifying to see my work in print."

After a summer of intense laboratory research, Lane decided that she didn't want to do bench research for the rest of her life. A couple of months later, she obtained the position of science editor at the *Stanford Daily*. "My experiences as editor confirmed to me that science journalism was it."

She worked at the *Dallas Morning News* during the summer of 1997 as a Kaiser Family Foundation Fellow. Here she wrote about public health and medical research. "I find that my background in biology is really helpful in discriminating between newsworthy stories and those that aren't," she says. "In addition, being trained to analyze data has been helpful in finding news that is not immediately apparent. Most helpful, however, has been my experience in journalism, such as familiarity with the jargon, how to interview, and a newspaper style of writing."

What general advice would you give a person thinking about embarking on a career in science writing?

I think that I was able to get my foot in the door as quickly as I did because I was enthusiastic. I know that that doesn't sound very tangible, but I think that employers appreciate it. What I've learned is that you've got to do what you want to do. Then, success follows. But, definitely get experience at your school newspaper. Investigate the fellowships and programs available. It takes a lot of work to get started; sometimes it's a little discouraging, but if it's really what you want to do, it's worth it.

What practical advice would you give on how to prepare and market oneself for a career in science writing?

I definitely recommend taking journalism classes, to learn the vocabulary and the style. The writing style is vastly different from academic writing. I took one journalism class on news writing and reporting and am finding that it was helpful. Also, try teaching a beginner class in your own subject area. This may help you to learn how to explain something that you might think of as obvious. That's one of the most important things you have to learn. Again, before actually entering the business, get experience. For example, many local papers welcome interns, and many of the institutes at the NIH have writing internships.

Ricki Lewis, Freelance Science Writer and College Life Science Textbook Author

Lewis received her Ph.D. in genetics from Indiana University, Bloomington in 1980. "I have very little formal training in journalism, just one graduate course I took when I grew tired of working with flies with legs grow-·ing out of their heads," says Lewis. "I've always enjoyed writing, but was drawn to it anew in grad school when I found the Ph.D. program and the world of science becoming progressively narrower. First I knew biologists, then geneticists, then developmental geneticists, then developmental geneticists working on flies. I felt the walls caving in, and that journalism course, with students and guest lecturers from many disciplines, was a breath of fresh air. I was hooked."

Lewis primarily writes college biology textbooks (general biology, human genetics, and anatomy and physiology) as well as news articles for such publications as *Science, Genetic Engineering News, BioScience,* and *The Scientist.* "I do need the depth of knowledge and the ability to ask good questions that my Ph.D. training provided," she notes. "For example, if someone I was interviewing mentioned reverse transcriptase, or signal transduction, or apoptosis, I wouldn't need to look it up or ask for a definition. What getting a Ph.D. teaches you is how to keep on learning, how to retain what you learn, and how to connect ideas."

One drawback to the freelancing life, she says, is that it gets lonely. "I see my editors only a few times a year. I imagine that no one uses my books, when actually thousands of college students probably hate my guts. But a major benefit has been that I work at home, which was wonderful when my kids were very little. If one of them had a strep throat, I didn't have to answer to anybody."

What general advice would you give a person thinking about embarking on a career in science writing?

Try writing an opinion piece for a local newspaper. I did this for years. It is fun, and you can try out different writing styles and topics, and accumulate a clip file. Realize that your first few assignments, and maybe more than a few, will be "on speculation," which means that you do the work and then the editor decides whether it will be published. It sounds unfair, but unless you're Isaac Asimov, you have to pay your dues.

Stop writing in the passive voice. It took many patient editors to finally get through my thick skull how to write in the active voice. Taking a journalism course would be enormously helpful. I wish I'd taken more.

What practical advice would you give on how to prepare and market oneself for a career in science writing?

Emphasize your technical background—degrees, research interests—but also show that you've done things that relate to everyday people. For example, while in grad school, I wrote a column on interesting animal facts for the student newspaper, then wrote for real newspapers and magazines. Show that you are eclectic, adaptable, and have diverse interests. Stress that your Ph.D. taught you how to learn. Earning a Ph.D., and especially writing that dissertation, gives a scientist excellent researching tools.

Katy Human, Science Journalist with the Boulder Camera, Boulder, CO

"While I was studying for my Ph.D. at Stanford University, no month went by when I wasn't considering some other option," recalls Human. Environmental and science education at an outdoor school in Vermont, working as a naturalist in a National Park, teaching at a small liberal arts college, and a career in writing were all possibilities, she says. "I've always enjoyed writing. I remember feigning disgust at the numbers of papers we had to write in college. In truth, I loved it. I loved the research, and I loved the writing."

A few years into her Ph.D. program, she attended the AAAS Mass Media program, which led to an internship at the *Dallas Morning News* during the summer of 1995. She returned to Stanford to finish her Ph.D. in ecology in 1996, after which she worked as an editor for the magazine *Earth*. Most recently she moved to the *Boulder Camera*.

"At the *Camera*, I write stories for the weekly science/environment section of the paper, the local section, and often the front page. I write six to seven stories a week, many of them relatively long. I make *lots* of phone calls, visit researchers in their labs or in the field when I can, and shuffle through faxes and mail for story ideas. Having a science background helps make it easier to know what sorts of questions to ask. On the other hand, someone without science training might have a better perspective on some issues. Sometimes I forget to ask why a project is important enough to merit the tax dollars spent on it, because I love science and find it intriguing without the justifications many folks need."

She says that the skills needed for her job include an ability to adjust your questioning style to fit the need of the interviewee: "Sometimes it works to be aggressive and to play up your scientific background. Other times, you have to do more quiet listening, and ask subtly probing questions."

What general advice would you give a person thinking about embarking on a career in science writing?

I found the skills I used in teaching particularly useful in writing. Teaching takes a great deal of patient, careful, and clear explaining. I volunteered weekly at an elementary school in East Palo Alto, another experience in which I learned some great simplifying skills useful in writing. To gain the attention of fourth graders, you need to be simple, fun, and brief.

Volunteer to write for your university's paper or for the press office. At Stanford, the student paper had a "science bug" column. Students wrote in silly science questions (or the columnist made them up) and someone searched out the answers. I never did this, but friends of mine did, and they had a blast. This would be a good way to test out the water, to see if you're really interested in writing for a general audience.

What practical advice would you give on how to prepare and market oneself for a career in science writing?

Get experience. The AAAS Mass Media program is excellent. These types of programs help you network and introduce you to the key players in the field, as well as future employers. But you can do a lot of this on your own, too. Search for other fellowships. Most newspapers take interns every year. Find out what newspapers (or other types of publications you are interested in) cover science well, find out who the editor is, and write or call that person. Or call reporters directly. Ask for advise on getting an "in."

During my last year of grad school, I spent Christmas in Minneapolis. I called Jim Dawson, science reporter at the *Tribune* (I'd never met him before) and asked if he'd have time for coffee. We had a wonderful conversation, and he gave me some great ideas for networking. I also attended the AAAS and NASW annual meeting and talked with all sorts of people there. I visited my parents in DC and met up with John Travis at *Science News*, to find out about their internship program. I went to another meeting, the Council for Advancement of Science Writing, and networked more. Talk talk talk. Talk with people until your throat hurts!

Jim Kling, Freelance Science Writer

Kling received his M.S. in chemistry from Indiana University in 1996. "I started out with the intent of becoming a professor of chemistry, to pursue academic research," he recalls. "After getting my B.S. in chemistry, I worked at the pharmaceutical company Eli Lilly to get a feel for life and chemistry in 'the real world.' After about two years there, I went to graduate school at Indiana University to pursue a Ph.D. in organic chemistry. Along the way, I gradually realized that I had very little talent for laboratory research: I was much more comfortable reading scientific articles, taking classes, and doing 'chalkboard' chemistry, as opposed to actual lab work, with its accompanying frustration and broken glassware. I had a natural talent for writing, and I enjoyed reading about science from all disciplines, so it finally dawned on me to consider writing about science."

At the start of his transition to science writing, Kling wrote a few science columns for a local arts and entertainment magazine, and then was accepted for a six-month internship in the public relations office of the Cancer Research Institute in New York, prompting him to leave school with a master's degree. He has been freelancing since 1996 and is published in a wide range of publications including *Science*, *Nature*, *Biotechnology*, *The Scientist*, and *Inc.*

> *What general advice would you give a person thinking about embarking on a career in science writing?*
> The most crucial skill is to have a knack for quickly picking up an unfamiliar scientific field. You must be able to listen to sources and pick out the important points. Determining what is truly a

significant advance in a scientific field that is new to you is a true challenge, best met by calling several unconnected sources to confirm the legitimacy of a new study. It's really an art form. In the search for story ideas, you really have to be open-minded, taking in press releases, story tips, and news, and sifting through it all.

Read articles from wide-ranging journals, such as *Science, Nature,* and the *Proceedings of the National Academy of Sciences.* That will teach you to broaden your approach to science—many scientists would struggle as science writers because they want to remain focused on their field of training. That's fine if you can land a staff job at a trade magazine that focuses on your specific field, but otherwise can be tough.

Within your training, challenge yourself. You have an advantage if you did your training at a top graduate school. My own organic chemistry classes at Indiana University were very intense, and though I have yet to write about organic chemistry, the difficult reading and the intellectual exercise of mastering the fundamental principles of chemistry were a great training ground for what I do.

What practical advice would you give on how to prepare and market oneself for a career in science writing?

Don't just tell yourself: "I can do it!" Go out and write. Publish in the local newspaper or "street-corner" magazine to refine your skills. Then don't be bashful: send your resume and those clips to managing editors at science magazines that catch your interest. But don't be surprised if only 1 in 10 (or fewer) of them answer your note. When you get interest from a magazine, work hard to find a story, and then ace it. If an editor gets one good piece from you, he or she will ask for more, and you'll be on your way.

Classes may be good for some, but I never felt them necessary. Volunteering is great—it's essentially what you're doing when you write for the local newspaper or tiny magazine, since they rarely pay. You might also do work for a local museum, university public relations office, or a science-education initiative.

Resources

Professional Societies

National Association of Science Writers (NASW). The largest professional society for freelance and employee science writers of newspapers, wire services, magazines, broadcast outlets, and trade publications. Its membership also includes science writers and public information officers working at universities, in government agencies, and in some companies. Its mission is to "foster the dissemination of accurate information regarding science through all media normally devoted to informing the public." Contact:

National Association of Science Writers
PO Box 294
Greenlawn, NY 11740
516-757-5664
Fax: 516-757-0069
diane@nasw.org
http://www.nasw.org

Society of Environmental Journalists (SEJ). SEJ's membership includes more than 1,100 freelance and employee journalists at newspapers, television and radio stations, broadcast and cable networks, magazines, newsletters, wire services, and photo agencies, as well as educators and students, whose job is to inform the public about environmental issues. Contact:

Society of Environmental Journalists
PO Box 27280
Philadelphia, PA 19118
215-836-9970, 215-836-9972
sejoffice@aol.com
http://www.sej.org

American Medical Writers Association (AMWA). AMWA is the largest professional society representing biomedical communicators. It has more than 4,000 members in 24 countries. Providing professional education to members is one of the society's main goals. Contact:

American Medical Writers Association
9650 Rockville Pike
Bethesda, MD 20814-3998
301-493-0003
http://www.amwa.org/amwa

Council for the Advancement of Science Writing (CASW). CASW is a nonprofit educational corporation managed by science journalists and scientists. Since 1959, according to its brochure, the council has been working to "improve the public's understanding of science and technology by conducting programs designed to enhance the quality of science and medical reporting and writing, and to improve relationships between scientists and the press." Contact:

Council for the Advancement of Science Writing
PO Box 404
Greenlawn, NY 11740
516-757-5664

International Federation of Environmental Journalists (IFEJ). IFEJ, started in 1993, is a sister organization to SEJ, with many of the same goals and ideals. It presently has about 70 members from 25 countries. Contact:

International Federation of Environmental Journalists
14, Rue de la Pierre Levee
75011 Paris
France
011-33-14805-4607
Fax: 011-33-14923-9149
m.schweres@oln.comlink.apc.org
http://www.sej.org/ifej.htm

Association of British Science Writers (ABSW). According to the ABSW's Web site, the group "exists to help those who write about science and technology and to improve the standard of science journalism in the United Kingdom." Its members include print and broadcast journalists, authors, scriptwriters and producers, and others active in the field of communicating science and technology. Contact:

Association of British Science Writers
c/o British Association
23 Savile Row
London W1X 2NB
United Kingdom
absw@absw.demon.co.uk
http://193.54.210.193/eusja/writer.htm

European Union of Science Journalists' Associations (EUSJA). EUSJA is the umbrella organization for science journalist professional societies located in European countries. For example, ABSW is a member organization. Contact:

European Union of Science Journalists' Associations
Nina Morgan, *EUSJA News* editor
Rose Cottage
East End
Chadlington, Oxon OX7 3LX
United Kingdom

Phone and Fax: 011-44-1698-676530
michael.kenward@dial.pipex.com
http://193.54.210.193/eusja/

Canadian Science Writer's Association (CSWA). CSWA is comprised of nearly 275 members that include science and technology media professionals, communications officers, and technical writers and editors. Contact:

Canadian Science Writer's Association
40 Alexander St., Suite 1111
Toronto, Ontario
M4Y 1B5, Canada
416-928-9624
Fax: 416-924-6715
cswa@interlog.com
http://www.interlog.com/~cswa/

Editorial Freelancers Association (EFA). EFA is a professional organization of self-employed writers, editors, indexers, proofreaders, researchers, desktop publishers, translators, and others who work in the publishing and communications industries. Members are drawn from a variety of specialties, including science, medicine, and technology. Contact:

Editorial Freelancers Association
71 West 23 St., Suite 1504
New York, NY 10010
212-929-5400
Fax: 212-929-5439
http://www.the-efa.org

American Society of Journalists and Authors (ASJA). According to ASJA's Web site, the society is the "leading organization of independent nonfiction writers. The society includes more than 1,000 leading freelance writers of magazine articles, trade books, and other forms of nonfiction writing who have met ASJA's exacting standards of professional achievement." Contact:

American Society of Journalists and Authors
1501 Broadway, Suite 302
New York, NY 10036
212-997-0947
Fax: 212-768-7414
asja@compuserve.com
http://www.asja.org/

National Writers Union (NWU). NWU is a trade organization for freelance writers. Contact:

National Writers Union
National Office East
113 University Place, 6th Fl.
New York, NY 10003
212-254-0279
Fax: 212-254-0673
nwu@nwu.org
http://www.nwu.org

National Writers Union
National Office West
337 17th St., #101
Oakland, CA 94612
510-839-0110
Fax: 510-839-6097
nwu@nwu.org
http://www.nwu.org

Education and Training

In 1996, the University of Wisconsin, Madison Center for Environmental Communications and Education Studies published the *Directory of Science Communications Courses and Programs in the United States.* Disk or hard copy versions are available for $10.00. Contact:

Sharon Dunwoody
School of Journalism and Mass Communication
University of Wisconsin, Madison
821 University Avenue
Madison, WI 53706
dunwoody@facstaff.wisc.edu

AAAS's NextWave (http://www.nextwave.org) section on science-writing careers contains lengthy descriptions of four programs: the Johns Hopkins University; University of California, Santa Cruz; New York University; and Boston University.

NASW coordinates a mentors program at the annual AAAS meeting and maintains a listing of fellowships and workshops for journalists and internships for students. The association also holds career-development and issues-oriented workshops for members at its annual meeting, which is held in conjunction with the AAAS annual meeting. Descriptions of all these programs can be found on its Web site.

AMWA also sponsors workshops and continuing-education programs in biomedical communication at its annual meetings. The same is true for most of the other science-writing professional societies listed above.

Jobhunting and Networking

Most professional societies publish job listings, as well as links to on-line resources on careers, on their Web sites. Many also maintain listservs, on which members discuss professional issues.

NASW maintains a jobs email list for members to be notified of immediate job and freelance openings. The NASW Web site also contains an archive of publications that continually seek freelance material and an archive of individual jobs advertised through the mailing list. AMWA publishes the "Job Market Sheet" nine times a year, which lists available positions.

The NewsWise Web site (http://www.newswise.com/), a database of news releases from scientific, medical, and business research institutions, maintains a guide to more than 90 awards, grants, and fellowships for science reporters. It includes a description, and deadline and contact information.

☐ Public Affairs And Information

Another link in the chain of communicating scientific findings to a broader audience is a set of professionals known by many names: public affairs or information officers, press officers, and media relations or external affairs specialists, for example. They work in the public affairs and press offices at universities, medical centers, federal and state agencies, private companies, advocacy groups, think tanks, and professional societies. Via news releases and press conferences, tipsheets, alumni magazine articles, Web sites, and personal contact, public information officers (PIOs), a common collective term, are the conduit for researchers, policymakers, and other officials to reach journalists and the public with information about scientific discoveries.

Many in the field say a detailed understanding of the needs of both scientists and journalists is important. A scientific background isn't essential, but helps in appreciating the culture of the research community and the process of scientific discovery. For a PIO at a research center, scientific training is helpful in understanding the larger relevancy of the findings of a scientific study. Skills of diplomacy and negotiation are also required in some media liaison positions, especially when dealing with controversial and emotionally charged subjects like misconduct cases or AIDS research.

One-on-One with Public Information and Relations Specialists

Lynne Friedmann, Public Relations Consultant and Freelance Science Writer, Friedmann Communications, Solana Beach, CA

Friedmann has a B.A. in journalism with a minor in biology from California State University, Long Beach. Her first job after graduation was with a public relations agency whose client base was exclusively high-technology and biotechnology companies. After that she worked for several years as public information representative for the Developmental Biology Center at the University of California, Irvine. For the past 10 years, she has had her own science and technology communications business, representing such clients as biotechnology companies, university and nonprofit research institutions, scientific professional associations, science museums, environmental organizations, and zoological parks. "What all my clients have in common is some thread of science," says Friedmann. She provides a variety of services: science writing and editing; media training; writing press releases, feature articles, annual reports, and newsletters; handling conference support and crisis communications; and organizing news conferences.

Besides being a strong writer, she says that another important skill needed for her line of work is the ability to manage several projects simultaneously, along with good phone and people skills. "Increasingly, strong computer and Internet skills are a must," she adds.

"The biggest benefit to this kind of work is the variety of cutting-edge science that I'm literally paid to learn," says Friedmann. "The biggest challenges are working at home, which can create a sense of isolation, and working without a steady paycheck, which can create cash flow problems if I don't budget properly. I'm covered by my husband's insurance, but when I was single, finding an affordable healthcare plan was a headache."

> *What general advice would you give a person thinking about embarking on a career in science communications?*
> Scientific training is helpful because it teaches you how to ask

good questions and present information in a logical sequence. Unfortunately, scientists are taught to write in a scholarly fashion following hard-and-fast rules that have been culturally transmitted over three centuries. Getting scientists to switch from passive to active writing is the biggest challenge. I advise against quitting your job and embarking on a formal writing degree program, but instead taking selected classes to hone writing and reporting skills. Volunteering through professional societies, museums, environmental groups, or a favorite charity is an excellent way to gain real-world experience and amass the clips that prospective employers will ask to see.

What practical advice would you give on how to prepare and market oneself for a career in science communications?

Employers want to see evidence of strong writing skills. Work samples or published clips are a requirement before anyone will take you seriously.

Having a science background is a big advantage in working with science- and technology-based companies and organizations because you can hit the ground running. That training also provides a measure of credibility with the scientists with whom you work. Because science is advancing so rapidly, you're constantly reading to keep current. You have to manage employer and client expectations that you are an instant expert in every field of science.

Hal Kibbey, Writer, Indiana University, Bloomington Office of Communications and Marketing

Kibbey received a B.A. in physics from Cornell University in 1965 and an M.A. in the history and philosophy of science from Indiana University, Bloomington in 1969. He has also taken several courses in science writing from the Indiana University School of Journalism. "I decided to become a science writer when I discovered there was such a thing," recalls Kibbey. "I saw a position listed in Indiana University's weekly notice of job openings. I had already decided that I enjoyed science but didn't want to be a scientist or a scholar of any sort, though I had done well enough in both. I wanted to be a writer of some sort, but had no idea how to go about it." Additionally, growing up in a university family influenced his decision to want to work and live in a university community. (Kibbey's father was a mathematician and dean of research at Syracuse University.)

"Being a science writer for a university news service seemed to be the perfect solution, so I took the journalism courses that I was told I needed and did very well," he recalls. "I decided that I wanted to live in Bloomington, Indiana, so I went after the only job in town, the position of science writer at the Indiana University News Bureau," a position that he has held since 1979.

He says his job requires the ability to write simply and clearly about discoveries made by scientists in the physical and life sciences. "My training in physics makes it easy for me to understand the basic ideas involved in any such discovery, and the scientist doesn't have to spend a lot of time explaining terms and concepts to me," he says. "At the other end of my job, I need to be able to talk on the telephone easily with journalists, which means understanding their requirements and working conditions (the importance of deadlines, for example) and being able to choose the best way to present the scientific discovery. I need to be able to quickly interest a journalist in the story and then to answer whatever questions he or she may have about it."

Kibbey says he sees himself as a liaison between scientists and the media, requiring him to be on good terms with both sides. "Showing respect for the values and priorities of both sides is essential for doing that," he says.

> *What general advice would you give a person thinking about embarking on a career in science communications?*
>
> When a person trained as a scientist becomes a science writer, his or her knowledge of how scientists do their work is a big asset. It's much easier to interview a scientist when you know how the scientific method works, why the results of a pilot project with only a few subjects must be treated with great caution, and why scientists often announce findings that contradict what was previously considered established fact. On the other hand, scientific training seldom involves the sort of people skills that are needed by a writer to obtain cooperation from scientists and to gain the attention and interest of journalists and editors.
>
> *What practical advice would you give on how to prepare and market oneself for a career in science communications?*
>
> I was told at the beginning that an intermediate-level journalism course in basic news reporting was absolutely essential if I was to become a science writer, and I'm inclined to agree with that. My journalism classes in freelance writing and science writing also helped me to eventually get the job I have now: my class assignments were published as articles in the student newspaper, and thus provided me with essential clips.
>
> Obviously, to be a professional writer of any kind you have to be able to write. Internships are valuable if you can get them. I didn't have one because they didn't exist then, but when my office began taking interns, I worked with several of them. They were bright students, and I taught them as much as I could and enjoyed doing it.

Linda Sage, Associate Director for Research Communications, Washington University School of Medicine, St. Louis

Sage received her Ph.D. in biochemistry from the University of Leicester, England, in 1965. After a postdoctoral fellowship in the same department, she moved to the United States, where she left academia and raised two children. "During that time, I became a freelance writer, combining my interests in science and writing," says Sage. "I wrote for magazines and newspapers and also wrote a book, *Pigment of the Imagination: A History of Phytochrome Research*, which was published by Academic Press in 1992. My only formal training in journalism or writing was a few evening classes."

Sage took a job as a grant writer at a research institute in 1993 and joined the public affairs staff of Washington University at the end of 1994. She now writes and edits news releases and magazine articles about the faculty's research and interacts with national and local reporters.

> *What general advice would you give a person thinking about embarking on a career in science communications?*
>
> When we hire new science writers for our office, we look for good writing skills, a science background, a knowledge of journalism, and a pleasant personality. We find that two skills are very important: the ability to interview a faculty member and quickly grasp the details of his or her research and the ability to translate this information into a format that can be understood by and is interesting to the general public.
>
> *What practical advice would you give on how to prepare and market oneself for a career in science communications?*
>
> I would recommend a master's degree in science writing from a reputable program. If that isn't possible, a would-be writer could get some experience and clips by freelancing locally for a while. It also is helpful to attend workshops such as the Santa Fe Science Writing Workshop held each summer. Joining the National Association of Science Writers and attending its sessions at the AAAS meeting each February also is a good idea.

Stephanie Seiler, Account Supervisor, Investor Relations, Noonan/Russo Communications Inc., New York

Seiler received her Ph.D. in 1995 from the department of microbiology and immunology in the Albert Einstein College of Medicine, Yeshiva University, New York. "Although I enjoyed my research on the proteins involved in muscle development, I started to realize early on in my doctoral program that I might not be happy staying in academia," recalls Seiler.

She cites several reasons for this uneasiness: seeing many bright, capable friends who were working in prestigious labs having problems landing university research positions; seeing those who had already landed jobs unsatisfied, struggling to get grants, and working inordinate amounts of hours just to keep pace; a growing realization that she preferred to view science from a global perspective; and a growing desire to develop a career that would allow her to spend more time with people.

"I saw myself losing the broad view that I love about science," she says. "But I wasn't sure what options might be out there for me."

After finishing her Ph.D., she worked in the lab of one of her committee members at Einstein doing cardiology research. "He was aware of my desire to one day work outside academic research, and this was OK with him," she says. "Again, although I enjoyed the research and the work in his lab, I still wasn't satisfied. After a year, I decided to start in earnest to look for something else. I bounced some ideas regarding careers on Wall Street and related areas around with a friend who had moved from lab research into financial analysis for the biotech industry. He gave my name to a headhunter, who called me the next day." Seiler says she was also influenced by her sister, who received her Ph.D. in biology in the late 1980s and moved into biotech investment analysis in 1994.

She interviewed with Noonan/Russo and eventually started there in late 1996 with the investor relations group, working with large and small biotech firms to communicate their niche in various markets to potential investors. Soon after, she also began writing for the media group, preparing press releases for client companies aimed at investors and business and trade publications, as well as annual reports for smaller companies that do not have their own communications departments.

"I found out that I like the variety that this kind of work offers me," she says. "I've finally found a way to combine my interest and experience in science with my desire to approach science broadly."

> *What general advice would you give a person thinking about embarking on a career in corporate communications?*
>
> I've heard of stories where people look at you as a quitter or a failure if you "leave" research science, but my experience was quite the opposite. Everyone at Einstein knew about my desires and was excited for me. I think people are really starting to see that the job market is bad and that is helping to change attitudes.
>
> In general, if you come to the conclusion that academia or research is not for you, you really need to evaluate your motives. What don't you like about it? Is it lifestyle? Workstyle? Or, some-

thing else, as in my case? I wanted to pursue science more broadly. Understanding your own motivations will help you home in on what it is you do want to do. Just remember that very few decisions are cast in stone. Career change is really a process of self-evaluation.

What practical advice would you give on how to prepare and market oneself for a career in corporate communications?
Some of the skills that I brought with me to the job from my scientific training are attention to detail, that is, how to keep clear notes regarding my work strategy. This helps in project management. I now manage 10 accounts and must keep what I'm working on for each straight.

The ability to be self-critical is also important. I need to be able to gauge what approaches to communicating a company's message are working and which ones aren't.

In graduate school, through journal clubs, seminars, and meeting presentations, I also learned to become comfortable talking with many types of people, as well as how to ask questions. This is helpful to me now because I still have to make presentations. I also have to cold-call members of the financial community to discuss clients.

I'm surprised at the number of applications we get from Ph.D.s. The ones that are the most attractive have a clear objective that corporate communications is what they want to do. They've researched their options. They've talked with people, and in some instances, have begun to educate themselves with a few business courses, although this isn't necessary to land a job. One area that I did not get any training in before taking this job is finance. I'm now taking advantage of Noonan/Russo's tuition reimbursement plan and have taken courses in finance and other investment disciplines in the evening.

You might be more marketable if you have some extracurricular training, but I think more importantly, this communicates to potential employers that you are serious about making a change.

As in setting up a scientific study, evaluate and investigate the area you're interested in—read about it, talk to people already working in that area, surf the Web—before plunging head first into an endeavor.

Resources

Professional Societies

National Association of Science Writers (NASW). The largest professional society for freelance and employee science writers of newspapers, wire services, magazines, broadcast outlets, and trade publications. Its membership also includes science writers and public information officers working at universities, in government agencies, and in some companies. Its mission is to "foster the dissemination of accurate information regarding science through all media normally devoted to informing the public." Contact:

National Association of Science Writers
PO Box 294
Greenlawn, NY 11740
516-757-5664
Fax: 516-757-0069
diane@nasw.org
http://www.nasw.org

Public Relations Society of America (PRSA). PRSA is the largest professional organization for public relations professionals, with over 17,000 members. It represents people in business and industry, counseling firms, government, associations, hospitals, schools, professional service firms, and nonprofit organizations. Specifically, the technology, environment, and health special interest sections are relevant to science communicators. Contact:

Public Relations Society of America
33 Irving Place
New York, NY 10003-2376
212-995-2230
hq@prsa.org
http://prsa.org

Council for the Advancement of Science Writing (CASW). CASW is a nonprofit educational corporation managed by science journalists and scientists. Since 1959, according to its brochure, the council has been working to "improve the public's understanding of science and technology by conducting programs designed to enhance the quality of science and medical reporting and writing, and to improve relationships between scientists and the press." Contact:

Council for the Advancement of Science Writing
PO Box 404
Greenlawn, NY 11740
516-757-5664

Council for the Advancement and Support of Education (CASE). According to its Web site, CASE's members comprise professionals in alumni relations, communications, and philanthropy, which includes alumni administrators, fund-raisers, public relations managers, publications editors, and government relations officers. Contact:

Council for the Advancement and Support of Education
11 Dupont Circle, Suite 400
Washington, DC 20036-1261
202-328-5900
Fax: 202-387-4973
http://www.case.org

Education and Training

PRSA sponsors a mentor program, scholarships, student internships, the Public Relations Student Society of America, and continuing-education workshops at national and local chapter meetings. The society also publishes *Where to Study Public Relations,* which lists academic programs in the United States and Canada.

CASW offers seminars, workshops and continuing education to journalists, as well as fellowships and internships to budding science writers. These are listed on the NASW Web site.

CASE supports communications, fund-raising, and other training workshops throughout the year. They also offer some scholarships to attend such programs.

Jobhunting and Networking

Profnet Hiring Line, a weekly Internet list, describes job opportunities in communications. It includes openings at universities, corporations, and other organizations, and often also lists science writing and editing positions at university news bureaus, newspapers, and professional societies, as well as internships. Profnet is a media Internet service to which thousands of universities, medical centers, and other organizations subscribe. Journalists submit story and source queries to the service.

Subscriptions to Hiring Line are free to ProfNet members, and $26 annually to nonmembers. For more information contact:

Dan Forbush
Profnet, Inc.
100 North Country Road, Suite C
East Setauket, NY 11733
dan_forbush@prnewswire.com

The PRSA General Store, located on the association's Web site, lists several career search and networking publications put out by the society. One of these is *Career Opportunities*, a bimonthly newsletter listing job openings. PRSA also maintains a resume posting service for members.

Regarding networking, many public information officers discuss professional issues on the listserv PIONet, started in 1994 by science writer Roger Johnson, formerly a biochemist. For more information on PIONet, send a brief message to Roger Johnson at rjohnson@newswise. com.

CASE maintains a gopher directory of available jobs searchable by professional area and key words, and places ads from job seekers. *The Chronicle of Higher Education* also lists jobs for public information officers at http://chronicle.merit.edu.

☐ Journal and Magazine Editing and Publishing

It's difficult to generalize about the job situation for scientists in journal editing. Some journals employ part-time editors, while others use volunteers who spend a year or more in editorial positions. Still others use freelancers. Many of these differences depend on a journal's frequency, with weekly and biweekly publications naturally needing more editors. Those run by professional societies tend to operate more on a shoe string, so therefore employ more part-timers and volunteers. Competition for both full- and part-time positions, say editors, is stiff. Many of the senior positions are held by well-established researchers in a given field, so the scope and responsibility of these posts means they are usually not open to less experienced scientists. Freelance editors also find work editing book chapters, monographs, and reviews.

There are literally thousands of scholarly journals in the sciences. Each paper submitted by a scientist to a journal must be reviewed by a panel of peers, edited for grammar and adherence to a journal's style, proofed, and eventually published, usually weekly, biweekly, monthly, or quarterly. Most scientists on staff at a journal do not handle the day-to-day editing for grammar and style, so much as the assessment of a paper's content for the significance of its contribution to a field and its appropriateness for the journal in question. This involves dealing with authors, as well as a group of subject-matter reviewers. Many journal editors also commission authors for reviews and other contemplative pieces that normally appear at the beginning of an issue.

Scientists also head up specialty and trade magazines, which are somewhat different from the peer-reviewed journals in a given field, but nonetheless cater to a specific, usually scientifically trained and savvy audience.

To be successful, however, editors say that one must possess a broad knowledge of their field mixed with an eye for detail. For those that manage other editors and liaise with the production office and authors of a journal article, administrative skills are also important.

One-on-One with Science Editors

Rebecca Chasan, Editor, BioScience, *Washington, DC*

Chasan received her Ph.D. in molecular biology from the University of California, Berkeley in 1991, where she studied the maternal control of early development in the fruit fly. "Although I loved science in general and my graduate project in particular, I began to think about finding an alternative career when I was midway through grad school," she recalls. "I realized that I didn't have a passion for lab work. I also didn't relish the thought of eventually competing for one of the increasingly scarce faculty jobs. I recognized early on in graduate school that I particularly enjoyed presenting scientific findings, both my own and those of others, such as in journal clubs. I liked finding the 'story' that pulled together the facts and questions about a piece of scientific work and placing it in context."

"Strangely, it took me a while to recognize that it might be possible to use my interest in science communication to develop an alternative career! I didn't know any science writers or editors, and I really didn't know what such a career would involve. Finally, after I talked to enough people, a light bulb went on, and I began to think seriously of trying to make a career in science writing and editing. By that time, I was close to finishing up, and in my last year of graduate school I took a class on science writing at UC, Berkeley's School of Journalism."

After finishing her doctorate, she worked as the news and reviews editor of the journal *The Plant Cell* for four and a half years. Feeling a need to move on to a publication that was read by a more diverse audience, she took the job in 1995 as editor of *BioScience*, published by the American Institute of Biological Sciences (http://www.aibs.org). "I do very little writing in this position, but my experience in editing review articles at *The Plant Cell* prepared me well for editing the scientific overview articles that are the core of *BioScience*," she notes.

What general advice would you give a person thinking about embarking on a career in science writing and editing?

One very important skill learned in science training is problem solving, a skill that is critical for just about any career. And I think that in any career involving science, not just careers in writing and editing specifically, communication skills are essential. All scientists develop them to some extent through the process of giving talks and writing papers, but most people could benefit from improved communication skills. Whatever your career, chances are that it will involve persuading or otherwise reaching an audience in some way.

The most important part of my job is evaluating and editing scientific overview articles. I make detailed suggestions to authors about how to improve their presentations so that their articles will attract and engage readers unfamiliar with the field. My job entails a number of skills, some shared with researchers, some different. One is the ability to juggle a number of different tasks, both short and long term, and to solve the inevitable problems that constantly crop up. And, like any researcher, I spend a great deal of time contemplating the significance of scientific findings, although I do so from a much greater distance than a researcher would.

What advice would you give on how to prepare and market oneself for a career in science writing and editing?

You should demonstrate in your interview that you have a real passion for language and for expressing ideas, and your recommendations should attest to your writing and/or editing skills. If you are just switching into this career, it's especially important to come across as someone who very much wants to be involved in science communication.

Although there are many programs in science writing in which you can formally prepare for a career in science writing and editing, more important than having taken many classes in science writing is showing that you have the skills and desire to do this kind of work. Get at least a little experience before applying for a job in this field: take a journalism class or write articles for your university public information department on some interesting research on campus.

Exactly how to retool depends on your ultimate goal. Both volunteering and taking classes are useful approaches for a career in science writing or editing. It's important to focus on what skills you have that you would like to put to use in a new career and then to find a way to develop these skills. Remember that most employers won't hire someone with no experience other than a vague idea that they want to do a new job. You need to show an employer that you will bring solid interest and skills appropriate for the job, even if not extensive experience.

Julie Ann Miller, Editor, Science News, *Washington, DC*

Miller received her Ph.D. in neuroscience at the University of Wisconsin, Madison in 1975. "As I was finishing my scientific training, I decided that I would rather write about science than do research," she recalls. "I was at the University of Wisconsin in Madison, where they had a journalism school program in specialized reporting, which included science writing. I took journalism courses as I was writing my Ph.D. thesis and continued into the next year."

After completing her doctorate and the coursework for an M.S. in journalism, she landed the position of life sciences writer at *Science News*. She spent 10 years as a writer at *Science News*, then went to the Marine Biological Laboratory at Woods Hole, MA, where she was a fellow in their first summer science writing program in 1986. After returning to DC, she became editor of *BioScience*. In 1995 she returned to *Science News* as editor for that magazine.

"My job entails responsibility for the weekly publication of a science magazine," explains Miller. "I guide the writers in their choice of subjects and make decisions regarding the mix and fit of articles in the magazine. I work closely with the writers in editing their work and oversee decisions about art and layout. I also provide general direction for the publication, for example spearheading special efforts such as the 75th anniversary issue and our Web site (http://www.sciencenews.org). I serve as the liaison between the magazine staff and the larger organization, Science Service."

What general advice would you give a person thinking about embarking on a career in science writing and editing?

The general skills one needs to have for this type of career are a wide general knowledge of science, an ability to present ideas logically, the patience to pay attention to details, and the stamina to meet tight deadlines. An editor must have the ability to work closely with writers and an understanding of publishing practices and opportunities.

In turning to science writing, former scientists can draw on their knowledge of science and its special vocabulary. They also have training in thinking about problems logically. Moreover, they have inside information on how research is done, which can help them evaluate the importance of the results that scientists report and lead them to other scientists who can put those results in context.

Finally, having been scientists, they should have the confidence to ask basic questions and challenge leaps of faith without worrying about being considered unintelligent.

What practical advice would you give on how to prepare and market oneself for a career in science writing and editing?

The major preparation for a science writing career is to write for a general audience and get as much of that writing published as possible. I would recommend taking courses in science journalism because you will improve your skills and convince prospective employers that you have a commitment to this occupation.

You can write for the campus or local city newspaper, your professional society, the university public information offices, and small, general interest magazines. You will need to show that you can make your stories interesting as well as accurate.

Ellen W. Chu, Editorial Director, Northwest Environment Watch, Seattle

Chu received her Ph.D. in biology—specifically marine bird ecology—from the University of California, Santa Cruz, in 1982. "In graduate school, I found myself the resident editor on projects requiring report writing," she recalls. After completing her doctorate, she taught scientific writing and science journalism at the Massachusetts Institute of Technology from 1982 to 1984, then was editor of the journal *BioScience* for the next two years. For the next several years, she worked as a freelance book editor for Academic Press and others until 1993, when she launched *Illahee: Journal for the Northwest Environment*. When the University of Washington discontinued the journal in 1996, she became a writer, editor, and writing instructor in the Department of Environmental Health at the University of Washington. Here she put out the department's newsletter and wrote and edited other publications, from brochures and fact sheets to professional journal articles and reports.

In the spring of 1998, she took the job at Northwest Environment Watch, a nonprofit research and publishing center that fosters a sustainable economy in the Pacific Northwest. "I will be editing and directing production of the books and also writing grants. I'm looking forward to working with a set of outstanding authors and to using all my alternative backgrounds in this job. It will also be a great way to stretch my own writing skills.

"Sometimes I think my Ph.D. is useless, since you hardly need one to be a good science writer," Chu remarks. "But it has certainly been useful for the academic or technical assignments I've had. My scholarly background has also given me the chance to be coauthor, with ecologist James R. Karr, of a new book, *Restoring Life in Running Waters: Better Biological Monitoring* [Island Press, Washington, DC, 1998], in which both my ecological and editorial training were relevant," she adds.

What general advice would you give a person thinking about embarking on a career in science writing and editing?

The ability to learn and understand science is important. Scientists hate nothing more than science journalists who turn out stuff that's inaccurate. Conversely, a keen sense of words and how to make something interesting to a nonscientific audience—while retaining accuracy—is equally important. Knowing how and when to simplify, to amplify, and to use analogies is key, as well as sensitivity to content, to people, and to language. Somebody trained in science really has to get out of the scientific conceptual box. A would-be scientist-writer has to become truly interdisciplinary and get away from that mindset as well as the jargon. You have to realize that the narrowness and "focusedness" you learn as a scientist, especially as a lab scientist, will not serve well in a writing or editing career. The only place a myopic focus is useful is in knowing rules of style and grammar—and then so you can apply them or break them at will, not slavishly adhere to them.

Alternative careers in science can make you feel somewhat schizophrenic, unless you manage to find a job that allows you to integrate the many facets of your learning and the aspects of your job that you most value. One of my conflicts is that my science has often been sidelined. I used my scientific training when I was editor of *BioScience* and when I edit books and articles for the professional literature. But for some jobs, being a scientist is not part of the job description, except insofar as a science background helps you translate material into plain English. To manage any writing in my own scientific discipline is always a struggle and major conflict of time.

What practical advice would you give on how to prepare and market oneself for a career in science writing and editing?

The best preparation is to amass good writing or editing samples. Lots of people say they're interested in writing and editing but don't do it well. Write and edit, over and over, more and more. From what I've seen of those who take courses versus those who just do it, no course can match experience. Courses are good for the basics: If a science student wants to write or edit and hasn't a clue about standard publishing practice or grammar, then the student should take a course for the basics. But then the practice is what will help land a job.

I've always loved grammar and happened to be good at remembering grammar and style rules and loved learning them, somewhat like learning taxonomy, which I also loved. I got into editing by accident, just by doing it. I think the best people in any "alternative" science field will have a knack for something relevant to that field, whether it is teaching, writing, editing, or coming up with unique approaches to "packaging" a topic.

Gregory Gasic, Editor of Neuron, Cambridge, MA

Gasic received his Ph.D. from Rockefeller University in 1988, where he studied molecular genetics and developmental biology of fruit flies. From there, he did two molecular neurobiology and neurophysiology postdocs, one at Yale University from 1988 to 1989, and the other at the Salk Institute from 1990 to 1992. "As my father was a professor at the University of Pennsylvania in the Department of Pathology, I got to see first-hand what the grant-writing grind was like before I graduated from college," recalls Gasic. "And, by the time I was in graduate school and had helped him write five RO1 grants, I wasn't too crazy about it. Working as a full-time editor of a major scientific journal allows me to critically think about and contribute to science without the tedium or repetition that is a hallmark of laboratory bench research, specifically, doing the same experiments and writing several versions of the same grant to obtain funding."

Even though Gasic was successful at obtaining grant funding while a postdoc, he applied for a staff editor position at *Nature* and spent months in their London offices handling manuscripts for original research papers. Then he came back to the United States, where he worked for the journal *Cell* for a year.

In 1994, Benjamin Lewin, publisher of *Neuron*, decided that the journal should be run by a full-time editor and offered Gasic the position. Gasic has been the chief editor of *Neuron* for almost four years. "I enjoyed the ever-broadening duties each position afforded me," he says. "In my job, I have to think critically about papers that span a wide spectrum of science, primarily neuroscience." His primary responsibilities include overseeing the submissions of all original research-paper manuscripts, deciding which ones to accept and reject, and where to send them for peer review; dealing with appeals from authors regarding, for example, reviewers comments; suggesting topics for mini-reviews; and traveling to scientific meetings and lectures to keep up-to-date with current research.

In addition to the broad scope of science that he now deals with, the most rewarding aspect of his position, says Gasic, is that he can make a sizeable contribution to the process of science and the way discoveries are communicated to a larger audience.

> *What general advice would you give a person thinking about embarking on a career in science writing and editing?*
> What I and many others do as scientific journal editors is not so much deal with the details of editing for grammar and style, much as a copy editor would do, but we read for different aspects of a paper's content. We must be able to judge it for both the

importance of its findings and the larger context in which the paper makes a claim to fit, as well as its appropriateness for this journal. This requires people skills. An editor needs to be tactful, yet firm, in dealing with appeals and rebuttals from authors regarding reviews and outright rejections.

At Rockefeller, I received a broad education in the life sciences. If I had to choose one aspect of my scientific training that I find the most useful, it would be that this type of training has allowed me to tackle many subjects with confidence.

It's also important to note that competition is stiff in this area, not much different than for a tenure-track assistant professorship. There were over 300 applicants in our last search for an editor. Most journals do not have in-house, full-time, Ph.D. science-level editor positions.

What practical advice would you give on how to prepare and market oneself for a career in science writing and editing?

The best advice on how to prepare oneself for a position like mine is to start early in getting as varied an education as possible, because you'll need to be confident with knowledge in many fields, as well as be able to draw connections between them. As a graduate student—even as an undergraduate—attend diverse seminars and read broadly. As a graduate student, volunteer to help your advisor review papers. Sign up for seminars and classes that include critical review of peer-reviewed papers as a teaching method. By the time I was a postdoc I was reviewing about one to two papers a month. If an opportunity to do this comes across your desk, don't shrink from it. This is another way to help you to think critically, integratively, and broadly.

When we test applicants for a senior editor position, we ask them to critique an issue of *Neuron* on the spot, detailing the weaknesses and strengths of each article, and ultimately, taking a stand on whether they would have published the paper. So, part of this job entails thinking quickly on your feet to galvanize an intellectual position, which serves as the basis for making an editorial decision. This is a more abstract skill to learn, but can be practiced if you start presenting your research and conclusions early on to friends, at departmental seminars, or at lab meetings.

In general we look for people with broad scientific interest, critical acumen, and an ability to deal well with people.

Pamela J. Hines, Senior Editor, Science, *Washington, DC*

Hines received her Ph.D. in molecular biology from the Johns Hopkins University in 1983, after which she spent the next five years as a postdoc and staff researcher at the University of Washington. In 1989, she made the move to *Science* and has been there ever since.

"Even before coming to Johns Hopkins, I met people who had taken a different career route from the traditional academic path; one was a scientist-turned-patent-attorney," recalls Hines. "I found that I was more and more intrigued by their stories about 'life outside the lab.' I started to seek these people out." Although working as a basic researcher in academia was her goal, Hines says she kept an open mind regarding positions she would take in science.

"One day I saw an ad for an editor position at *Science*," she says. "I didn't know anyone there, but the description piqued my interest, so I applied. It's been a great fit for my interests and training."

As senior editor on *Science*'s science editorial staff, Hines and her colleagues are responsible for what gets published and what doesn't. "This entails evaluating submissions for their scientific content and context within a larger scientific point of view, not just the correct use of language and accompanying tables and figures," she says. It also entails working with authors during the editing phase, which Hines notes has its "own challenges." She covers papers that fall in such disciplines as plant biology, cell and molecular biology, neurobiology, development, evolutionary biology, ecology, and science policy.

> *What general advice would you give a person thinking about em-barking on a career in science writing and editing?*
>
> First, a curiosity about other people's research and intellectual choices helped me identify career directions of which I wasn't aware. It opened my view to opportunities I didn't expect. The willingness to explore new opportunities, a broad interest in science, and open-mindedness are specific qualities that have served me well in editing. Also, in my particular job, comfort with the written language is important and valuable, and not something that is particular to scientific training.
>
> *What practical advice would you give on how to prepare and market oneself for a career in science writing and editing?*
>
> One can take a lot of directions. You can just jump in as I did, or you can take it slower. Volunteer to write and edit for your professional society newsletter or magazine. Even if you start out doing this simply to try out a new area and eventually conclude that you may not make a career out of it, it's not wasted effort and you'll be making a contribution to your field in terms of professional service. With this experience you can hone your writing skills and learn how to communicate ideas in ways other than in the stylized format of scientific papers.
>
> Take courses in journalism, technical editing, and other types

of scientific communication. Even one such course would put you at an advantage over most scientists, whether you use those skills in a research career or in a writing career. The American Association for the Advancement of Science Mass Media fellowships is a great place to get experience. Link up with such science writing professional societies as the National Association of Science Writers.

Write for many kinds of outlets and ask for feedback. Ask people to make a complete mess of the manuscript and don't get too worked up over it. Use their feedback to improve your writing.

Read broadly, although I realize that time pressures make this difficult.

Set up a journal club where you critique papers. But remember there's a huge difference between analyzing a paper for its experimental details vs. the paper's over-all message, although both are critical. Asking such questions as: "Is it new?" or "Is it a surprising finding?" help to hone the analytical skills needed in a position such as mine.

Beth Schachter, Science Editor, HMS Beagle, New York

Schachter received her Ph.D. in molecular and cell biology from the University of Southern California in 1977. She was an associate professor of obstetrics and gynecology and of cell biology at Mount Sinai Medical School in New York City, where she headed a basic research laboratory and taught for 16 years.

She says that when it was time to look for a new job due to simultaneous problems with internal motivation and extramural funding, she chose not to leave the New York area. "Therefore I did not pursue what otherwise might have been a more normal career choice for one with a love for teaching, namely to look for jobs at undergraduate institutions. Rather, I began the next phase of my professional life by taking a path of least resistance. Through professional connections, I was contacted by a head hunter who worked mainly for medical education divisions of public relations and advertising firms. It is now quite common for pharmaceutical and biotech companies to outsource much of the writing that deals with medical education aspects of drug promotion. I was hired by such a med/ed house, officially as a writer, but also as a trainee in project development. So that was my entrance into full-time science writing."

In early 1997 Schachter began her current job as the science editor at *HMS Beagle* (http://biomednet.com/hmsbeagle), an Internet-based biomedical magazine. Her post involves choosing and procuring pieces for the magazine, copyediting, and contributing to the form and content of the magazine.

"This is an amazingly wonderful job for one with a broad range of scientific interests," she notes. "In fact, some days I feel like this is my ideal second career, since much of it is new while a lot of it builds upon my knowledge and interests. Am I still a scientist? I would say very much so, but I am a different sort now. Before, as an experimental researcher, I read things very differently than I am now starting to do. Slowly I am developing the critical eye of an editor."

Postscript: Due to corporate restructuring, Schachter left HMS Beagle in May 1998. She views her time at the webzine as a terrific internship and an entrée into the rapidly developing world of on-line scientific publishing and journalism.

> *What general advice would you give a person thinking about embarking on a career in science writing and editing?*
>
> Be realistic about your goals, which means don't set them too low as well as too high. Don't be afraid to expand how you think or use the skills you are learning in your scientific training. As a scientist, when I read the work of others, I wanted to absorb as much detailed information as possible, but now as an editor involved in identifying topics worthy of covering, I now look first at general concepts, then at specific details, as deadlines permit.
>
> *What practical advice would you give on how to prepare and market oneself for a career in science writing and editing?*
>
> Before sending out your CV, let a couple of trusted friends or colleagues check it for thoroughness and appropriateness for the particular job. For example, in preparing mine for my writing positions, I minimized the fact that I trained a large number of college and postgraduate pre-med students.
>
> Before going out on interviews, read a couple of books on the area in which you're interviewing. If you hear or read the same message repeatedly, take it seriously. Once you have received an invitation for an interview, make it a two-way dialogue. Be prepared to ask questions as well as to give answers. That means that you should do a background check on any potential employer, so that you know their strengths and limitations. During any interview, listen carefully. What you selectively choose to ignore will come back to haunt you!
>
> Also, be honest about what you know how to do and note that you are interested and capable of learning new things. That's all textbook stuff, which is why I now see the value in reading the textbooks.
>
> But how can a potential career switcher go about retooling and getting experience for a career in science writing and editing? There

are many programs to help scientists train for writing/editing positions. In New York City, I know of programs such as internships at *The Sciences*, the magazine put out by the New York Academy of Sciences. Also, consider contacting your local natural history museum, public relations department at local medical centers, and marketing and public relations divisions of pharmaceutical companies. Be prepared to do freelance work in order to learn about editing and publishing. Having a Ph.D. or other formal training in science should ultimately put you in a strong position.

Resources

Professional Societies

Council of Biology Editors (CBE). According to CBE's Web site it "aims to improve communication in the sciences by educating authors, editors, and publishers," by facilitating communication among those who publish findings from life science research. The council was created in 1957 by a joint action of the National Science Foundation and the American Institute of Biological Sciences. Contact:

Council of Biology Editors
60 Revere Dr., Suite 500
Northbrook, IL 60092-1577
847-480-9080
Fax: 847-480-9282
cbehdqts@aol.com
http://cbe.org/cbe

American Medical Writers Association (AMWA). AMWA is the largest professional society representing biomedical communicators. It has more than 4,000 members in 24 countries. Providing professional education to members is one of the society's main goals. Contact:

American Medical Writers Association
9650 Rockville Pike
Bethesda, MD 20814-3998
301-493-0003
http://www.amwa.org/amwa

Association of Earth Science Editors (AESE). AESE has about 300 members who are editors at journals, government geological surveys, commercial firms, and consultancies; journal managers; and others concerned with publication in the earth sciences. Contact:

Association of Earth Science Editors
c/o American Geological Institute
4220 King St.
Alexandria, VA 22302-1502
703-379-2480
Fax: 703-379-7563
agi@agiweb.org
http://www-odp.tamu.edu/publications/AESE/aese.htm

European Association of Science Editors (EASE). EASE is open to editors of scientific publications, publications managers, and others in science communication. Contact:

European Association of Science Editors
EASE Secretariat
c/o Jenny Gretton
PO Box 426
Guildford GU4 7ZH
United Kingdom
Phone and Fax: 011-1483-211-056
secretary@ease.org.uk
http://www.ease.org.uk

Society for Technical Communication (STC). STC is a professional organization of more than 20,000 members worldwide that includes writers, editors, illustrators, publishers, educators, students, engineers, and scientists. Their Web site is the main resource for information on education, training programs and seminars, fellowships, and jobhunting and networking in technical communication. The site includes links to local chapters, regional and international conferences, seminars, publications, special-interest groups, and educational resources and programs. Employment information is searchable by region and job type. The site also has links to jobhunting tips, job-searching resources on the Internet, and a resume-posting service. Contact:

Society for Technical Communication
901 N. Stuart St., Suite 904
Arlington, VA 22203-1854
703-522-4114
Fax: 703-522-2075
membership@stc-va.org
http://www.stc-va.org

Association of American Publishers (AAP). AAP is the principal trade association of the book publishing industry, with about 200 members in the United States. Its Professionals/Scholarly Publishing Division covers scientific, medical, technical, and scholarly books and journals. Contact:

Association of American Publishers
71 Fifth Ave.
New York, NY 10003-3004
212-255-0200
Fax: 212-255-7007
http://www.publishers.org

Society for Scholarly Publishers (SSP). SSP is a professional organization open to anyone interested in scholarly publishing, which includes those in science, technology, and medical publishing. Contact:

Society for Scholarly Publishers
10200 West 44th Ave., Suite 304
Wheat Ridge, CO 80033
303-422-3914
Fax: 303-422-8894
ssp@resourcenter.com
http://www.edoc.com/ssp

Editorial Freelancers Association (EFA). EFA is a professional organization of self-employed writers, editors, indexers, proofreaders, researchers, desktop publishers, translators, and others who work in the publishing and communications industries. Members are drawn from a variety of specialties, including science, medicine, and technology. Contact:

Editorial Freelancers Association
71 West 23 St., Suite 1504
New York, NY 10010
212-929-5400
Fax: 212-929-5439
http://www.the-efa.org

Education and Training

CBE sponsors short courses, but does not maintain listings for fellowships, internships, or academic programs. AAP has links to seminars, its newsletter, conferences, and special interest committees on its Web site. AMWA also sponsors workshops and continuing-education programs in biomedical communication at its annual meetings.

The STC Web site and the site of the Association of Teachers of Technical Writing (http://english.ttu.edu/ATTW/) list Ph.D., M.A./M.S., and B.A./B.S. major, minor, and certificate programs that give courses and confer degrees in technical and scientific editing and writing.

The Board of Editors of the Life Sciences runs a certification program for scientific editing. For information on eligibility and application materials, contact:

Barbara B. Reitt
Secretary for Examination Administration
560 Nall Farm Rd.
Highlands, NC 28741
Phone and Fax: 704-526-9138

Jobhunting and Networking

CBE sometimes publishes job announcements in the back of its newsletter, *CBE Views*, and plans to post jobs on its Web site soon. Nine times a year, AMWA publishes the "Job Market Sheet," which lists available positions.

Job advertisements appear in *Publishers Weekly* (http://www.bookwire.com/pw), the *Chronicle of Higher Education* (http://chronicle.merit.edu), and at CareerPath (http://www.careerpath.com), the on-line listing of the Sunday classified sections of all newspapers in the United States. Search using the keywords "editorial" and "publishing." The *Literary Market Place* is a telephone-book-like directory that lists contact information for all publishers and has a section on science-book publishers and can be found in most large libraries. Many publishers also suggest contacting the Association of American University Presses for further help in the job search (see p. 118).

The STC, AMWA, and CBE annual meetings are all good places to network and learn of jobs by word of mouth, say editors. Each concentrates on a different discipline or outlet: STC is mostly computer software-oriented; AMWA is for biomedical writers and editors; and CBE draws primarily editors from peer-review journals.

☐ Book Editing and Publishing

Like scientist-journal editors, researchers who have moved into book publishing say that being able to focus on the big picture of a scientific topic is one of the most attractive features of working in publishing. The satisfaction of shepherding a concept for a book through the manuscript drafts to the final product is another plus.

In general, the popular and scholarly science publishing industry can offer a variety of positions for scientists, including sales and marketing, production, and different types of editorial roles. Scientists in this field have to blend their knowledge and appreciation of science with their familiarity with the book publishing process, with books within a market segment, and with ideas for future book projects.

One common editorial position held by scientists is that of acquisitions editor. These editors seek out and sign up new book contracts. Publishers say scientists are aptly suited to recruit other scientists for book projects because they speak the same language and probably have similar experiences.

Former scientists also become developmental editors. These editors work very closely with scientist-authors during the editing, reviewing, and publishing phases of a book project. They essentially act as the researchers' guides through the publishing maze. Again, familiarity with the subject matter of a book helps facilitate this part of the process.

There is variability within the industry as to what constitutes an appropriate educational and experiential background for science publishing. Opinions vary as to whether graduate training in a science is necessary; in fact, according to some editors, having a background in the area in which you are working can be frowned upon. Therefore, you should be aware of these differences and tailor your approach to the company or industry segment in which you're interested. This is where informational interviews with someone already in the field will be helpful.

Scientists who now work in publishing say that it requires a complex blend of people, schmoozing, organizational, managerial, and, of course, communication skills, as well as patience and the ability to focus, to be successful. In general they suggest learning basic skills by getting involved with on-campus newsletters or with university presses, which often are open to unpaid volunteers.

One-on-One with Scientists Now Working in Book Publishing

Peter Cannell, Director and Science Editor of the Smithsonian Institution Press, Washington, DC

Cannell received his Ph.D. in evolutionary biology from a joint program between the City University of New York and the American

Museum of Natural History in 1987. After getting his degree, he spent a year and a half at the Smithsonian's National Museum of Natural History as a postdoctoral fellow in the division of birds, before moving over to the Smithsonian Institution Press.

"Beyond my formal training I have always had an interest in natural history in the broadest sense, and spent a great deal of time in graduate school understanding and pursuing interests in different fields, perhaps to the detriment of my thesis progress," recalls Cannell. "Even in college, whereas I knew my major interest was biology, I was a joint major in art history and geology. So, I guess the take-home message is: be interested in everything."

As science acquisitions editor, he says one of the most important on-the-job skills is to be able to see the forest for the trees. "You have to be able to sense where a field is going, or potentially going, almost before the people in the field, who tend to be focused on pieces of it," explains Cannell. "You need to be able to find those rare people that can also see, and present, the broader picture. As M. Lincoln Schuster, cofounder of Simon & Schuster, said, 'Don't pass judgement on a manuscript as it is, but as it can be made to be.' He also said something else that is true to my experience: 'the greatest joy and highest privilege of a creative editor is to touch life at all points and discover needs still unmet—and find the best authors to meet them.' You need to be able to join the author in providing the vision, but be willing to disavow credit."

> *What general advice would you give a person thinking about embarking on a career in science publishing?*
>
> Be interested in everything. Try to experience everything, including some training in business. Be open to alternate career possibilities. Be open to changes. Science tends to push you more and more into narrow specialties. Publishing and some other professions like teaching require you to browse broadly over science at large. What fun! I recall that when I took my doctoral degree comprehensive exam, a friend commented that never again would our knowledge be as broad. I'm happy to say that's not true.

> *What practical advice would you give on how to prepare and market oneself for a career in science publishing?*
>
> Volunteer. Go to meetings. Talk to people. Experience things. Practice getting to the heart of things—beyond the main body of data. What is someone's argument? Do they know that is their argument, or are they enmeshed in the data? Can you help them get to the bigger idea? If so, you might be a publisher!

Carol Lewis, President, LLH Technology Publishing, Eagle Rock, VA

Along the way, Lewis has received training and experience in English, comparative religions, electrical engineering, elementary education, and drafting and design. "All of that eventually led me to a position as a draftsperson with a small consulting engineering firm in Columbia, MD in 1975," she recalls. "Engineering was a real challenge, one that I found I liked, so I ultimately went back to school full-time to finish my degree in electrical engineering. After graduation, I worked for several years as a 'real' engineer, and loved much about it, but then found that I hadn't totally killed off my liberal-arts self and it was trying to reassert itself.

"Books and writing were big loves of mine from an early age (I started out as an English major before switching to religion), so I looked for something that might combine them with my engineering interests," she says. After stints as a freelance technical writer, Lewis eventually became an acquisitions editor for Academic Press, obtaining titles for them in the areas of electronics and electrical engineering. She met her current business partner there, and in 1990 left Academic Press to start their own technical publishing business, HighText Publications.

Now Lewis is president of her own (with two partners) technical publishing business called LLH Technology Publishing. LLH specializes in books on engineering and electronics, and some Internet publishing. "This type of work requires the willingness to wear a lot of hats," she remarks. "I mostly handle editorial functions: soliciting proposals for new book and software products, reviewing them, deciding whether to offer a contract, and then shepherding each project to completion, but I also have a great deal of input into marketing and advertising decisions, financial reporting, and hiring decisions, as well as a myriad of other miscellaneous matters that come up in the course of running a business."

What general advice would you give a person thinking about embarking on a career in science publishing?
Any scientific or technical discipline is suited for publishing, as any discipline will have its own body of printed work to support it. A strong educational background in the subject matter you are publishing is essential. For those interested in working for an established publishing company as an editor, the primary skills needed in addition to a knowledge of the subject matter are being comfortable with people, being a good "schmoozer," being able to convince prospective authors to commit themselves to a project, and having a sense for what type of information other professionals

Sydor. "One of the best things that I think any former grad student with experience in research can bring to this kind of position is the ability to be extremely detail-oriented, while still keeping the big picture in mind."

What general advice would you give a person thinking about embarking on a career in science publishing?

Graduate school teaches you an enormous number of skills that you probably take for granted. Think about what you can do; no matter how small it seems, put it on your resume and be confident. If you can get through grad school, then there are a lot of other things you can do.

It is easy to feel demoralized because you no longer want to do something that probably took a large commitment to start in the first place. There is nothing wrong with changing your mind.

It is important to give potential employers positive reasons for your career change. Don't talk about what you hated and want to get away from. Talk about why you think the new job will be more fulfilling.

There is a huge list of transferable skills that you learn in graduate school, especially in science. A few that I use all the time are: computer skills, writing experience, presentation skills, organizational skills, analytical reasoning, and creative problem solving skills.

What practical advice would you give on how to prepare and market oneself for a career in science publishing?

Talk to people in the field. Try to get some freelance work to establish a reputation. Lots of freelance work is available in this field. Call people in the editorial department directly.

But most important is to be confident about your transferable skills. What really matters is the ability to work with people and to stay on top of the details. Anyone who can do those things well (and grad school often teaches you those things) can do well in publishing.

People skills are often overlooked in the lab environment. Work on these, as they are important almost everywhere else.

How to gain experience in a new area varies a great deal from field to field. For me, the most important thing was talking to people in the field (from the top to the bottom of the hierarchy) and just jumping right in with both feet. Set up informational interviews with scientists already in the field and talk with publishers at scientific meetings.

Robert Harington, Senior Editor, John Wiley & Sons, Inc., New York

Harington received his doctorate in biochemistry from University of Oxford in 1989. After that he went to work directly for a small publisher called Current Medical Literature in the United Kingdom until 1990. Here he learned to copy edit manuscripts and develop review articles with researchers.

"Halfway through my doctoral program, I decided that working on one detailed project at a time was not what I was looking for," recalls Harington. "I wanted to approach science from a broader perspective. I was finding that I was more intrigued by making larger connections than honing in on narrow questions. I attended a conference in New York along with my supervisor and other doctoral students in the group. My supervisor helped launch a new journal and at that launch, I was introduced to the publisher. That was my first introduction to the world of publishing. From my discussion with the editor about her career, I decided that this move would satisfy my desire to work in science as more of a generalist than a specialist."

During the early 1990s, Harington worked as an acquisitions editor for Edward Arnold and Cambridge University Press in England. After this he moved to the United States, where he worked in the same capacity for the Johns Hopkins University Press. Two years ago, he moved to Wiley, where he is now a senior editor in the life sciences responsible for 16 journals and many book projects.

> *What general advice would you give a person thinking about embarking on a career in science publishing?*
> Some regard scientific training as central to the job. This type of training can certainly teach you how to ask questions, read and understand technical literature, and make connections among disparate findings.
> What you need as an acquisitions editor is a certain amount of fearlessness to make cold calls to prominent researchers with whom you're interested in engaging in a book project. You need the skills of a salesperson to, for example, "sell" the company you represent to a potential author. So personal skills are important. But how much of that is really taught in graduate school?
> You also need to have an entrepreneurial instinct to judge what might make a saleable, interesting book.

> *What practical advice would you give on how to prepare and market oneself for a career in science publishing?*
> There's a shortage of experienced life science editors, and as a result, they are often approached by recruiters. That's good news if you're interested in moving into publishing, but how do you first get experience or find out if this is an area for which you're well suited?
> Working as a copy editor, as I did at the start—whether on a freelance basis or as a staff person—is sometimes a route into scientific and technical publishing, but this is very different from

what I do now as an acquisitions editor. If you know someone at a publishing house, write and offer yourself as a copy editor. Or, you could offer to be a reviewer of technical article manuscripts for journal publishers. Presses often have internships, some paying, others not. Use the Web or such publications as *Writer's Digest* or *Publisher's Weekly* to familiarize yourself with the scientific and technical publishers.

My boss, who is not a researcher, started out as a sales representative. That's an excellent route into publishing for people who come from a nonscientific background; this path could also work for scientists looking for a way into publishing.

Resources

Professional Societies

Association of American Publishers (AAP). AAP is the principal trade association of the book publishing industry, with about 200 members in the United States. Its Professionals/Scholarly Publishing Division covers scientific, medical, technical, professional, and scholarly books and journals. Contact:

Association of American Publishers
71 Fifth Ave.
New York, NY 10003-3004
212-255-0200
Fax: 212-255-7007
http://www.publishers.org

Society for Scholarly Publishers (SSP). SSP is a professional organization open to anyone interested in scholarly publishing, which includes those in science, technology, and medical publishing. Contact:

Society for Scholarly Publishers
10200 West 44th Ave., Suite 304
Wheat Ridge, CO 80033
303-422-3914
Fax: 303-422-8894
ssp@resourcenter.com
http://www.edoc.com/ssp

Association of American University Presses (AAUP). AAUP is a cooperative nonprofit organization of university presses, including those that handle science and technology titles. Contact:

Association of American University Presses
584 Broadway, Suite 410
New York, NY 10012
212-941-6610
Fax: 212-941-6618
aaupny@netcom.com

American Medical Publishers Association (AMPA). AMPA is the professional organization that represents those working for medical publishers. Contact:

American Medical Publishers Association
14 Fort Hill Rd.
Huntington, NY 11743
Phone and fax: 516-423-0075
jillrudansky-ampa@msn.com
http://www.am.pa.com

International Association of Scientific, Technical, and Medical Publishers (STM). STM represents publishers who publish books, journals, and databases in science, technology, and medicine. It represents 276 imprints, mostly in the United States, United Kingdom, Germany, and the Netherlands. Contact:

International Association of Scientific, Technical, and Medical Publishers
Muurhuizen 165
3811 EG Amersfoort
The Netherlands
011 31 33 465 60 60
Fax: 011 31 33 465 65 38
http://www.stm.springer.de

Education and Training

There are summer institutes for people who want to enter publishing, listings of which may appear in the following publications:

* *Book Publishing Training Programs: 1995 Directory*, Association of American University Presses, New York, 1995
* *Editing Fact and Fiction: A Concise Guide to Book Editing*, Leslie T. Sharpe and Irene Gunther, Cambridge University Press, New York, 1994, pp. 215–222.

- *A Guide to Publishing and Bookselling Courses in the United States,* Peterson's Guides, Princeton, NJ, 1992.

AAP has links to seminars, its newsletter, conferences, and special interest committees on its Web site.

Jobhunting and Networking

Job advertisements appear in *Publishers Weekly* (http://www.bookwire.com/pw), the *Chronicle of Higher Education* (http://chronicle.merit.edu), and at CareerPath (http://www.careerpath.com), the on-line listing of the Sunday classified sections of all newspapers in the United States. Search using the keywords "editorial" and "publishing." The *Literary Market Place* is a telephone-book-like annual directory that lists contact information for all U.S. publishers. The international version lists all those outside the United States. These have sections on science-book publishers and can be found in most large libraries, but is only useful if you already know the name of the publisher you're looking for.

Many publishers also suggest contacting AAP for further help in the job search. For example, its Web site includes links to dozens of publishers, who in turn have links to job listings and can be a potential source of freelance work.

To break into this field as a freelancer, publishers suggest that you volunteer to edit a project with your professional society's journal, for example, to get some examples for your CV. They also suggest taking copy editing courses to gain the necessary credentials and experience. Then send your CV, with a follow-up call, to university presses, scholarly presses, and association publishers (American Chemical Society, American Physical Society, and the American Mathematical Society, for example). These outlets keep files of freelance editors to whom they outsource work.

There are also outside prep houses to whom publishers outsource entire book projects for editing and production. These outlets hire freelancers, especially for science-and-technology-oriented books. *Literary Market Place* may have a separate listing for prep houses.

☐ Other Outlets

There are many other writing and editing outlets for people with scientific and technical training: grant writing and fund-raising, marketing communications, software documentation, and multimedia and the Web, to name a few.

Alan Muirhead, Freelance Science and Technical Communicator, Philadelphia, PA

Muirhead received his Ph.D. in chemistry from the University of Illinois, Champaign-Urbana in 1972. For most of his career, he worked for DuPont, including nine years as a research chemist, followed by eight years in technical marketing, which included customer training, product testing, telephone support, and writing data sheets and promotional brochures. He was also a manager of technical marketing and of the telephone technical-support center.

"When the company decided to move the telephone center in 1995, I chose to exit the company and became a freelance technical writer," he explains. "Communication was a common thread throughout all my positions and something I liked to do. After more than two years, it's still a good decision."

He now writes promotional brochures, software manuals, and computer-system validation documents for large manufacturers with a strong base in science and technology. "I have to understand the client's needs, learn the product or technology I'm writing about, communicate my plans and progress to the client, and write and deliver the documents."

What kinds of general advice would you give a person thinking about embarking on a career in science and technical communication?

Check it out first. Talk to technical writers. Find out what their joys and frustrations are. Understand what the local market opportunities are. For example, as a freelancer, ask yourself: "Will it be easy or hard to get the first few jobs and build a portfolio?"

The ability to write is an obvious skill needed to be a technical writer. The ability to communicate may be less obvious, but I have seen good writers fail because they could not communicate with the client. It also helps to have a fair amount of project-management skill, not formal, but the ability to identify what needs to be done and then go out and do it. For freelancers, some self-motivation and the ability to withstand rejection also help.

What practical advice would you give on how to prepare and market oneself for a career in scientific and technical communication?

I've found the Society for Technical Communication to be very helpful. I joined as I changed careers, and have gotten a lot of good advice and made some new friends. I was quickly "volunteered" to edit the local chapter newsletter, which has given me more writing experience as well as opened a network for job leads and technical advice.

As far as marketing my abilities goes, I emphasize my previous experience in product development, customer support, and management, which communicates to my clients that I also can understand the perspectives of the users, the developers, and the people who are paying to get the job done. And, I promote my ability to learn quickly, as evidenced by the wide range of things I've done.

Resources

The Society for Technical Communication is a professional organization of more than 20,000 members worldwide that includes writers, editors, illustrators, publishers, educators, students, engineers, and scientists. Their Web site is the main resource for information on education, training programs and seminars, fellowships, and jobhunting and networking in technical communication. The site includes links to local chapters, regional and international conferences, seminars, publications, special-interest groups, and educational resources and programs. Employment information is searchable by region and job type. The site also has links to jobhunting tips, job-searching resources on the Internet, and a resume-posting service. Contact:

Society for Technical Communication
901 N. Stuart St., Suite 904
Arlington, VA 22203-1854
703-522-4114
Fax: 703-522-2075
membership@stc-va.org
http://www.stc-va.org

CHAPTER 6

Informatics

An explosion of information in broad areas of science—biomedicine, chemistry, and ecology—is opening new doors for life and physical scientists who have an interest in computers and the organization of scientific data, as well as computer scientists interested in other areas, for example, genetics and biochemistry.

The flood of data from the Human Genome Project and similar efforts, along with technological innovations in computer databases, has laid the groundwork for the development of bioinformatics, a burgeoning discipline that involves the collection, management, analysis, and interpretation of data generated from large-scale genome sequencing databases throughout the world. The need for people trained in computational chemistry, a disciplinary cousin of bioinformatics and computational biology, has also been growing.

Changes in healthcare such as the advent of health maintenance organizations and an ever-increasing number of clinical trials has also led to the expansion of an allied discipline called medical informatics. This consists of managing the clinical information obtained from drug trials and patient records.

While bioinformatics and medical informatics are where most researchers-turned-informatics-specialists are employed, two other areas warrant close attention for the future. First is the collection, maintenance, distribution, and analysis of information from scientific journal articles. Once the domain of library scientists, more people with scientific training are being sought for this type of work. One is Marie McVeigh, editor for life sciences at the Institute for Scientific

Information (ISI) in Philadelphia. She has a dual B.S. in biophysics and English literature and an M.S. in cell biology from the University of Pennsylvania.

"I view my scientific training as an apprenticeship where I learned tools that could apply to other fields," says McVeigh. "Scientific training is an apprenticeship for doing science. It is up to the individual to realize that certain of those skills can be translated to a business environment. I've always been interested in publishing and am now applying that interest and my training in life science to manage ISI's database of thousands of life-science journals. In the last three years we have been hiring more people with scientific training. But on the whole, ISI does not turn over editorial staff very much: there were only three new hires in the last three and a half years, including me. All three of us have significant backgrounds in science, but that isn't really enough to make a statement about a trend at our company. But what I can say is that more and more scientists have been approaching me in the last few years to ask about making the move from the bench *to* publishing."

She says her science background is essential for understanding the relationships between disciplines, and hence their journals; for organizing the life-science journals in the most logical and up-to-date way, so researchers can easily find what they're looking for; and anticipating new products, such as a molecular medicine database.

With the increasing interest in preserving Earth's biodiversity, databases describing the spatial and temporal relationships of plants and animals are being collected more than ever by investigators all over the world. This type of biological information is just starting to be stored

---

CHARACTERISTICS OF A SWITCH TO A CAREER IN INFORMATICS

These attributes may not strike every reader the same way. Depending on your background and interests, you may view some of these as either attractive or unappealing.

- You need to be comfortable with computers, computer programming, and thinking in terms of algorithms to answer scientific questions.
- It's a growing, but competitive field.
- You could work in a variety of settings and capacities.
- You get to work with the practical applications of science.
- You get a chance to work with cutting-edge ideas.
- You need to be able to keep abreast with the research in two distinct fields.

and accessed in a systematic way. Environmental scientists with a knowledge of both these databases and computer systems may play a significant role in designing future biodiversity information systems.

☐ Bioinformatics

Because bioinformatics is so closely tied to the pharmaceutical and biotechnology industries, many of the present and future jobs at all levels are thought to be in industry, but many caution that the field is attracting many good people, so is already becoming very competitive. A small handful of teaching and research positions are also opening up at universities that are setting up centers to train the next generation of bioinformatics specialists. Presently, many are concerned about a "brain drain" from budding academic programs into industry because that's where most of the jobs are predicted to be. But many of the fledgling academic programs already have close ties to industry.

"As novel drug targets are generated by genomics-driven research, bioinformatics will be important in selecting those targets most appropriate to the drug-development process," says Maria Betty, a senior scientist at Wyeth-Ayerst Research, Inc. "Rational target selection, and interpretation of the vast quantities of data in public and private sequence databases, requires individuals with strong biology backgrounds and computational skills to work closely with both bench scientists and computer scientists." AAAS's on-line careers forum, NextWave, profiled several bioinformatics specialists in 1996 (http://www.nextwave.org).

Leaders in the field come from all sorts of backgrounds, says Jim Ostell, chief of the information engineering branch at the National Center for Biotechnology Information in Rockville, MD. "Some come through an academic route, developing models of biological systems with computers; others are people who as graduate students took care of the lab's computers by default or interest and are now applying that skill full time; still others are software developers who picked up some biology along the way or biologists who are proficient in computer science." Another group is mathematicians and biostatisticians who write algorithms to search or analyze genome-related data.

Still others, like Mark Gerstein, an assistant professor of molecular biophysics and biochemistry at Yale University, are specifically trained in bioinformatics. He received his Ph.D. in biophysics and bioinformatics in 1993 from Cambridge University, United Kingdom. His current research concentrates on analyzing genomes in terms of protein and nucleic-acid structure. "So often, four or five years into a Ph.D. program students are in a situation that bears no resemblance to what they expected before they entered," notes Gerstein. "I suggest that anyone interested in bioinformatics—in an academic or industrial setting—first get experience in what it will be like."

He advises prospective bioinformatics specialists to start by taking courses that will get you to work with a computer. "Interacting with a computer as your main research tool is a lot different from working at the bench running gels or experimenting with mice," he remarks. "This can be the deciding factor in whether or not you like this field. You have to be comfortable with computers and programming and have a natural affinity for analyzing scientific problems from a computational perspective."

Read on for the personal stories and practical advice of a few scientists who decided to apply their scientific training to work in the field of bioinformatics.

One-on-One with Bioinformatics Specialists

Maria Betty, Senior Scientist at Wyeth-Ayerst Research Inc., Princeton, NJ (http://www.bioplanet.com)

Betty completed her Ph.D. in molecular biology at Oxford University in the United Kingdom in 1994. "By my final year there, I knew a career in academic research was not for me," she recalls. "The constant pressure to write papers and grant applications, along with low salaries and long hours, were a sufficient deterrent. I applied for positions in industry and was offered a job at Wyeth Research (UK) working on postreceptor signaling in depression. Shortly after I started at Wyeth, the parent company announced its decision to close the UK research division. A small number of people were offered the opportunity to relocate to the United States. I took up this opportunity and migrated across the Atlantic Ocean.

"I had first begun to think of bioinformatics as a possible career alternative whilst working towards my doctorate. I was always the person in the group who people came to when they had problems on the computer, be it with a word processing or DNA analysis package. My Ph.D. on the molecular biology of the nicotinic acetylcholine receptor called for a considerable degree of sequence analysis. I quickly became the lab expert and realized I derive a great deal of satisfaction from messing around on computers. This, I think, is key to becoming a bioinformatician: you have to like computers and be content to play around on them for hours on end, often producing what seems like very little."

In her present job, she once collaborated with a research fellow at the National Center for Biotechnology Information who was doing some consulting work for Wyeth. "At this point I had already decided I wished to make the transition," says Betty. "I signed up for UNIX courses, and started my own Web page to learn HTML and CGI programming. Working with the NCBI fellow, I learned some more sophisticated analysis techniques and received encouragement and advice on what skills I would need to become employable in bioinformatics.

"I came to realize that whilst I had gained a great deal of useful experience, I wasn't acquiring the depth of knowledge necessary to give me a competitive edge over other molecular biologists wishing to make this transition. I decided to take the plunge and inform my manager of my desire to become a bioinformatician, and fortunately for me the gamble paid off. Management recognized the need for bioinformatics support within the department." Betty currently works with the Wyeth bioinformatics group.

What general advice would you give a person thinking about embarking on a career in informatics?

The most emphatic advice I can give to someone wishing to make the transition from biology to bioinformatics is to get hands-on experience using the relevant computer programs and analyzing genes. Seek out opportunities at your workplace to work on bioinformatics- and genomics-related subjects, and to interact with others working in these fields. If you have just finished your degree, look for summer jobs or internships, even if the work seems mundane, such as checking automatic sequence data. It will give you invaluable experience.

What practical advice would you give on how to prepare and market oneself for a career in informatics?

Experience with gene analysis software is extremely important, but unfortunately it won't make you very marketable since there are hoards of molecular biologists out there who already have this experience and are applying for the currently limited numbers of jobs. In-depth computational skills will give you a competitive edge. The easiest way to acquire these, if your circumstances permit, is to take a course in computational biology.

In addition to extensive knowledge of the run-of-the-mill molecular biology packages (GCG, BLAST, etc.), you should try to acquire Web-related skills, including HTML and JAVA; programming skills, especially Perl (C++ is a bonus); and become familiar with a variety of operating systems (especially UNIX). Experience using relational databases such as Sybase 11 and Oracle 7 and knowledge of SQL, a database query language, is also highly advantageous.

One area of bioinformatics that is set to expand is the determination of relationships between molecular structure and amino-acid sequence. If you wish to enter this field, you will need to learn all you can about structural biology and modeling, mathematical optimization, computer graphics theory, and linear algebra. If you are already working as a biologist and want to expand your computational skills, try investigating local universities and colleges; many of them offer basic courses in UNIX, C++, HTML, and Java.

The list sounds somewhat daunting, but don't despair—very few people possess all these skills when making the transition. In a nutshell, you will need to be able to readily pick up, use, and understand the tools and databases designed by computer programmers and to communicate biological science requirements to computer scientists. By acquiring at least a subset of these skills, you will be in a position to demonstrate to a prospective employer your ability to meet these criteria.

John Greene, Senior Staff Scientist, Bioinformatics Research, Gene Logic, Inc., Gaithersburg, MD

Greene completed his doctorate in genetics at Harvard University in 1989, after which he did a postdoc at NIH studying transcriptional regulation in early development. "I could see how depressing the academic funding situation was getting," he recalls. "I wanted to try to make an impact on human health, so I looked for a job in industry. After a 10-month stint with an antisense DNA company with more ideas than dollars, I was offered a position at Human Genome Sciences (HGS) as a molecular biologist in the protein therapeutics group."

While there, he filed for patents on several novel genes and coauthored eight papers, but as he puts it: "Something was still missing—the thrill was gone and benchwork had become drudgery. One day, I saw a posting for an in-house job for a bioinformatics scientist. The director of bioinformatics—Mike Fannon, who is now VP of Bioinformatics and CIO—took me to lunch the next day after I indicated some interest and got me fired up about entering bioinformatics in a way I hadn't been excited in almost a decade."

At first, Greene was unable to secure a transfer, but a spark had been lit. He began to look into outside opportunities in bioinformatics, and in the midst of his investigations, HGS asked him to act as scientific liaison for their corporate partners. Eventually he was offered and took the position of bioinformatics scientist in 1996 for HGS.

In January 1998, Greene moved up to a Senior Scientist position in bioinformatics at nearby Gene Logic, Inc., to work with Keith Elliston, Senior VP of R&D. "Dr. Elliston was formerly Scientific Director of the Merck Gene Index and head of Bioinformatics for Merck Research

Laboratories and is one of the best-known figures in industrial bioinformatics," he notes. "He was a major reason for my move."

Greene acts as the bioinformatics research analyst for a collaboration with Proctor and Gamble Pharmaceuticals on genes that are differentially expressed in congestive heart failure. He also leads a team developing a database of rare expressed sequence tags (ESTs) and is interested in the bioinformatics involved with gene chips.

Greene notes that his job entails a little of everything: analyzing gene sequences; programming, mostly using HTML and Perl to manipulate sequence text and build Web tools; using SQL to prepare specialty reports; acting as a liaison to corporate partners; evaluating new technologies and new sequence analysis programs; and helping to recruit new people to the group.

"It's almost never dull!," he concludes.

What general advice would you give a person thinking about embarking on a career in informatics?

Although right now the gap between demand and supply is huge, I think that's going to change. Most of us in the field get called by recruiters fairly often. But the problem is that most people don't have practical industry experience. It's a conundrum. Right now, industry would like to hire top-line molecular biologists who are also accomplished, professional-level computer programmers, but those people are already in desirable positions.

The infrastructure still needs to be built in many companies, so for the time being computational skills will outweigh biological skills. Sadly, many of these groups have few biologists on staff, and the computer people aren't familiar enough with the biology side of things. However, once the informatics tools are designed and built, someone has to use them, and at that point, I'm betting you will see many more hires of biologists skilled in using the tools and knowing how to combine them.

What practical advice would you give on how to prepare and market oneself for a career in informatics?

I wouldn't go too far overboard on programming skills, but some are necessary. It would be very difficult to be both a good biologist and a professional programmer. But having said that, don't forget to master the Genetics Computer Group (GCG), also known as the Wisconsin package, and take advantage of all the tools now available on the Web. (The advent of the Web has opened up the ability to rapidly prototype Web tools for extracting and writing information to databases.) Note I said master—just because you used GCG once to assemble a sequence and do some analysis doesn't make you a bioinformatics expert. Certainly learn some programming and database skills so you can relate to the professional computer people.

I'm obtaining a Certificate in Information Systems from George Washington University, so I can have a broader understanding of the computer systems we use. But don't neglect solid biological research so you can understand what the real problems are and help convert the torrent of information into useful concepts and discoveries.

The best people are either professional computer people who have learned a good deal of biology, or biologists with a solid computer background. Learn HTML, UNIX, SQL, Perl, and Java, and as much as possible about relational databases.

Tony Kerlavage, Director of Bioinformatics at The Institute for Genomic Research (TIGR), Rockville, MD

Kerlavage received his Ph.D. in biochemistry in 1981 from the University of California, San Diego. From there he did a postdoc at the University of Pennsylvania and then started work in the lab of Craig Venter (founding president and director of TIGR) at NIH, where he studied neurotransmitter receptors using classical techniques. Kerlavage describes his move into bioinformatics as more of an evolution than a conscious transition into an allied field. "One day in 1986, we were reading the journals and we saw that someone had cloned one of the receptors we were working with," he recalls. "I remember it vividly: The whole group was sitting in a room reading this manuscript and at the end of the meeting we decided to drop everything we were doing and teach ourselves molecular biology to clone other genes for these various receptors. Once we started generating the DNA sequence data, we had to somehow analyze it. At that time most people in the lab were fairly computer-phobic. This was shortly after the first Macs and early PCs were available and I was dabbling around on those. So I just started exploring what tools were available to deal with the information we were producing. As we did more and more of this, the analysis of the sequences sort of naturally fell into my lap. So I'm basically self-taught."

By the early 1990s, the group started producing massive amounts of ESTs, pieces of DNA sequences that mark expressed proteins. "When we started scaling up with the EST sequencing, we were operating on a very different scale, and the computer operations had to scale up as well," remarks Kerlavage. As part of that scale-up Kerlavage had to learn Sybase, a relational database management software for designing the layout of databases. He took a training course in relational databases design offered locally by Sybase. In 1992, when many in Venter's lab left NIH and founded TIGR, Kerlavage says that the group underwent another scale-up in terms of personnel and computers.

What general advice would you give a person thinking about embarking on a career in informatics?

The interest, drive, and dedication needed to learn something completely new has to be there first to move into bioinformatics—or for that matter any allied science career—successfully. It won't work for everyone.

It's also important to be in an environment like TIGR where the data are being generated. In essence, people here are forced to react very quickly to problems. So out of necessity they learn what they need to learn by working closely with a team of experts from varied backgrounds to solve a problem. They're learning the new skill within a context. Because this type of on-the-job training is becoming essential to gain experience in bioinformatics, TIGR is exploring options for setting up such a program with local universities.

What practical advice would you give on how to prepare and market oneself for a career in informatics?

For a long time there was no formal training in this area. The term bioinformatics was only coined a few years ago, and people are still debating its definition. Now some of these programs are starting to spring up. Typically what they're doing is bringing people in and giving them an education in both computer science and life science, although some are more directed at one side or the other. So you certainly can come at this field from either side. Considering the diversity in backgrounds of people we've hired here at TIGR, that's true. For example, some with a strict biology background who know their way around a computer have come in and learned the necessary computer tools. They have taught themselves how to write simple scripts to carry out tasks, but they're not using the more high-powered languages like C++ or Java. They're using Perl, a popular language in bioinformatics. It's fairly easy to pick up and a lot of biologists have learned this. So learning programming languages like Perl would be extremely valuable. Go to a local bookstore and pick up books from which to teach yourself these languages. You can also find formal classes. Java is also really taking hold in the bioinformatics world. But I'm not so sure that this is easy for the average person to pick up.

Teri Klein, Associate Adjunct Professor, Department of Pharmaceutical Chemistry at the University of California, San Francisco

Klein received her Ph.D. in medical informatics from the University of California, San Francisco in 1987. Her research concentrated on mapping unknown receptor sites. Prior to starting her doctoral program in the early 1980s, she worked as a life science researcher in corporate and academic labs.

"Along the way toward deciding to go on for a Ph.D., I became interested in solving biological questions which could be addressed using computers," she recalls. "Although I now work mostly in bioinformatics and biomedical computing, the medical informatics degree gives me the freedom to work in the broad area of computer-related health science issues. Within my program I was taught everything from basic programming to operating systems, all of which apply to classical clinical medical informatics as well as bioinformatics."

Klein is now involved in developing rational approaches to drug design and understanding the structural basis of disease. In particular, her current studies include the genetic collagenous disorder osteogenesis impefecta and the molecular mechanisms of mutagenesis and DNA repair.

What general advice would you give a person thinking about embarking on a career in informatics?

Get an experiential and educational foundation that is sufficient to bridge the gap between both computer and biological/chemical sciences. For example, if you're a life scientist, do a postdoc in a lab that concentrates more on the theoretical aspects of biological systems, not one that uses traditional bench or wet-lab approaches. For example, for what I do now—designing drugs based on biological structure—I need to understand the disease process from the biological side and how to use design and visualization tools from the computer-science side. This also means that you need to be motivated to keep abreast of changes in two fields.

What practical advice would you give on how to prepare and market oneself for a career in informatics?

The field is pretty wide open now. With the hundreds of genome-based databases out there, there's a wealth of data to be explored and analyzed. There are many positions advertised at universities and in industry, with more posts being offered in the private sector at the moment.

The National Center for Biotechnology Information sponsors training fellowships and the facilities to get practical experience in both areas. In graduate school, take advantage of resources on your campus and the Internet. Gain exposure by attending such conferences as the Pacific Symposium on Biocomputing or the Intelligent Systems for Molecular Biology.

Mark Graves, Assistant Director of Bioinformatics, Iconix Pharmaceuticals, Mountain View, CA

Graves received his Ph.D. in computer science from the University of Michigan in 1993, after which he held a postdoctoral fellowship at Baylor College of Medicine in Houston in the Department of Cell Biology, where he worked on computational molecular biology. "I've always been interested in ways to organize complex information, as well as genetics," says Graves. "Combining the two seemed natural."

At Baylor, he audited all the graduate-level genetics courses that were offered and interacted with the life science as well as the computational-biology faculty. After his postdoc he became an instructor in the Department of Cell Biology at Baylor for almost two years. Then he worked at Mercator Genetics, a biotech startup, doing positional cloning in the hunt for disease genes. In 1997, when Mercator was bought out by Progenitor, another biotech company, Graves started consulting independently for companies that needed his bioinformatics expertise. He then joined Iconix, a start-up company combining chemical and genetic approaches to drug discovery.

What general advice would you give a person thinking about embarking on a career in informatics?

From a computer-science background, you'll have to be willing to expand the thought processes and skills you learned in computer science to be able to work in the biological sciences. I'm excited about learning how to solve new problems. To me, it has been a freeing experience, to not always have to think linearly, as one does in mathematics and traditional computer-science applications.

A couple of instances come to mind. For example, in trying to represent within a database if one piece of DNA has successfully joined to another piece of DNA in an experiment, a trained computer scientist might decide that the way to represent the answer to a yes/no question like "Did A hybridize to B?" is with a yes/no answer. However, most biologists would be unsatisfied with this approach. They will be looking for some form of experimental evidence, for example, the strength of the hybridization signal. The problem is that the hybridization experiment might have a 30 percent error rate that the biologist would also like to track.

In one project I worked on, there were 40 concepts that needed to be captured in a computer and all but one required some deviation from a straightforward, yes/no representation.

Another example of the different thought processes occurs in developing software. Software engineers are taught to proceed from the abstract requirements, through design, to implementation. Biology, however, starts with concrete examples, analyzes and experiments with them, then creates a model.

Biologists are trained to work in this more ambiguous, fluid environment, which is foreign to the computer scientist. It is learning to think in both paradigms that I find fascinating and necessary to succeed.

What practical advice would you give on how to prepare and market oneself for a career in informatics?

Coming from a computer-science background, I suggest auditing life science classes. Even undergraduate courses will get you into the subject matter enough to be able to converse with the biologists you'll be working with. This will give you a foundation and get you familiar with the jargon of the subject matter. Try to land an internship or fellowship with someone already in the field. Also, spend some time in a wet lab: run some gels, learn how to do PCR, help a friend with an experiment.

☐ Medical Informatics

The amount of information generated by the medical and healthcare professions has mushroomed in the last decade, from more and more complicated medical records to digitized cadavers. And, the field of medical informatics, which entails managing and applying that information, has grown along with it. Medical informatics specialists are employed at universities, hospitals and medical centers, pharmaceutical companies, contract-research organizations, and managed-care organizations. Not all medical informatics specialists are M.D.s; many in fact come from nursing, pharmacy, basic research science, and library science. Some people work with what is called decision support—using digitized information on the Web or an expert system, for example—to make better diagnoses. Another area is clinical-information management, in which patient care is improved by analyzing computerized medical records to constantly refine procedural guidelines.

According to Russ Altman, an assistant professor of medical informatics at Stanford University, medical informatics consists of clinical informatics (information systems and theory to aid in the optimal delivery of clinical care to patients) and bioinformatics (application of computational technologies to problems in molecular biology). But, he says, this is not a common distinction. "Most people equate medical informatics with clinical informatics, and keep bioinformatics administratively separate. We believe that there are a strong set of similarities in the methods used by the two subdisciplines, and in the ways in which students should be trained in these areas. Thus, our students graduate with a solid knowledge of both fields, but an emphasis on one or the other."

Read on for the career advice from some who are working in medical informatics in an academic environment.

One-on-One with Medical Informatics Specialists

Mark Frisse, Associate Professor of Medicine, Medical Informatics, and Computer Science and Associate Dean and Director of the Bernard Becker Medical Library at Washington University, St. Louis, MO

Frisse received his M.D. from Washington University in 1978, after which he practiced as an internist and oncologist for over 10 years. During this time he also became the editor of the *Washington University Manual of Medical Therapeutics*. In 1987 he completed his M.S. in medical computer science from Stanford, and returned to Washington University. In 1997 he received his M.B.A. from Washington University.

Frisse cites three factors that influenced his transition into medical informatics: One, a change in Medicare billing that made it important for the first time for people to really pay attention to what clinicians were doing. "Cost containment issues, I believed, would drive computers and hospital information systems. Two, I used my first word processor, a WANG, and saw what you could do to produce good text. Three, I became exposed to digital radiology systems, and wondered: If they can send X-ray images around, why can't I send images of books?"

These influences eventually led to postdoctoral informatics training at Stanford University. Upon returning to Washington University in 1987, he recalls, "there were few people who knew both medicine and computing, so I became involved in a number of activities that most physicians considered uninteresting at the time: planning for ambulatory facilities, communications infrastructures, etc. It was a real eye-opener. I remained active clinically, so it was a stretch to maintain knowledge in all areas. I'm now an associate dean and a library director. I run a library and information technology service composed of about 50 people in more traditional library roles and 25 people doing computing and networking. The skills required for this type of position are organizational development, financial planning, diplomacy, and collaboration.

What general advice would you give a person thinking about embarking on a career in informatics?

I believe formal training is important. This means classwork, not just paradigm hopping. Informatics is much more than what government agencies decide to fund from year to year, but all too frequently the funding issues become dominant over training. One must look at education as a long-term investment and commit to it. Unless one is going into a purely clinical/administrative position, one must ally oneself with a strong engineering program. Even in the clinical arena, one *must* have more business skills than most (if not all) formal training programs currently offer.

I have an M.D., extensive clinical credentials, an M.S. from Stanford and, most recently, an M.B.A. I cannot imagine functioning without all of these degrees, or, more concisely, without the knowledge I obtained from these three disciplines. I learned early from a mentor that some of the best contributions can be made by leaving one's home discipline, absorbing oneself in a different discipline, and then returning and applying the new perspective to one's original career. I believe that.

What practical advice would you give on how to prepare and market oneself for a career in informatics?

There is no substitute for formal training both in computer science, information technology, more broadly defined, and business management. And, there is no substitute for mentored administrative experience . . . none.

In my view, the key is to distinguish oneself as an extremely well trained and experienced professional from a health professional who knows how to build Web pages or such. Unfortunately, although I believe intensive training is essential, there is little evidence that the clinical marketplace can distinguish between those who are intensively trained and those with superficial knowledge. Often organizations seek healthcare professionals who can articulate technical terms to clinical peers. I believe the research marketplace has a much greater ability to distinguish between those who talk in superficialities and those who know their stuff.

Russ Altman, Assistant Professor of Medical Informatics at Stanford University

Altman received his M.D. in 1990 and Ph.D. in 1989, both from Stanford University. "I started in bench lab work, but realized that I liked theoretical computer work better," he recalls. "So I switched from experimental structural biology to medical informatics, with an emphasis on molecular biological computing. My time is split in a manner that is consistent with traditional academic medical positions. Eighty percent of my time is devoted to research and 20 percent to clinical medicine, along with some administrative responsibilities."

What general advice would you give a person thinking about embarking on a career in informatics?

Strive for excellence in whatever you do, and keep track of your accomplishments in the alternative endeavor, so you can talk about them in job interviews and highlight them on resumes. Communication skills and evidence that you can work on a team are always key. Also, it is helpful to hone any mathematical or computer skills, since these tend to be useful in many different settings. After getting a degree, I think on-the-job training is the most key. I'm not convinced that certificates other than degrees themselves are worthwhile. Get your degree, and then start doing useful things, no matter what the task.

What practical advice would you give on how to prepare and market oneself for a career in informatics?

Working on an informatics project and cultivating collaborative experiences is important. It helps to know the domain—medicine or biology—as well as having technical experience in computer science, statistics, and mathematics, but you don't need a degree in both to be useful to a collaborative effort.

I have recently come up with the idea of a "transition experience" to give people some idea about what to look for in their next professional step. When you want to enter a new field in which you don't have previous credentials, you need to find a job that you can obtain on the strength of your "old" credentials but that lets you gain skills and experience in the new field, providing you with "new" credentials. Thus, a computer scientist could join a biology project as a computer person, but slowly get more involved in the biology side. Similar for biologists wanting to get involved in bioinformatics.

Also, letters from previous mentors are extremely important. They can testify to all the key attributes I mentioned previously. I guess the old saying is true: do what you love, and good things will follow.

David Lobach, Assistant Research Professor and Former Postdoctoral Fellow in Medical and Bioinformatics at Duke University Medical Center

Lobach completed a joint M.D.-Ph.D. in immunology from Duke in 1987. From 1987 to 1994, he worked in clinical settings in the areas of internal medicine and endocrinology. He also conducted research in molecular genetics. Then he enrolled in the Duke University Graduate School in Biomedical Engineering for a two-year M.S. in bioinformatics. "I moved to this field because it is more applied," he explains. "I could better see the direct benefits of my work, especially in improving quality of patient care. I'm also very interested in computers." He now does medical informatics research to develop decision-support systems for applying clinical information to patient care.

> *What practical advice would you give on how to prepare and market oneself for a career in informatics?*
> If you're looking for another way to contribute to your field, there's a great need for people who know how to make better use of clinical information. Getting a formal degree is a good way to get up and running. Applied internships associated with a formal program give one exposure to the real world and insight into what the field is all about.

Resources

Professional Societies

American Medical Informatics Association (AMIA). This is the main professional society for medical informatics professionals. Contact:

Gwyn Roberts
Director, Membership & Marketing
American Medical Informatics Association
4915 St. Elmo, Suite 401
Bethesda, MD 20814
301-657-1291
Fax: 301-657-1296
gwyn@mail.amia.org
http://www.amia.org

International Society of Computational Biology (ISCB). The ISCB was formed in 1997 with 540 members. Attendees of the International Conferences on Intelligent Systems for Molecular Biology (for the 1998 meeting: http://www-lbit.iro.umontreal.ca/ISMB98), the Pacific Symposium on Biocomputing (http://www.cgl.ucsf.edu/psb/), and the Meeting on the Interconnection of Molecular Biology Databases (http://ari.ai.sri.com/~pkarp/mimbd.html) were all charter members. Contact:

Larry Hunter, President
301-496-9303
hunter@nlm.nih.gov
http://www.iscb.org

Education and Training

Fellowships

Centers for Disease Control. Two-year fellowships in public health informatics are competitively available to candidates with either a public health background and a strong interest and/or experience in computer systems or prior training and/or experience in informatics and an interest in applying that knowledge in the public health arena. A master's degree (or doctorate) in a relevant discipline is required. Contact:

Cheryl Guthrie
Postgraduate Research Program - CDC
Education and Training Division
Oak Ridge Institute for Science and Education
P.O. Box 117
Oak Ridge, TN 37831-0117
423-576-8503
http://www.cdc.gov/epo/dphsi/informat.htm

or

Centers for Disease Control
Division of Public Health Surveillance and Informatics
Epidemiology Program Office
MS C-08
1600 Clifton Road NE
Atlanta, GA 30333
404-639-3761
soib@cdc.gov

GenBank Fellows Fellowship Program. This program is a National Center for Biotechnology Information (NCBI) initiative to improve the quality of the GenBank database and provide training in bioinformatics. Candidates are selected from scientist applications with Ph.D., M.D., or equivalent degrees, strong backgrounds in biology, and an interest in applying computational tools to research problems in molecular and structural biology, genetics, and phylogeny.

Applicants for GenBank Fellows positions need not necessarily be U.S. citizens. Appointments are made either within the NIH Intramural

Research Training Award Program or within the Visiting Fellows Program of the Fogarty International Center. Stipends are determined according to the number of years of postdoctoral experience. Contact:

David Landsman
NIH/NLM/NCBI
8600 Rockville Pike
Building 38A, Room 8N807
Bethesda, MD 20894
301-496-2475
Fax: 301-480-9241
info@ncbi.nlm.nih.gov
http://www.ncbi.nlm.nih.gov

Alfred P. Sloan Foundation-U.S. Department of Energy Joint Postdoctoral Fellowships in Computational Biology. There are several up-to-two-year postdoc fellowships for new Ph.D.s in computational molecular biology related to the study of human and other genomes in academic departments or other laboratories in the United States or Canada selected by the applicant. Contact:

Michael S. Teitelbaum
Sloan-U.S. Department of Energy Joint Postdoctoral
 Fellowships in Computational Biology
Alfred P. Sloan Foundation
630 Fifth Ave., Suite 2550
New York, NY 10111
http://www.sloan.org/science/CMB.html

National Library of Medicine Fellowship in Applied Informatics. These are one- or two-year fellowships for physicians, nurses, health science librarians, researchers, administrators, and others involved in healthcare activities with a B.S., M.S., and/or Ph.D. or enrolled in a program leading to such degrees. The program encourages midcareer and junior applicants. Fellows are trained in informatics as it applies to both clinical and basic research, and patient care. Contact:

Office of Extramural Outreach and Information Services
National Institutes of Health
6701 Rockledge Drive, MSC 7910
Bethesda, MD 20892-7910
301-435-0714
Fax: 301-480-0525

askNIH@odrockm1.od.nih.gov
http://www.nlm.nih.gov/about_nlm/organization/extramural/appfellow.html

Educational Programs

Bioinformatics. There are a few universities that offer formal educational programs in bioinformatics and computational biology. Some of their Web sites listed below describe training fellowships and provide links to bioinformatics news, events, tools for research, and career information.

W. M. Keck Centers for Computational Biology. Two centers for graduate and postdoctoral training in computational biology:

University of Pittsburgh-Pittsburgh Supercomputing
  Center-Carnegie Mellon
Pittsburgh, PA
http://www.cs.pitt.edu/keck/Frames/Welcome.html

Baylor College of Medicine-Rice University-University of Houston
Houston, TX
Marc Archambault, Director of the Keck Center in Houston, TX
march@bioc.rice.edu
713-527-4752
http://www-bioc.rice.edu/

Rutgers, The State University of New Jersey-University of Medicine and Dentistry of New Jersey. Ph.D. program in computational molecular biology. All students receive financial support, including a fellowship stipend and tuition remission (http://cmb.rutgers.edu/).

University of Pennsylvania Center for Bioinformatics. B.S. degree through the Schools of Arts and Sciences and Engineering, M.S. in Biotechnology with a track in computational biology and bioinformatics, and doctoral and postdoctoral programs in computational biology.

Center for Bioinformatics
University of Pennsylvania
1312 Blockley Hall
418 Guardian Drive
Philadelphia, PA 19104
215-573-3105
Fax: 215-573-3111
http://cbil.humgen.upenn.edu/cbiweb

George Mason University. Ph.D. program in bioinformatics and computational biology as applied to molecular biology and ecology.

George Michaels, Program Coordinator
Institute for Computational Sciences and Informatics
George Mason University
103 Science and Technology-I, MS 5C3
Fairfax, VA 22030-4444
703-993-1998
gmichael@gmu.edu
http://www.science.gmu.edu/~michaels/Bioinformatics

Washington University Institute for Biomedical Computing. Summer internships and graduate-level courses.

David States, Director
700 South Euclid Ave.
St. Louis, MO 63110-1012
314-362-2135
Fax: 314-362-0234
states@ibc.wustl.edu
http://www.ibc.wustl.edu/CMB

Boston University BioMolecular Engineering Research Center. Postdocs, graduate training, and workshops (http://bmerc-www.bu.edu/bmerc-main. html).

Stanford University's interdepartmental Medical Information Sciences training program. Postdocs and graduate training in bioinformatics, specifically genomics. Contact:

Russ B. Altman
Section of Medical Informatics
Stanford University Medical Center
251 Campus Drive, MSOB X-215
Stanford, CA 94305-5479
650-725-3394
Fax: 650-725-7944
russ.altman@stanford.edu
http://www-smi.stanford.edu/people/altman/bioinformatics.html
http://www-smi.stanford.edu/projects/smi-web/academics/

University of Washington Department of Molecular Biotechnology. Interdisciplinary graduate programs in biological, physical, and computational sciences.

Graduate Studies Coordinator
Department of Molecular Biotechnology
Box 357730
University of Washington School of Medicine
Seattle, WA 98195-7730
molbiotk@u.washington.edu
http://weber.u.washington.edu/~mbt/graduate2.html

University of California, Santa Cruz. Graduate and undergraduate-level bioinformatics class (http://www.cse.ucsc.edu/classes/cmp243).

EMBL—Structural Biology, Biocomputing Unit, Heidelberg, Germany. Ph.D. program (http://www.embl-heidelberg.de/ExternalInfo/PhdProgramme/PhD3Biocomputing.html).

Birkbeck College, London, UK Department of Crystallography. M.Sc. in molecular modeling and bioinformatics.

Malet St.
London WC1E 7HX
United Kingdom
011-44-071-631-6800
http://www.cryst.bbk.ac.uk/~jody/courses/bioinf_cont.html

University of Manchester School of Biological Sciences. M.Sc. in bioinformatics and computational molecular biology.

The Graduate Office
School of Biological Sciences
1.30 Stopford Building
University of Manchester
Oxford Rd.
Manchester M13 9PT
United Kingdom
011-44-061-275-5608
http://www.biomed.man.ac.uk/gradschool/msc/bioinf/bookbio.html

University of York, United Kingdom. M.Sc. and postgraduate diploma in biological computation.

University of York
PO Box 373
York YO1 5YW
United Kingdom
011-44-0-1904-432888
Fax: 011-44-0-1904-432860
http://www.york.ac.uk/depts/biol/gsp/masters/bc/biol_com.htm

AAAS's Nextwave (http://www.nextwave.org/server-java/SAM/virtual. htm) lists several on-line learning centers that offer Internet-based courses.

Medical Informatics. The National Library of Medicine encourages and supports training programs in medical informatics. Over 20 such programs exist at several universities throughout the country. For more information on this, look on the National Library of Medicine Web site: http://www.nlm.nih.gov.

A selected list of leading medical informatics training programs is also maintained by Stanford University's interdepartmental Medical Information Sciences training program at http://www-smi.stanford.edu/ projects/smi-web/academics/. It contains hotlinks and contact information for all programs.

The National Library of Medicine also sponsors "Medical Informatics," a one-week summer course at the Marine Biological Laboratory to train fellows in the application of computer and information science to medicine. Contact:

Marine Biological Laboratory
Woods Hole, MA
admissions@mbl.edu
http://www.mbl.edu

Jobhunting and Networking

"There's no shortage of jobs in this area right now because there's a whole industry springing up around genomics," remarks Kerlavage. "Now everyone is trying to hire their own informatics team, and in addition to that there are new companies forming to specifically fill that niche. These firms are set up to build software tools to make mining DNA sequences easier at pharmaceutical and biotech companies."

Jobs—especially ones based at universities—are advertised in such pertinent scientific journals as *Science* and *Nature*. At scientific meetings there are often job fairs that sometimes have bioinformatics jobs advertised. Kerlavage and others in the bioinformatics field say that most of the jobs in the field are advertised through the professional grapevine. "There's a lot of word-of-mouth job information at meetings, especially for industry-based jobs," he says. "A lot of companies exhibit at these meetings, putting up looking-to-hire notices on the bulletin boards. The boards get covered the first day of the meeting."

Maria Betty's Web site (http://www.bioplanet.com) contains links to some bioinformatics job vacancies and to bioinformatics employers' homepages, especially those in industry. Also check out the employment links on the ISCB and AMIA Web sites.

The Web site of the International Conference on Intelligent Systems for Molecular Biology (for 1997 meeting: http://www.ebi.ac.uk/ismb97) also has lots of career and networking information, including a description of the job fair held at its annual meeting, travel fellowships, mirror Web sites, previous ISMB conferences, and links to other bioinformatics and related conferences. These are annual conferences held all over the world that bring together biological, chemical, and computational scientists interested in computational biology. 1998 marks the sixth year of the gathering.

"Recently a whole industry of bioinformatics recruiters has developed," says Chris Overton, director of the University of Pennsylvania Center for Bioinformatics. "These headhunters are aggressively searching for qualified people. Many such recruiters have come to Penn to interview our graduates at job fairs that we've set up. People are also starting to move around from one place to another so many jobs are first heard about through personal contacts."

Technology Transfer

According to a 1997 report by the Association of University Technology Managers (AUTM), universities in the United States issue about 1,500 patents per year, with about 200 universities engaged in technology transfer. This is six times the 250 patents issued from universities in 1980, prior to the Bayh–Dole Act, which enables universities, federally funded research programs, and small businesses to own and patent inventions discovered in federally funded research programs.

Technology transfer managers help shepherd an idea conceived in the public sector—at academic or government research centers—to commercialization in the private sector. They deal with the disclosure of an invention, the patenting and licensing of the commercialization rights, and the eventual publication of the research describing the new discovery.

Professionals in this area, employed in universities, medical centers, and federal research labs, come from both academia and the private sector. In a university setting, the majority of professionals do not have a business background, whereas in industry, most do not have university tech transfer experience, although may hold advanced degrees in the sciences.

In general, most tech transfer professionals in industry are senior management, not entry level. Many work in acquisitions and licensing groups and are not research scientists, although they may at one time have worked within an R&D group in a company. Some scientists working within the business side of science have some type of tech transfer role (see Chapter 8).

147

According to the AUTM, new graduates will probably have an easier time finding a job in a university tech transfer office versus one in industry. Generally the positions that entail licensing and development in a corporate setting—especially in large companies—are held by people who have considerable experience within the company or relevant experience in licensing.

"Take a licensing course from AUTM," advises Christina Liu, a technology transfer fellow at the National Cancer Institute who has graduate training in both biology and business. "It's worth spending the money to get the experience and to have it on your resume to show potential employers you are serious about a career in tech transfer. It's also a great opportunity to network." Liu also mentions that it's hard to get on-the-job training in many areas of intellectual property without a law degree because of the proprietary nature of the work, so she recommends the AUTM workshops as another way to get exposure to the field.

In general, tech transfer professionals describe themselves as being forward-looking and keenly interested in a broader picture of basic research, its practical application, and where that is headed. Read on for more about the individual experience and advice of six scientists at various points in their careers who are now technology transfer professionals in academic settings.

One-on-One with Tech Transfer Professionals

Liana Moussatos, Manager of University & Government Licensing in the External Science & Technology Department at Bristol-Myers Squibb Pharmaceutical Comp., Princeton, NJ

Moussatos received her Ph.D. in plant pathology from the University of California, Davis in 1989. She then worked as a postdoc in the Department of Cellular and Molecular Physiology in the Yale University School of Medicine until 1994. "I began to take an interest in alternative careers during my postdoc when I noticed that even world-famous researchers were not getting their NIH grants renewed and attributed this to the changing whims in Washington."

At the end of her postdoc, she landed a technology transfer fellowship with the National Cancer Institute "to learn the changing whims in Washington and how to transfer new research discoveries into products that benefit society."

At the end of her fellowship in 1996, she was hired as a Licensing Assistant at Memorial Sloan-Kettering Cancer Center. "Although my

---

CHARACTERISTICS OF A SWITCH TO A CAREER
IN TECHNOLOGY TRANSFER

These attributes may not strike every reader the same way. Depending on your background and interests, you may view some of these as either attractive or unappealing.

* Most positions are not entry level.
* You get to work with the broad aspects of science.
* You get to work with the practical applications of science.
* You get a chance to work with cutting-edge ideas.
* You can work with diverse types of professionals.
* It's a one-way switch.

---

title was licensing assistant, I only did one license because there was a strong need for database upgrading and developing a home page and I had the necessary computer skills," says Moussatos. "The need for technology transfer staff with computer skills is very high and it is rewarding and fun to create something that helps everyone in the office do their job better. However, there is no career path in these positions. Advancement comes from gaining experience in closing deals involving money.

"About seven months into my position, I realized that in order to become good at negotiating deals, I needed industry experience. I started telling my contacts about my thoughts and they gave me leads, resulting in interviews at biotech, pharmaceutical, and venture-capital companies. This led to my accepting my current position at Bristol-Myers Squibb in December 1997."

What general advice would you give a person thinking about embarking on a career in technology transfer?

Get experience negotiating deals. While interviewing I was always asked how many license deals had I closed and how much money was involved. However, it is also who you know in the business so keep in touch with your mentors and make new contacts at Association of University Technology Managers and Licensing Executives Society (LES) professional meetings. To get your feet wet, take AUTM's Basic Licensing course.

What practical advice would you give on how to prepare and market oneself for a career in tech transfer?

Remember resumes are not curriculum vitae. Limit them to one page and organize them by your skills.

Regarding interviewing, just be calm and don't talk too much. You are there to ask questions just as much as tell them about yourself.

Kathleen Denis, Vice President of Technology Development for Allegheny University of the Health Sciences, Philadelphia, PA

Denis received her Ph.D. in immunology in 1981 from the University of Pennsylvania. Her first experience with technology development began at a diagnostics firm, Specialty Diagnostics, in Santa Monica, CA, where a mentor involved her in technology acquisition transactions. This coincided with her first experience patenting her own technologies on novel methods for producing human monoclonal antibodies. In 1991, she began consulting for the University of Pennsylvania Center for Technology Transfer. This experience led to her present position, where she now heads the Office of Technology Development for the Allegheny Health, Education, and Research Foundation.

Denis says that she has always had an "informal interest in the business of science." She describes her position as serving "the interface between researchers and the outside commercial world." She manages the interactions involved in commercializing technologies developed at Allegheny. This includes contracting for industry-sponsored research; negotiating other contracts with industry such as confidentiality, consulting, and material transfer agreements; and managing the patenting and marketing of technologies developed by researchers at Allegheny, as well as evaluating new technologies that Allegheny would like to bring into their hospitals and laboratories.

What general advice would you give a person thinking about embarking on a career in tech transfer?

Do some consulting either on a reasonable recharge or low or no cost for a technology development office at an academic institution. This would probably be your best bet to get started, as these offices are often understaffed and have more work than the individuals can handle. Before doing this or right around the time of first looking for a consulting-type position, I would advise either attending a meeting of the Association of University Technology Managers or their basic licensing course. These are reasonably priced opportunities to learn more about the field, to begin to speak the language, and to begin to meet other people in the field.

What practical advice would you give on how to prepare and market oneself for a career in tech transfer?

I believe someone interested in a career in technology transfer needs to have a certain personality type. You need to be action-oriented and interested in interpersonal relationships. It is very difficult to be successful in technology transfer without creating relationships. Our work goes far beyond the agreements we negotiate. We really create relationships between ourselves, our administration or faculty investigators, the investigators at commercial entities, and the business-development people at commercial entities. Also, one has to have a knack for problem solving, negotiation, and the ability to keep very complex materials straight and to work on them simultaneously. Without those skills, there really is no preparation that can be made for this career. With those skills, an individual could then tailor a resume to more or less emphasize any technology evaluation experience, experience with patenting, experience interacting with industry, or negotiating agreements to benefit their job search.

The advantage of having a science background in technology transfer, and particularly a Ph.D.-level science background, is that you will get more respect from your faculty investigators if you have a Ph.D. The Ph.D. in many ways gives you the ability to critique scientific work and ask appropriate questions to help separate the wheat from the chaff. One disadvantage is that you tend to get overly enamored with the technology. A technology can be absolutely spectacular, but if no one wants to buy it, it will not be of much use to a tech transfer office.

One of the major trade-offs is more psychological than real: the loss of respect of your colleagues once you leave pure research. But, I feel that less and less as the years go by. A related issue is you now become part of the establishment. You're an administrator, rather than a scientist. You're often viewed as part of the enemy camp by individuals who previously would have been your colleagues. I try to combat that by joining them rather than beating them. I am very sympathetic to faculty needs and their culture. I try to patiently explain the difference between their wants and needs and those of their industry counterparts. They are usually quite willing to accept you more as a colleague if you use that approach. I also like to maintain a faculty appointment at the institution. This helps me stay in touch with a department fairly closely and provides an opportunity for teaching.

I read scientific publications, more general ones, and ones in my former area of research. I also attend scientific meetings every few years in my former discipline or a related one.

Doug Heller, Project Manager, ARCH Development Corp., Chicago

Heller received his Ph.D. in organic chemistry in 1996. "I have always had an interest in the practical or applications side of science and how technology can benefit society," says Heller. "As a graduate student, I also came to appreciate my people and communication skills and realized I would better realize those talents in a business environment than in a strictly research one."

Heller is currently a project manager with the technology transfer office for the University of Chicago—ARCH. "I have cradle-to-grave responsibilities for the technology transfer process," he says. "I scout for research which might have commercial applications; perform the first-round screening to assess commercial potential; and then—should it pass initial scrutiny—plan and manage for its commercialization. I manage the patent process, do the research and marketing to identify and attract business partners, and negotiate license agreements. A small percentage of deals involve starting up a company around technologies. In these cases, I help write business plans, procure funding, and assist in assembling the package of resources (management and facilities, for example) to launch the start-up. I am also responsible for managing a preexisting portfolio of patent and license cases."

What general advice would you give a person thinking about embarking on a career in technology transfer?

There are a number of general skills that one gains, especially in a Ph.D. program, that I think translate well to nonscientific arenas. The ability to cope with disappointment and uncertainty is one. The ability to be self-directed and create structure and a plan, when there are many options and directions in which to proceed, is another.

Specific technical knowledge in a scientific area that happens to be hot business-wise—biotech, for example—can be a powerful asset. Certainly my technical training is one of my strongest assets, and allows me to fairly quickly read and understand proposed scientific ideas. As a graduate student, the skills I gained from constantly reading the scientific literature and knowing how to go about finding information—basic library research skills, really—have translated well to the kinds of market research and analysis I now do.

Familiarity with academic culture is another asset when it comes to interactions with faculty. People management in general is a big component of technology transfer. Being comfortable interacting with a wide variety of people and being able to appreciate their perspectives is a critical skill.

The ability to quickly discern if a project is worth working on seriously is another important skill. Tech transfer is a big juggling act and can get unmanageable if one doesn't triage opportunities well.

What practical advice would you give on how to prepare and market oneself for a career in tech transfer?

Strong interpersonal skills are necessary. Technology transfer is more about listening and relationship building than about the technology per se. I would recommend that job applicants emphasize their people skills. Marketing can involve a lot of cold calling, so being comfortable with starting conversations with strangers is important.

I would highlight in an interview or cover letter any experience with managing a project or working as part of a diverse team. Any sales experience whatsoever would be another thing to emphasize. Any evidence of entrepreneurial inclination and experience would be another aspect to talk up. Knowledge of business and markets in one's technical area is another obvious way to show your interest in tech transfer.

You can get fairly up to speed on the players in a particular field by reading trade magazines and the general business press. As for training in technology transfer, I would recommend that the person read outside of their particular area of expertise, and start picking up on what may be trends. A series of biotech journals, variously titled *Trends in . . . Biotechnology, Genetics*, etc., is one suggestion.

Familiarity with patents is another useful skill. As a graduate student, I made it a point to read patents in my particular field. The technology transfer industry organization, AUTM, has meetings periodically, which can be a great opportunity to network and learn about the field. Volunteering with a university technology transfer office is yet another way to gain exposure.

Sandra Shotwell, Director of the Office of Technology Management at the Oregon Health Sciences University (OHSU), Portland, OR

Shotwell received her Ph.D. in biology from Caltech in 1982, after which she did a postdoc at Stanford University in neurobiology from 1982 to 1984. In the mid-1980s, she moved into the area of technology transfer when Stanford decided to formally commit to commercializing biotech-related inventions from its researchers' innovations.

"I had many motivations to direct my career towards tech transfer," explains Shotwell. "Bench research wasn't a great fit for me. The focus was too narrow. With tech transfer, I could use more of my skills. Now I combine my knowledge of science and my people skills with newly gained experience in federal regulations, patent law, and negotiation."

In her present job, she manages OHSU's tech transfer office, which includes staffing, budgeting, and strategic planning. She also manages to keep her hand in basic licensing and spinning off new technologies into start-up companies.

What general advice would you give a person thinking about embarking on a career in technology transfer?
The transferable skills that I learned in my scientific training that

I now use as a technology transfer professional are the ability to analyze and solve problems, technological and subject matter expertise, and verbal and written presentation skills. More importantly, in a way, is to consider what I didn't learn in my scientific training: how to make a deal, how business is conducted, marketing, and negotiating. I learned those skills, as well as patent law, and federal laws and regulations pertaining to technology transfer and the Food and Drug Administration, on the job. There is much to learn on the job, many subtleties of which are not possible to touch on in the summary courses now available.

What practical advice would you give on how to prepare and market oneself for a career in tech transfer?

Demonstrate interest by joining AUTM and LES, taking their basic licensing courses and attending meetings. This shows serious interest to potential employers and offers situations to make contacts within the field and for jobhunting.

To really get experience in tech transfer, you need to learn by doing it; it's really an apprenticeship approach. Some offices take on interns to do research-oriented jobs; this might be a good way for a graduate student to get a foot in the door and to learn what is involved in commercializing scientific discoveries. Others consult with tech transfer offices, working on a project-by-project, contractual basis. Contact the tech transfer offices at your university and see what opportunities they may have or be open to. It never hurts to ask!

Frances Toneguzzo, Associate Director for Technology Licensing, Office for Technology and Trademark Licensing at Harvard University, Cambridge, MA

Toneguzzo received her Ph.D. in biochemistry from McMaster University, Canada in 1978. After two postdocs, one at the University of California, Berkeley and another at Harvard University, she started working as a research scientist at DuPont, where she gradually moved up to a supervisory position as a group leader. After DuPont, she worked for a smaller company developing instruments, and after a brief stint as a consultant, started her own company with two colleagues based on clinical diagnostics. She came to her present position at Harvard in 1993.

"A combination of strong technical background and intimate knowledge of the biotech industry, as well as a general interest in exploring ways for academia and industry to collaborate, led me to my position at

Harvard," explains Toneguzzo. "This position has a variety of aspects. First is the importance of establishing and maintaining solid working relationships with faculty. After all, that is where the technology transfer process starts."

She also evaluates technologies for commercial utility, oversees patent filing and prosecution, markets inventions, and negotiates license agreements. "Lately I've been spending most of my time negotiating agreements," she adds.

What kinds of general advice would you give a person thinking about embarking on a career in technology transfer?

A strong analytical ability in combination with industry experience should give one the ability to look at the big picture and not focus on the details. I have heard this as an argument against hiring Ph.D.s for tech transfer positions; that is, they would spend too much time on the scientific minutiae and miss the big picture. But in my experience that is an absolute fallacy. Also, the ability to present rational and logical arguments—also learned from scientific training—is critical for win–win negotiation strategies.

What practical advice would you give on how to prepare and market oneself for a career in tech transfer?

I believe that strength in a technical area and knowledge of industry are the two most important background qualities. Negotiation and business strategies can be learned on the job, however, establishing good working relationships with faculty is key. Having a technical background helps a great deal in that.

Knowledge of the industry is also important in developing reasonable licensing strategies. Again, that is not something that can be learned on the job. AUTM offers a basic licensing course, which is extremely useful. Negotiation seminars also abound and would be useful. Some tech transfer offices look very favorably on people with M.B.A.s. This is probably not a bad degree to get since it can open up many doors in industry as well.

Martin Rachmeler, Former Director of the Technology Transfer Office at the University of California, San Diego

Rachmeler was a faculty member in the department of microbiology-immunology at Northwestern University from 1962 to 1989. He further assumed responsibility for research services administration in 1977 in the office of the Vice President for Research. One of his responsibilities in the new position, in addition to continuing to teach in the medical school, was technology transfer, which was relocated from the legal department. "I seized upon this area because it was an opportunity for me to live vicariously with other scientists while not performing any research myself," he notes.

Rachmeler's training in tech transfer was both formal and informal. In addition to his experience and training in science and research, he took courses given by various groups, including LES, AUTM, the Patent Law Institute, the John Marshall Law School in Chicago, and the Franklin Pierce Law School in Maine.

"A good part of my training came on the job and by interacting with attorneys and licensing colleagues in industry and at professional society meetings," he says. His job as director of technology transfer entailed educating investigators, evaluating invention disclosures and copyright materials disclosed to the office, marketing and filing patent applications on commercially viable inventions, registering copyrights, and licensing intellectual property to industry for the UCSD community. Rachmeler retired in early 1998.

What kinds of general advice would you give a person thinking about embarking on a career in technology transfer?

It is an exciting possibility, but one needs a good many skills in order to practice this profession. A good knowledge of science is essential, as is an understanding of patent and licensing laws. Knowledge of the business communities with whom you will interact is also necessary. You will use your scientific knowledge when interacting with investors, with business colleagues to whom you're trying to license the technology, and with attorneys. The patent and licensing laws form the basis of a large portion of the activity in which you will be involved. You will be discussing with patent lawyers the actions they are preparing on behalf of your institution or company. Therefore, you must be able to communicate with the attorneys, as well as be able to explain the actions to your inventors and to the community at large.

Writing licenses is the mainstay of your activity and understanding the basis for the terminology used. Being able to put the understandings of all parties on paper is absolutely necessary. Inventions must be marketed to potentially interested parties, and notwithstanding the variety of databases available, the greater your knowledge of the marketplace, the easier it will be to find an investor.

Once you have located a potential licensee, you must be able to negotiate appropriate terms for the license such that it benefits your institution, as well as the licensee. It would be useful to have taken one or more of the formal courses in negotiating. You will, of course, learn some of these skills on the job.

Being able to communicate well, both orally and in writing, is essential for all aspects of technology transfer. All of the knowledge that you gain from formal training and through experience and interactions with others is for naught if you cannot communicate your ideas.

What practical advice would you give on how to prepare and market oneself for a career in tech transfer?
It is indeed rare to find someone who has succeeded in this arena without a good scientific background. Research experience allows one to understand the actions of inventors and to be able to communicate with them more effectively. Research experience in industry is very useful in that it not only enhances your scientific knowledge but also may give you a general outlook on that particular industry as well as similar ones. I would take every opportunity that I could to enhance my knowledge of patent and business laws necessary for licensing. Formal courses are provided by law schools, commercial organizations, and some professional societies. Attending professional society meetings is not only useful for enhancing one's knowledge, but also for making contacts among your licensing colleagues—from academia, the legal profession, and industry.

Technology transfer professionals are drawn from many areas: Ph.D. graduates, bachelor's and master's degree science graduates with M.B.A.s, industry scientists, and J.D.s with science backgrounds are among some of the backgrounds I have seen. Learning on the job is more of the rule than the exception, so it is important that you present yourself with as much knowledge as you may have, but more importantly, as someone who has the capacity and desire to learn more. Technology transfer is a growing profession, so there are opportunities. There are a few schools now providing programs in technology transfer; however, if you have some of the background listed above and want to get in the field, there are openings in industry, academia, the nonprofit sector, and the legal professions.

Resources

Professional Societies

Association of University Technology Managers (AUTM). AUTM is a professional society whose goals are to assist administrators of patent and copyright offices at universities to license and patent new technologies and to encourage the production of inventions by university faculty. Its Web site includes links to conferences; courses; university technology offices; government agencies, organizations, and companies involved in tech transfer; related on-line resources; and professional-development tools. It also lists educational programs and job opportunities in industry, government, and academia, and links to other sources that list opportunities like the *Chronicle of Higher Education* and the National Technology Transfer Center. Contact:

Association of University Technology Managers
49 East Ave.
Norwalk, CT 06851
203-845-9015
Fax: 203-847-1304
autm@ix.netcom.com
http://www.crpc.rice.edu/autm/

Licensing Executives Society (LES). LES is an international professional society whose members are engaged in professional and business activities related to the transfer of technology and intellectual property rights. The society sponsors seminars, workshops, and training courses. Contact:

Licensing Executives Society
1800 Diagonal Road, Suite 280
Alexandria, VA 22314-2840
703-836-3106
http://www.les.org

Education and Training

The AUTM Web site lists links to B.S. and M.S. degree programs relevant to technology transfer, as well as fellowships, seminars, nondegree certificate programs, and summer institutes. Both AUTM and LES offer such courses as basic licensing, but, say tech transfer professionals, there's no substitute for on-the-job experience.

Although there are no formal degree programs in tech transfer per se, several organizations sponsor fellowships and internships, as well as training programs in allied areas like intellectual property law and entrepreneurship:

AAAS—Critical Technologies Institute Science and Engineering Fellows Program. AAAS sponsors one- to two-year fellowships for candidates with a minimum of five years of industrial experience to midlevel and senior executives. Fellows spend one year at CTI, a Washington, DC-based, federally funded research and development center within RAND, a policy think tank. Contact:

AAAS Fellowship Programs
1200 New York Ave., NW
Washington, DC 20005
202-326-6600
Fax: 202-289-4950
science_policy@aaas.org
http://www.aaas.org/spp/dspp/dspp.htm

National Institutes of Health (NIH); National Cancer Institute (NCI) Technology Transfer Fellowship Program. Fellowships are open to physicians, lawyers, Ph.D.s, and individuals with master's degrees in a wide variety of disciplines for specialized training in technology transfer as it applies to the prevention, diagnosis, and treatment of cancer.

There is no one contact name and address for these fellowships. Each program and office within NCI manages its own program. Contact names for all of these, as well as available openings, occasionally change. Visit the NCI Web site (http://www.nci.nih.gov/ttran/ttfp/ttf.htm) for the most up-to-date application information.

Other NIH institutes. Related programs are sponsored in other NIH institutional offices such as the two-year Intramural Research Training Associates fellowships that train fellows how to handle such processes as material transfer agreements and Competitive Research and Development Agreements, or CRADAs; however, there is no central place to get information. NIH officials suggest contacting individual institutions or looking on the NIH training and education Web site: http://www.training.nih.gov.

NIH Office of Technology Transfer (OTT). This NIH office sponsors summer internships that are often filled by Ph.D.s, M.B.A.s, and J.D.s. However, the spots are highly competitive. The office coordinates all patenting, marketing, and licensing activities relevant to the technology transfer process. Interns are given an opportunity to participate in the technology transfer process at the NIH by assisting OTT staff in various functions related to accomplishing the mission of transferring NIH technologies to the private sector. Interns help assess the commercial potential of inventions and participate in the development and implementation of marketing strategies; they assist in the negotiation of licenses, the review of patent portfolios, patent prosecution, and researching policy issues. Internships are unpaid, however, academic credit may be available through your school. Contact:

Carol C. Lavrich, Technology Licensing Specialist
Office of Technology Transfer, NIH
6011 Executive Boulevard, Suite 325
Rockville, MD 20852
301-496-7735 ext. 287
Fax: 301-402-0220
carol_lavrich@nih.gov
http://www.nih.gov/od/ott/

National Technology Transfer Center (NTTC). This center links U.S. companies with federal research laboratories to guide government-sponsored research into commercially relevant technology and products. NTTC sponsors training courses and technical apprenticeships. The latter program places graduate and undergraduate students from historically Black colleges and universities and minority institutions in apprenticeships with technology-based companies and federal and university technology transfer offices. Contact:

National Technology Transfer Center Training Courses
316 Washington Ave.
Wheeling, WV 26003
800-678-6882
Fax: 304-243-4395
train@nttc.edu
http://iridium.nttc.edu/nttc.html

NTTC Entrepreneurial Technology Apprenticeship Program
Nicole Kedward
Program Associate, ETAP
National Technology Transfer Center Training Courses
316 Washington Ave.
Wheeling, WV 26003
800-678-6882
nkedward@nttc.edu

Look on the NTTC Web site for information on how to apply, eligibility, features of the program, and sites that sponsor apprenticeships.

Jobhunting and Networking

The LES, AUTM, and NTTC Web sites contain links to job openings in government, academia, and the private sector; however, these links are accessible to members only. The AUTM Web site also links to individual job openings and related announcements in the *Chronicle of Higher Education*'s weekly "Academe" and to openings in the federal government.

To begin to familiarize yourself with the field's lingo and currently debated issues, tech transfer professionals suggest participating in tech transfer chat groups and reading patent and technology transfer issue-oriented publications. The AUTM Web site links to the Techno-L discussion group, the Intellectual Property newsgroup, as well as all sorts of publications. To start networking and familiarizing yourself with the details of technology transfer, many also suggest conducting informational interviews with people at tech transfer offices.

8

CHAPTER

Business

Whether you are interested in running your own business or managing the marketing and development of a new product, there are a wide variety of situations in the business world in which scientists are making major contributions. For many researchers who are applying the transferable skills they learned in graduate school—problem-solving and communication skills, for example—to the world of business, the match is not one of convenience, but of choice.

"Researchers are superbly suited for any area of business because scientific training teaches you analytical and logical skills," says Don Doering, a research fellow in the Wharton School of Business at the University of Pennsylvania in Philadelphia. Doering received his Ph.D. in biology from the Massachusetts Institute of Technology's Whitehead Institute in 1992. "Business is an incredibly diverse area. You can have a career in business where you are purely in an analytical role such as in financing or investment banking to a very people-oriented position like sales or customer services."

Many say they are attracted to the field because they derive satisfaction in their role of translating basic scientific knowledge to solving everyday practical problems. Others say that a job environment that provides constant change, and in some cases an element of risk, appeals to them. "Change in a business career can be rapid and frequent," says Doering. "That covers both moving into different roles within one organization and changing from one company to the next in a progressive way."

For James Reddoch, working in business versus scientific research

---

CHARACTERISTICS OF A SWITCH
TO A CAREER IN BUSINESS

These attributes may not strike every reader the same way. Depending on your background and interests, you may view some of these as either attractive or unappealing.

- You could work in a variety of settings and capacities, from people-oriented sales positions to analysis-oriented ones.
- You can work with diverse types of professionals.
- You get to work with the broad aspects of science.
- You get to work with the practical applications of science.
- You get a chance to work with cutting-edge ideas.
- Often job settings change, some with an element of risk, as in entrepreneurship.
- You may hear some criticism that you sold out.
- You must be comfortable with some imprecision and a shorter time scale in decision making.
- It's a one-way switch.
- You must be comfortable communicating in a new style.

---

represents an opportunity to make new types of discoveries, as one integrates several disciplines to create new commercial alliances and partnerships. Reddoch was a postdoctoral fellow in therapeutic radiology at the Yale University School of Medicine and now works as an analyst for Gerard Klauer Mattison, an investment banking firm in New York.

For Doering, part of the attraction for moving into the area of commercializing new technologies is its inherent complexity. "In some ways solving problems in business is much more involved than in basic science," he says. "In science you control all the variables, but one. Sure, such concepts as: 'Buy low and sell high' aren't complicated. But, because you can't control what the competition is doing, what the economy is doing, or the market, you have a more complex problem made of softer variables. That's why business is interesting intellectually to me."

No matter what a person's motivation, it is somewhat hard to make clear distinctions between the different areas of business that employ scientists and people with technical training. They fall into many categories: sales, marketing, product development, business development and administration, entrepreneurial activities, and financial and market analysis. Some areas of business like sales and marketing are amenable to entry by newly minted Ph.D.s without further education or experience, unlike others such as entrepreneurship and management that require more background.

Sales and marketing entail mixing scientific, communication, and people skills to sell and market products and services. Many scientists who have moved into business from research or right out of school started in sales or marketing. They used their technical knowledge of a product to better market it to a customer, and at the same time learned the ins and outs of an industry on the job. People working in this area also apply their technical and business knowledge of a certain field to research and develop future products.

Business development and administration involves work in medical, pharmaceutical, chemical, and other technology-oriented firms negotiating collaborations with inventors, investors, and other collaborators. Generally those in development have been working in industry for some time. Their job is to produce a business plan that will put the company in a favorable position with partners and investors. This takes a savvy blend of negotiating and communication skills, along with knowledge of the product and its future market.

Still another area, entrepreneurship, blends marketing, development, and administrative skills. An entrepreneur makes things happen, like creating new companies. The typical entrepreneur, if there is one, has experience in several areas: sales and marketing, product development, business development, and management. Essential in entrepreneurship are vision and, perhaps more important, the ability to communicate that vision.

Finally, there's working as an analyst. An increasingly familiar scenario involves physicists, chemists, and biologists who are now using their analytical skills to examine the commercial viability of new ideas and financial markets for large-scale technical corporations, investment companies, venture-capital firms, and business consultancies. For example, venture-capital firms—companies that represent people looking to invest in emerging technologies or products—need former researchers to analyze the science behind the business plans they receive. By the same token, the scientists need to understand the business side of the science presented in the plans.

Crossover areas related to commercializing scientific discoveries include technology transfer, patent law and examination, and intellectual property rights negotiation. See Chapters 7 and 9 for more on these related career paths. Larger businesses employ patent lawyers to manage their intellectual property dealings. These businesses often have technology transfer departments. Engineers and scientists will often work within these departments or closely with the lawyers in the patent offices to handle specific intellectual property questions.

"Some jobs will provide greater opportunities to actually use a science background than others," says Sara Beckman, former codirector of the Management of Technology program at the University of California, Berkeley. "Product marketing, for example, often requires significant scientific knowledge." Financial analysis, on the other hand, she adds, may require much less specific scientific knowledge, but much more knowledge of finance.

"Roles within areas of business are also varied," says Doering. "Scientists can play a role in any business interface where an understanding of technology is needed." This could mean working with customers in understanding their needs, which feeds into business development, product design, and company strategy. This could also mean interfacing with lawyers and government agency officials, or with people who work on such operational and strategic issues as how long it takes to develop a certain product.

Scientific training may get you an interview within the world of business, but it is the general understanding of how science works, not the specific facts of, say, a particular signal transduction pathway, that is most useful. "If you are interviewing for a position in business, emphasize that your scientific training also taught intellectual discipline, problem-solving skills, a quantitative way of breaking down issues, the art of data interpretation, and good communication skills," concludes Reddoch.

Read on for the advice and experience of several scientists working in the business side of science, including marketing managers, entrepreneurs, analysts, and educators.

One-on-One with Scientists Working in Business

Bradley Sheares, Vice President, Anti-Infectives Business Group for Merck & Co., Inc. in West Point, PA

Sheares received his Ph.D. in biochemistry from Purdue University in 1982, after which he was a postdoctoral fellow at the Center for Cancer Research at MIT for four years. From there he took a job as a research fellow in the Department of Biochemical Regulation at the Merck Research Laboratories, a post he held for almost three years. Then in 1990, he took part in the Merck Marketing Management training program, after which time he became product manager for AIDS/Developmental Products with the Hospital Products Marketing Group. He moved over to product management in late 1991. In his present position he was responsible for the 1995 U.S. introduction of Crixivan, a protease inhibitor used to treat AIDS patients.

When he was studying for his Ph.D., Sheares says that he never thought he would spend the rest of his career at the bench, but his interest in business didn't come until later. "I've always thought of myself as a scientist," he says. "I enjoy the structure and discipline that's involved in scientific problem solving; but, I didn't want to isolate that interest to the lab."

Moving into an industry position was a big decision, he remembers. "I was 30 years old, never had a 'real' job, and we had a baby on the way. I took a look at academic life and my situation and the grant situation, and thought: 'All-in-all a post in industry would offer me more opportunities scientifically and otherwise.'"

He did bench research at Merck for about four years, where he was exposed to the business side of pharmaceutical science. "This appealed to me," he says. "It brought all of the aspects of pharmaceutical science—basic research, clinical research, development, sales, marketing, manufacturing—together for me."

What general advice would you give a person thinking about embarking on a career in business?

Pursue what you're interested in. As you go through your education, many people find out that what they're doing and will be doing is very different than they expected. It's more likely that you'll do well, if you do something you like. But that's important advice for all careers.

Also, don't worry about what you read regarding trends. Don't chase the trend du jour. If you're good at what you pursue, you'll do well.

Be an honest judge of yourself in assessing the skills you need. Recognize what you need for what you're interested in and then match, realistically, what you have to what's needed. During this process, constantly ask yourself: "Can I see myself doing this?"

In my case, there's a difference between laboratory research and business that must be reckoned with. In the lab, you're able to replicate and test ideas to the nth degree, but in business you have to make decisions on a shorter time scale based on less information. So, you must become comfortable with a measure of imprecision. Sometimes scientists get hung up on details. You need to develop your intuitive and risk-taking side.

One more thing: an alternative career is—except for the rare case—a one-way move, so you must really be sure that's what you want to do.

What practical advice would you give on how to prepare and market oneself for a career in business?

It's important to develop your credentials in your first area of expertise. You'll need credibility in the area from which you're coming. You'll need to establish with interviewers that you're not just switching careers because you're floundering. Come from a solid foundation. Everyone can appreciate accomplishment in any career area.

Talk to people in various areas of business: administration, marketing, sales. Set up informational interviews. Do your homework. Talk about your own skills and experiences and how they would fit into the area in which you're interested. Prepare. Prepare. Prepare.

Scientific training teaches you how to think about a complex problem, tenacity, self-motivation, confidence, and problem solving. Scientists are trained to identify a question, research it, and come up with reasonable approaches to test different theories to answer it. All of these are skills that can be applied to any career area.

Lisa Spiro, Manager, Marketing and Planning at Genentech Corp. in South San Francisco, CA

Spiro has a B.A. from the University of California, Berkeley in physiology. After graduating in 1985, she began working at Scripps Research Institute in San Diego, where she conducted research in immunologic approaches to treating cancer. After a few months, a postdoc fellow she worked with at Scripps who left the institute to take a position at a small start-up biotechnology company, Telios Pharmaceuticals, persuaded her that there were greener pastures working in industry. "So off I went on my new adventure," she recalls.

"At Telios, I became interested in the business side of the company, and especially noticed the lack of business people with science training as well as the lack of science people with business training. The two groups really did not communicate all that well, which sometimes led to incongruent goals. I realized there was a great need to fill that gap, especially in the area of new product development."

After receiving an M.B.A. from the University of San Diego in 1993, she took the position as new product development analyst at Telios. This position involved analyzing market trends in various therapeutic areas, including tissue regeneration, cardiovascular, arthritis, and ophthalmic markets to develop new products.

Spiro has been with Genentech since 1994. "At Genentech, I perform a similar function, but have more resources to test many of our assumptions about the market by performing market research with our target customers. Skills that are important in this job include being a team player (we work with almost all functions in the business—clinical, research, finance, business development, manufacturing, and regulatory affairs) and developing good communication skills (we do a lot of presentations to senior management to recommend drug-development strategies)."

What general advice would you give a person thinking about embarking on a career in business?

If you have a scientific background and are analytical by nature, take some marketing classes or get more formal training with an M.B.A. Without a graduate business degree, it will be harder, but not impossible to break into this type of job. Aside from that, doing an internship at a biotech company would definitely help. You could start in a market research function and work your way up from there. There are accreditation programs in many universities that offer marketing programs.

While I say there is a tremendous opportunity to fill this gap between scientists and business people, each of these groups doesn't always recognize the need—keep in mind that you will not always be recognized for helping to bring these two together.

What practical advice would you give on how to prepare and market oneself for a career in business?

Definitely play up your scientific experience, as well as any business experience. It is important to bring out any drug-development experience you have or know about, that is, how drugs go from the research lab to testing in humans to the FDA for approval. Something that is highly valued at Genentech is to be able to grasp the big picture, that is, strategic thinking and how a particular strategy vs. another could aid in the success of a drug in development.

I see my job as being scientific, as well as business-oriented. It is important to understand the biology of the therapies that we are working with and to be able to speak intelligently about current treatments, future treatments, and new discoveries in research. Bottom line is that having a scientific background makes things a lot easier, because the learning curve is less steep. Also, a big part of our audience is physicians and other healthcare workers. Formal business training is also important, that is, knowing basic forecasting techniques, how to perform market research, and an overall understanding of business issues. Most important, you must be analytical and have a good grasp of numbers, since a lot of numerical analysis is involved in market research.

In that sense, I think that having some science training, whether it be nursing or undergraduate biology, chemistry, or a related subject, along with an M.B.A. or some formal business training is required for a position like mine.

Julie Rehm, Associate Department Manager at Battelle Memorial Institute, Cleveland, OH

Rehm received her Ph.D. in chemistry from the University of Rochester in 1996. Before coming to Battelle, Rehm was an NSF postdoctoral fellow in polymer science at Xerox Corp. in Rochester, NY. Her responsibilities in her present position include being the chief financial officer for the department, a technical project manager, and personnel manager for the Great Lakes Industrial Technology Center, a NASA regional technology transfer center managed by Battelle.

"I chose the career path that I did because I was no longer interested in working in a research lab," says Rehm. "Although I enjoy research, I found it to be very isolating and I wanted to interact with people and scientists with varying backgrounds. I realized that I would rather manage science than spend time in a lab doing experiments."

What general advice would you give a person thinking about embarking on a career in business?

The biggest piece of advice I have for fellow scientists is network, network, network. Start early in your career and always build upon your current network. Hone networking skills, which include written and verbal communication. Hone marketing skills and any activities that can improve your leadership ability and your ability to debate. Be enthusiastic and open to learning new concepts, and most importantly, be flexible! Engage challenges, don't avoid them.

The other piece of advice I have, which is related to networking, is to talk to as many people as you can who have a job (or had a job) in the field in which you are interested. They will be able to give you valuable advice and help you decide if you are choosing the right career for yourself. Writing letters, sending emails, making phone calls, one-on-one informational interviews, and a trip to DC (that I paid for myself) were the networking tools of choice for me. I mostly interacted with science policymakers working in the federal government and at private think tanks.

What practical advice would you give on how to prepare and market oneself for a career in business?

Volunteering worked for me. Had I not volunteered to be (a) President of the Rochester Chapter of the Materials Research Society and (b) a nonpaid intern for a member of Congress in my district in Rochester, NY, I probably would not have been able to land the job I have right now. The skills and competencies I honed while doing these include leadership, teamwork, the ability to think on my feet, project management (meaning how to delegate tasks and follow through on assignments), organization, and multitasking, as well as general administrative skills like phone etiquette. Taking classes in economics and business administration couldn't hurt either, but I think experience more than makes up for lack of classes.

Han Nachtrieb, Vice President for Human Resources at the Fred Hutchinson Cancer Research Center in Seattle

Nachtrieb received his B.A. in chemistry from the University of Washington. "My first job out of school as an environmental engineer taught me that getting something from the bench to a large-scale reality was a human endeavor as much or more than it was science," he recalls. "Within that context, I realized that I was a good listener, could integrate a team's ideas, and motivate others to pursue those ideas. I was also aware of how difficult finding a job with a Ph.D. was at the time." But, he adds that a career outside of science was never a plan: "I got my first HR job almost by accident and fortunately my employer was supportive; they sent me back to get an executive M.B.A. This made it possible to really develop the managerial and business skills necessary to handle the scope of my current position. Science is still my most important love; I still read the journals and anytime my work really bugs me I go talk to a scientist—the sense of excitement and purpose comes back."

He describes his present job as "trying to make this organization a good place to be and resolving intractable interpersonal problems." The skills involved, lists Nachtrieb, include working well with all sorts of people, patience, quick thinking, creativity, the ability to see globally, empathy, and resilience. "On the other hand, a feeling of closure on a project is rare," he notes. "The fun of discovery is absent and the paperwork and lack of any private moments can be daunting."

What general advice would you give a person thinking about embarking on a career in business?
Training in the scientific method usually makes for an outstanding thinker. If interpersonal and communication skills are developed, I'd maintain that such persons can do just about anything they set their minds to. Regarding retooling and getting experience, that varies from person to person. My advice would be to get some outside perspective about oneself and then fill in the gaps that that perspective shows exist.
Then network. For this, professional organizations can be invaluable, for example, the Washington Biotech and Biomedical Association brings together scientists, bankers, and sales folks. I

see people overusing "hard data" sources like Web lists and over-looking the human network.

What practical advice would you give on how to prepare and market oneself for a career in business?
Find an environment that will provide quick growth—as in learning experiences—and responsibility. One that will allow you to make survivable mistakes and one with good mentors. It's almost less marketing than targeting. Spending time searching for the right company and the right person to work for is very important, more important than say, tailoring a CV.

Janice M. LeCocq, Chief Executive Officer, Gryphon Sciences, South San Francisco, CA

LeCocq received her Ph.D. in medical anthropology in 1980 from Stanford University. From the early 1980s on, she worked as a securities analyst for Montgomery Securities, an investment banking firm. Her clients were biotechnology and medical-devices companies. After about four years she moved into corporate finance at Montgomery, where she worked to secure funding for life-science companies. She became a partner at Montgomery in 1986.

In 1990 she joined ICOS Corp. as the executive vice president for finance and administration. Then in 1994 she went to a biotech startup called Gryphon Sciences, where she is chairman and CEO. Gryphon uses a proprietary protein-synthesis technology to provide rapid access to gene products for use as research reagents in drug discovery.

"I love being on the cutting edge of what's going on in life science today," says LeCocq. "It's extremely exciting to try to develop technologies that can lead to ground-breaking medical products. It provides intellectual stimulation, worthy results, and a chance for financial independence."

What general advice would you give a person thinking about embarking on a career in business?
Emphasize the skills in which scientists should excel: critical analysis, problem solving, objective review of what's known and what isn't, and where the next action should be. Technical expertise is often very fungible. But, every job is essentially a sales job, so great communication skills are also critical.

Many scientists are used to working relatively independently, or interacting mainly with other scientists, so you need to be able to effectively communicate with a wide range of people and to understand their objectives. A good place to start is often literally selling the products of the industry you're targeting. Instrumentation and laboratory equipment sales, where technical expertise and laboratory experience is highly valued, is a good way to learn the business.

What practical advice would you give on how to prepare and market oneself for a career in business?

Provide the reviewer of your work experience with concrete examples of how you can or have brought real value to the organizations in which you have worked, not just a list of skills. Emphasize the impact of those skills. For businesses, the best value is one that can be translated directly or at least solidly indirectly to financial or market value.

Steve Lupton, Associate Director of Corporate Development at Targeted Genetics Corp. in Seattle, WA

Following his B.A. degree in biochemistry from the University of Oxford in 1981, Lupton worked as a research technician at the Imperial Cancer Research Fund in London. Then in 1983, he started in a graduate program in molecular microbiology at SUNY Stony Brook, eventually moving to Princeton University with his advisor, where he received his Ph.D. in molecular biology in 1986.

After completing graduate school, he worked as a staff scientist in the molecular biology group at Immunex Corp., a biotech company located in Seattle. In 1989, he joined a group set up by Immunex to spin out a new biotech company focusing on gene therapy called Targeted Genetics. "I became Director of Gene Expression, and staffed up my lab," says Lupton. "In mid-1996, the company reorganized its molecular biology operations, and I became Associate Director of Corporate Development." In the fall of 1996, he entered the Executive M.B.A. program at the University of Washington to gain a formal business education.

"From the point I joined Targeted Genetics, I have been involved in various aspects of biotech business development," says Lupton. "So moving from lab management to corporate development was an easy transition for me."

His present job includes developing marketing materials for internal research and development programs, presenting these materials to prospective investors and corporate collaborators, evaluating technology licensing opportunities, scanning issued patents and patent applications for relevant developments, negotiating material transfer and collaborative agreements, preparing competitive assessments of technologies under development, gathering information on competitors and their products, and attending meetings relating to corporate development.

"The ability to deal with many different ongoing projects at the same time is an important skill," says Lupton. "So are the abilities to maintain order in the face of a barrage of information and to quickly assess the relevance of a piece of information."

What general advice do you have for a person thinking about embarking on a career in business?

The best advice I have given other people considering making a career change is to spend a great deal of time thinking about the end result you want. What type of job do you want to be doing in 10 years? Are there any people you can identify who are doing that type of job now, and can you go and talk to them about it? Some people's idea of a career change is to go to graduate school to get a Ph.D. or an M.B.A., and this becomes the goal. They don't think through to what they want to do after they get the Ph.D. or M.B.A. Consequently, they just drift into something, and they end up unhappy with what they get.

What practical advice would you give on how to prepare and market oneself for a career in business?

I don't think my line of work is different from any other area when it comes to looking for a job, interviewing, etc. The one skill that might be useful to emphasize is the ability to explain complex scientific or business concepts in simple terms to people with little experience or expertise. People in my line of work often find themselves acting as a bridge between scientists and business people. So the ability to talk to both groups is important.

Thomas Piccariello, President, Synthons, Inc., Blacksburg, VA

Piccariello received his B.S. in biology in 1979 and his Ph.D. in organic chemistry from Virginia Tech in 1989. He worked as a metallurgical and electrochemical technician from 1979 to 1983; as a postdoctoral fellow in wood science and forest products at Virginia Tech from 1989 to 1991; as a research assistant professor in pharmacology at the University of Virginia from 1991 to 1993; and as a senior scientist for a pharmaceutical firm in Charlottesville, VA from 1993 to 1996.

"As an undergraduate I was interested in running my own business and as a graduate student realized that by diversifying my studies I could acquire the necessary skills to start a contract-research company," recalls Piccariello. "I incorporated Synthons while I was a graduate student, but felt I needed more experience, in science and business, before I took the plunge." Synthons prepares research and pilot-scale synthetic chemicals for large corporations, virtual companies, law firms, specialty chemical brokerage houses, and biotech companies.

Following his graduate studies, he says he maintained a "watchful eye" for opportunities to start his own company. From 1993 to 1995, he managed the research lab for a pharmaceutical firm at the Virginia Tech Corporate Research Center (VTCRC). "While in this milieu, that is, directing research efforts with a biotech company among other high-tech start-up companies, I was able to gauge the potential success for my contract-research company. In 1995, I asked Herb Cork, director of the Business Technology Center (BTC) at Virginia Tech, for help with various business issues. We teamed up with Jim Hiney of the Technology Law Offices at Virginia Tech, my present corporate counsel, to see me through the initial contract negotiations.

"In 1995, I felt that the timing was right to strike out on my own, which I did in 1996. Initially, in order to keep the cash flow respectable, I was doing everything. That included marketing, customer relations, quotes, proposals, reports, accounting, experimental design, and the actual work, including washing the dishes. Fortuitously, I did not have a large volume of business in the beginning. In the last year, I have hired loyal, hard-working people who now do 75 percent of the day-to-day work and even more of the marketing. I have also enlisted the help of consultants who share a lot of the responsibility on accounting, law, and engineering."

What general advice do you have for a person thinking about embarking on a career in business?

I have surmised that in this present highly competitive job market scientists are turning to alternate disciplines more frequently. Marketing has proven to be a rewarding career for scientists because their scientific training gives them an edge from a product-development point of view. They thus become a unique conduit between R&D and sales, management, and marketing. This would also be excellent experience for scientists who may want to start their own company.

What practical advice would you give on how to prepare and market oneself for a career in business?

For those scientists who are looking for an alternative career, the path I chose is certainly a viable one. It is very important to have a good business plan that not only addresses the science but also the marketing, management, accounting, and financing. Courses and seminars on business-plan development may be helpful, but I do not know for sure because my business plan was fashioned after an outline I received from a friend. There are software packages available that will take you through the process, and I have heard that they are very helpful, but I think they are fairly close to the hard copy outline I worked from. The hard part about my plan, which I'm redoing now, is gathering marketing data. Again I was fortunate because the BTC has assembled a team of business students who are helping me determine potential customers and competitors. The students are also helping with the organization of the plan.

I should also point out that operating in Virginia has distinct advantages where Virginia Tech, its BTC and VTCRC, and the state of Virginia's Center for Innovative Technology (CIT) have been very helpful in starting my business. These are the kinds of organizations one should tap into before starting a science-oriented business.

Probably the two most important things to remember when embarking on an entrepreneurial journey is to get extremely organized and don't be hesitant in seeking help from places like universities and business-development centers like CIT, BTC, and VTCRC. Finally, I would be remiss if I did not mention that the support I received from my family, particularly my wife, was invaluable for me during the anxious nascent months.

James Reddoch, Analyst for Gerard Klauer Mattison, an Investment Banking Firm in New York

Reddoch received his Ph.D. in biochemistry and molecular genetics from the University of Alabama at Birmingham (UAB) in 1997. There he ran a program called the UAB Industry Roundtable that brings together speakers with Ph.D.s who work outside academia and graduate students. The group continues in his absence. While a graduate student, he became interested in the business side of science by watching a faculty member friend take a university spin-off company public. Reddoch recently completed a postdoc in therapeutic radiology at Yale University and is now working as a biotech-industry analyst for Gerard Klauer Mattison, an investment banking firm in New York.

> *What general advice would you give a person thinking about embarking on a career in business?*
> There is a great deal of job diversity in business for people with a science background. The difficulty is in making the transition. It really requires some maneuvering to get firms to accept you as someone who can do something other than bench work. By "maneuvering," I mean emphasizing those aspects of your work experience that can immediately add value to their effort, be it finance, marketing, sales, forming collaborations with other firms, or whatever. Most interviewers have the misconception that scientists either cannot do something else or will require extensive retrain-

ing. In truth, more than maneuvering, making the transition requires doing homework, because your real focus should be on how your experience can be molded to contribute to their mission. And "molded" does not have to mean "conformed." Depending on the company, bringing in new ideas (within reason) may register well with an interviewer.

In interviews, converse on a professional level about what the position will entail on a daily basis and in general. Speak about your experience by stating your accomplishments as succinct facts. Do not dwell on the science, as interesting as it is, unless prompted. Keeping the discussion in the realm of facts (about your relevant experience, the open position, and where the two intersect) prevents the interview from getting lopsided and fends off questions like: "So, what makes you think you're qualified to do securities analysis?" It may also shield you from loaded questions like: "So, what do you consider to be your greatest strength? weakness?"

It helps to do a good bit of informational interviewing to become familiar with the language of the people who do the work. I spent four days in New York talking to friends working on Wall Street and every securities analyst that would see me. Most said that new hires came either from industry or from a finance background. Although that sounded discouraging at first, I knew that if they were considering science types from industry then they were prepared to hire people without explicit financial training. I assumed they were interested in industry types because those people would know something about the process of product development, so I played up my involvement in the Industry Roundtable as well as my thesis research on late-stage cancer therapeutics in an attempt to mold my experience into something meaningful to their work. This was met with encouraging looks, and I was kind of hoping that at least one encounter would be magically transformed from an informational interview to an actual "job available" interview. That did not happen at the time, but I still highly recommend at least a couple of rounds of informational interviewing before deciding to make the switch. My own data-gathering experience allowed me to meet some nice people who have since been very helpful and I learned a lot about the typical analyst's educational background, daily routine, salary, etc., as well as the job's mix of science and business.

What practical advice would you give on how to prepare and market oneself for a career in business?

Cast your skills in a new light. Rather than highlighting your electrophoresis skills it may be more appropriate to highlight your communication skills, or administrative skills in the context of a student group, or managerial skills in training an incoming student. I would encourage alternative-career jobseekers to familiarize themselves with announcements for jobs at the science–business interface and use the same words in cover letters, resumes, and even interviews. For example, I once saw an announcement for an analyst position with a private merchant bank in California. It described how the ideal candidate would have "strong financial skills, a strong scientific background, and a degree in a financial, business, or scientific discipline." Duties would include "data collection, analysis of biotechnology and pharmaceutical industry trends, and competitive analysis of companies and technologies." If there's anything a scientist has been built to do, it's collect data and analyze trends. But rather than protein levels following varying doses of an inhibitor, it's cash flow, for example, that you've got to be talking about.

"Candidates must be familiar with basic financial modeling and corporate valuation models, and have a strong background in a biological science. They must be willing to learn quickly, be able to juggle multiple projects, work independently, and thrive in a fast-paced environment," read another part of the advertisement. Use these words, with specific examples from your work history as evidence, to convince your interviewer that you are the right person for that position. Let announcements like this one guide you in knowing what the company wants.

Another thing I would remind jobhunters is that there is a big difference between a CV and a resume in terms of what you include and emphasize and where you put it and how you state it. For example, publications are critical when applying for an academic job, for which a CV is most applicable; however, for a marketing job, publications are not as critical. When applying for a marketing position, one would want to flesh out some accomplishments that have some applicability to business, for example, success with problem solving in a group setting or an innovation that saved the lab some money or a seminar you gave on your work to a lay audience.

John Rice, Director of Medical Technology, Senmed Medical Ventures, in Cincinnati

Rice received his Ph.D. in microbiology and virology in 1976 from Ohio State University. For the next 13 years he worked at Battelle Memorial Institute, in Columbus, OH. His research broadly encompassed using the tools of biotechnology for the development of new vaccines, drugs, and diagnostics. During his last five years there, he moved into research management and business development as a department head.

"During this time, I got a taste for the business side of science and decided this would be a great way for me to facilitate translating basic science research into relevant applications," says Rice. "My position now is the best of both worlds." He has been with Senmed, a venture-capital firm that invests in medical technology-based companies, since 1989. He is responsible for analyzing technological innovations for potential commercialization. Working closely with university scientists, entrepreneurs, and technology transfer specialists, he identifies emerging areas of science that may lead to profitable business opportunities. He then manages the early stages of the investment process.

What general advice would you give a person thinking about starting a career in business?

If you decide to move into any aspect of the business of science, your intimate technical knowledge of your discipline will become rapidly obsolete. That's what you lose, so you have to be comfortable with being more of a generalist in your approach to your career.

But on the other side, the analytical skills—the ability to test the validity of an idea—learned in scientific training is an underlying competence that can be applied to any aspect of a career in business, whether it's sales, marketing, management, or entrepreneurial activities.

What practical advice would you give on how to prepare and market oneself for a career in business?

What you don't get exposure to with most scientific training is business experience. To get that training, many people go back for an M.B.A. or a law degree. Some gain experience on the job, by apprenticing at venture-capital firms where they do much of the due diligence leg work in checking out the quality of science, patents, and people involved in the venture while at the same time gaining exposure to the valuation and negotiation processes involved in venture-capital investing.

Another route is to do research for industry where you'll be exposed to the perspective of doing targeted, applied investigations for a private-sector firm. This helps in understanding the pursuit of science from that perspective.

I think that people are better off getting formal training, which includes everything from business-management short courses to accelerated executive M.B.A. programs. These programs help you identify what management skills you'll need to hone, such as shepherding projects to completion within strict deadlines. They also help you develop familiarity with such critical business issues as valuation, financing strategies, market analysis, and management competence.

Don Doering, Research Fellow, Wharton School of Business, University of Pennsylvania, Philadelphia

Doering received his Ph.D. in biology from the Massachusetts Institute of Technology's Whitehead Institute in 1992. While a graduate student, he worked with technical licensing executives and received a patent for a small electrophoresis device that was licensed, manufactured, and marketed. After graduating, he incorporated himself and became a consultant for evaluating the commercial viability of new technologies for such clients as biotech companies, investors, and research labs.

He narrows his reasons for heading in this direction instead of a traditional research postdoc to three areas: "The people that I knew that were not only excellent at basic research but happy doing it had a really deep interest in the molecular details of a particular scientific question. I didn't see myself as deeply interested in the details of molecular biology as I needed to be to motivate the kind of excellence that I expected from myself and that the work demanded. Secondly, I felt that I had innate skills—managerial, people, communication skills— that I could eventually see being used as a PI, but in the near term couldn't see being used to full advantage as a postdoc. The third thing is that there were societal problems that I wanted to be involved with more directly. Biomedical research is certainly in that realm, but with my skills and interests I also wanted to work in other areas. Although consulting was not so much an ambition in its own right, it was a way that allowed me to start to explore the variety of career opportunities in business for scientists."

Through his freelance consulting, Doering encountered a socially responsible venture fund called Calvert Social Venture Partners (CSVP), and started work there in 1993 assessing early-stage investment opportunities in such areas as environmental, reproductive-health, and agricultural biotechnologies.

"When I started out in business consulting, I realized that the primary asset that I could bring to a project was my understanding of technology and ability to translate what it's all about to a lay audience," says Doering.

"The further I went along, I also added comments to what I was reviewing—whether it was a description of an invention or a nascent business plan—regarding managerial, organizational, marketing, and business issues. Progressively, I developed a better understanding of the business aspects of commercializing technological innovations."

After a year at CSVP, he met an entrepreneur with a plan to start AquaPharm Technologies Corp., a supplier of health and nutritional products for the aquaculture industry. After a while, Doering decided that he wanted to join the company, and when CSVP invested in AquaPharm, he joined as its founding vice president in late 1993. His responsibilities covered strategic planning, as well as assessing technologies for licensing potential. He left AquaPharm in 1996, when it closed.

"After three and a half years on the entrepreneurial hot seat, I traveled and came to Penn in the spring of 1997 as an independent research fellow in Wharton's Emerging Technologies Management Research Program. I teach and analyze how companies organize, strategize, and manage technologies in fields that are made highly uncertain by rapidly changing technologies, for example, the Internet, telecommunications, transportation, or biotechnology.

"In leaving science there are obviously a lot of wonderful things about academic life that I left behind and miss. I felt that an academic career in a business school would give me the intellectual challenge that I had known in basic science, but because business is of a practical nature, it would also be a way for me to bridge my different skills, experiences, and interests."

What general advice would you give a person thinking about embarking on a career in business?

One of the most important things for any career change is to first understand what it is that you really like about science, what it is that's unsatisfying to you, and what you would like to incorporate or not incorporate in your next career. I think scientists are superbly suited for any aspect of business. Science teaches you analytical and logical skills. We're often misled during graduate school to view the training as simply how to, say, run gels and columns and grow cells and animals, but really at the heart of all of that is experimental design. Scientists learn how to take a problem, break it down, create a strategy to solve it, look at the results, analyze the results, and come up with the next strategy.

What practical advice would you give on how to prepare and market oneself for a career in business?

What's important is finding out if you're interested in business. There are a lot of opportunities in graduate school or your own free time to test your interest and skills in business and management. It could be something as simple as organizing the purchasing and stocking of your lab. Or your technology licensing office might need people to research new technologies. Or, organize and run a seminar series. You could become involved in your church, volunteer organization, sports group, club, or a family business to see if you enjoy fund-raising, planning, and organizing. Any of these activities can become a claimable achievement on your CV or in a cover letter or interview that demonstrates managerial skills and interest. I think people often mistake that the experience has to be profound, competitive, or formal.

Scientists will be hired because of potential. With a graduate degree, you've demonstrated that you're smart, can work hard, and have analytical skills. But beyond that you need to show potential employers that you have drive and interest to work in business. I think these informal activities can demonstrate this.

Also, read the trade journals to gauge your interest in any field. Pick up *The Wall Street Journal* or *Business Week* and read it and make sure you find it appealing.

Go out and talk with people already working in business, for instance, other scientists now employed in some aspect of business in which you think you might be interested. Ask yourself: Does what this person does on the job match my expectations? What do they now do that they didn't get from their scientific career?

Of course, many people get a formal business education, most commonly an M.B.A. But what I did as a consultant and with the venture capitol group—analyzing case after case—is not that dissimilar from what you would do for an M.B.A., so that's another way to gain experience.

Sara Beckman, Former Co-Director of the Management of Technology Program at the University of California, Berkeley Haas School of Business

Beckman received her Ph.D. in industrial engineering from Stanford University in 1987. She worked at Hewlett Packard from 1985 to 1993 and has taught at Berkeley since 1987. "I left HP during a major reorganization of the corporation that reoriented the group I managed," says Beckman. "I felt that the transition provided an opportunity to explore other options."

What general advice would you give a person thinking about embarking on a career in business?

I worked in industry for a number of years, during which time I reviewed resumes and hired people. First of all, I believe that the most important part of changing careers is to be sincere about the desire to enter the new career field and to show that sincerity through activities undertaken. In the case of someone wanting to go into manufacturing, I suggest that they become American Production and Inventory Control Society-certified. They have a certification program that allows you to learn about and show your proficiency in various manufacturing management techniques.

Certainly, any chance they have to do part-time, volunteer, summer work in their field should be spent doing so. Reading books about the subject helps, or attending appropriate career fairs.

What practical advice would you give on how to prepare and market oneself for a career in business?
I encourage people seeking to change careers not to throw away all of what they have done, but to leverage it into a new position. If I put a Ph.D. biologist in a marketing position in a company in the biology field, for example, I would expect that person to be able to interact with the scientists in the company as well as customers and partners outside the company. Students who were CAD programmers before coming back to get an M.B.A. might use that skill to market CAD programs. That way they get to do marketing, which was their new career option, but can sell their technical experience in the job search process.

Resources

Professional Societies and Trade Organizations

Association of University Technology Managers (AUTM). For people interested in biotech business development, there are numerous links on the AUTM Web site that list technology transfer and business-development offices at universities and companies. Also see Chapter 7 for more information on this business-related area. Contact:

Association of University Technology Managers
49 East Ave.
Norwalk, CT 06851
203-845-9015
Fax: 203-847-1304
autm@ix.netcom.com
http://www.crpc.rice.edu/autm/

Licensing Executives Society (LES). LES is an international professional society whose members are engaged in professional and business activities related to technology transfer and intellectual property rights. The society sponsors business-related seminars, workshops, and training courses. Contact:

Licensing Executives Society
1800 Diagonal Road, Suite 280
Alexandria, VA 22314-2840
703-836-3106
http://www.les.org

American Entrepreneurs for Economic Growth. This is a national organization of venture-capitol-backed companies. Contact:

American Entrepreneurs for Economic Growth
1655 N. Fort Myer Drive, Suite 700
Arlington, VA 22209
703-542-3743
Fax: 703-524-3940
sgreene@aeeg.org
http://www.aeeg.org

National Venture Capital Association. This is an umbrella organization for 200 professional venture capitol organizations. It hosts networking and educational programs, among its many activities. Contact:

Daniel T. Kingsley, Executive Director
National Venture Capital Association
1655 North Fort Myer Dr.
Suite 850
Arlington, VA 22209
703-524-2549
Fax: 703-524-3940
http://www.nvca.org

Biotechnology Industry Organization (BIO). This is the largest trade organization for the biotechnology industry. Contact:

BIO
1625 K Street, NW
Suite 1100
Washington, DC 20006-1604
202-857-0244
Fax: 202-857-0237
http://www.bio.org

Many scientific sales representatives have organized groups of independent technical sales, service, and marketing professionals. Some examples are the New England Scientific Manufacturers Association in the Boston area, the Technical Sales Association that represents NIH sales associates in the Baltimore–Washington, DC–Virginia area, and the Philadelphia Area Scientific Sales Association (PASSA). Many hold meetings, often with training sessions in new scientific techniques; publish newsletters; mount biotech industry exhibits; and host social events for networking among colleagues. These venues may be a good place to talk with people already in scientific sales and marketing about their profession. The groups' leadership changes from year to year, so members suggest that scientists interested in sales and marketing should ask sales representatives that visit their labs, purchasing agents in the companies from which they order equipment and supplies, or representatives at exhibit halls at scientific meetings about local associations.

For more information on PASSA, contact:

Philadelphia Area Scientific Sales Association
Jonathan Mensch, 1998 President
PO Box 402
Kulpsville, PA 19443
PASSAInc@aol.com

For more information on TSA, contact

Technical Sales Association
c/o Global Trade Productions, Inc.
Two Skyline Place
5203 Leesburg Pike, Suite 1313
Falls Church, VA 22041
703-671-1400
Fax: 703-671-7695
gtpi@aol.com

Education and Training

Although many people in business say they get most of their training on the job, there are quite a few places to get formal instruction in business administration, development, and entrepreneurship.

General Educational Programs in Business Management

Executive MBA Council. This is the oversight group for M.B.A. programs designed for professionals already on the job. Its Web site lists contact information for member schools. Contact:

Executive MBA Council
35 Broad St., Suite 200
Atlanta, GA 30303

404-651-3760
Fax: 404-651-1439
http://www.emba.org

The International Association for Management Education, formerly the American Association of Collegiate Schools of Business (AACSB). This is the leading accrediting agency for bachelor's, master's, and doctoral programs in business administration and accounting. Its Web site lists over 300 schools accredited at the M.B.A. level, as well as other educational and training information. Contact:

AACSB—The International Association for Management Education
600 Emerson Rd., Suite 300
St. Louis, MO 63141-6762
314-872-8481
Fax: 314-872-8495
http://www.aacsb.edu/

Business Management Degree Programs Specifically Geared for Scientists and Engineers

University of Illinois M.B.A. program
410 Kinley Hall
1407 West Gregory Drive
Urbana, IL 61801
800-MBA-UIUC
Fax: 217-333-1156
MBA@uiuc.edu
http://www.mba.uiuc.edu

Johnson Graduate School of Management
Cornell University
315 Malott Hall
Ithaca, NY 14853-4201
607-255-2327
800-847-2082
MBA@johnson.cornell.edu
http://www.gsm.cornell.edu

Sloan School of Management, Massachusetts Institute of Technology. Leaders for Manufacturing Program is a small program of about 45 mid-career students. This is a partnership between 13 U.S. manufacturing firms and MIT's School of Management and Engineering. Contact:

School of Management and Engineering
Suite E40-422
MIT
77 Massachusetts Ave.
Cambridge, MA 02139-4307
617-253-1055
Fax: 617-253-1462
http://web.mit.edu/lfm/www

Pennsylvania State University. Penn State's accelerated M.B.A. program, a combined B.S. in general science and M.B.A. in five years. Contact:

Donald W. Genson, Executive Director
428 Classroom Building
Pennsylvania State University
University Park, PA 16802
814-863-0284
dwg9@psu.edu

University of California, Berkeley, Haas School of Business. The Management of Technology program allows students who are getting M.S. degrees in Engineering or M.B.A.s to obtain a certificate in the Management of Technology. The focus is on providing the management tools required to work in high-technology industries. Contact:

Sara L. Beckman
Haas School of Business
University of California, Berkeley
350 Barrows Hall
Berkeley, CA 94720
510-642-1058
Fax: 510-642-2826
beckman@haas.berkeley.edu

Northwestern University Center for Biotechnology. M.S. degree option that covers studies in both science- and biotechnology-related business courses. Contact:

Center for Biotechnology
Northwestern University
1801 Maple Ave.
Evanston, IL 60201-3135
http://www.nucb.nwu.edu

Educational Programs for Entrepreneurship. The Ewing Marion Kauffman Foundation's Center for Entrepreneurial Leadership's Web site links to a site called entreWorld (http://www.entreworld.org), where it lists contact information for 20 Centers for Entrepreneurship within the United States. Most of these are based at universities. The site also lists internships sponsored by schools and foundations, and the National Consortium for Entrepreneurial Centers, a group of universities and entrepreneurial councils that assists entrepreneurs and their companies.

The Foundation sponsors two other programs that help budding entrepreneurs learn necessary skills and make contacts. One is the Kauffman Fellows Program. This program is a joint venture between the Kauffman Center for Entrepreneurial Leadership and venture capital firms. Two-year fellowships pair fellows from business, science, and engineering backgrounds with venture-capital firms. The second is Fast Trac, a business development, education, and assistance program for entrepreneurs to get their businesses off the ground. Contact:

Kauffman Foundation
Center for Entrepreneurial Leadership, Inc.
4900 Oak St.
Kansas City, MO 64112-2776
816-932-1400
info@emkf.org
http://www.emkf.org

Jobhunting and Networking

There's a growing number of sources on the Web for jobhunting at the interface of science and business. In addition to the business-related listings in your city's classified newspaper sections and the job advertisements in trade magazines like *Genetic Engineering News* and *The Scientist,* Reddoch suggests that an hour spent using a Web search engine, combining search terms like "business," "biology," and "biotechnology" will enable you to find most of the applicable Web sites out there.

Some of these include:

- *MedSearch Healthcare Careers,* which includes searchable job archives in industry and the nonprofit sector (http://www.medsearch.com);
- *MedZilla,* which lists jobs and candidates in the fields of biotechnology, pharmaceuticals, healthcare, and medicine (http://www.chemistry.com/);

(*text continues on p. 191*)

Mitchell Blutt, Executive Partner, Chase Capital Partners

Blutt received his M.D. from the University of Pennsylvania in 1982, after which he took his residency in internal medicine at the Cornell University Medical College/New York Hospital in New York City. "My transformation from M.D. to physician-venture capitalist wasn't really about a job search," explains Blutt. "It was more of a realization that the face of medicine was changing. When I was living in Manhattan I was exposed to Wall St. for the first time. I came to realize that being a physician was not as autonomous a career as I once thought, and this was in a largely pre-HMO world. I also realized that it wasn't doctors that were driving medical discoveries, it was drug companies, at least in the U.S."

As part of the Robert Wood Johnson Foundation Clinical Scholars program, a two-year fellowship for medical residents to combine clinical experience with aspects of healthcare, Blutt wrote a thesis on entrepreneurship at academic medical centers. In conjunction with this program, he also obtained an M.B.A. from Penn's Wharton School of Business. "Within Wharton, I was naturally exposed to the world of capitalism, but what really impressed me was that this power was driving healthcare," says Blutt. "At the time, as a budding physician, I felt vulnerable not knowing what this field entailed.

"In the summer of 1987, I was encouraged by Dr. Samuel P. Martin, a prominent physician and visionary, to pursue a summer internship in venture capital at Chemical Venture Partners (CVP; now Chase Capital Partners) which was part of Chemical Bank," he recalls.

After he finished his M.B.A., he started with CVP. "I wanted a mix of business with the traditional combination of research, seeing patients in the clinic, and teaching," says Blutt. "I've managed to blend all three for the last 10 years." Blutt works at Chase, as well as teaches and sees patients one afternoon a week at Cornell.

Blutt receives many requests for information regarding his career transition. Reprinted here with his permission is a letter that he sends to people seeking career advice.

```
Dear Colleague:
   Presumably, as a consequence of the rapid evolu-
tion of our healthcare environment, the pace of
inquiries I receive from medical students, physi-
cians, and other scientifically trained professionals
who are interested in entering the financial and
business community has continued to increase beyond
my ability to more personally respond. I would,
however, like to share some thoughts and advice with
you.
```

- **Communicate with your personal contacts.** The transition you are contemplating is not obvious to the business community. A personal contact who knows you beyond your resume would be best equipped to give you a first opportunity.
- **Understand your objectives.** If you want an unrelenting travel and time-intensive work style with a deal-making orientation, Wall Street (e.g., investment banking, venture capital) may be suitable. If you want a research-oriented business opportunity, the pharmaceutical or biotechnology industries may be more appropriate. If you want a management-intensive experience, the health services industry could be right. Try to develop these priorities before endeavoring too far into your pursuit.
- **Get over it.** We've all toiled for many years with various endeavors accumulating years of education, credentials, and status. Being a physician is an excellent adjunct to being a fine healthcare industry professional, but it's by no means an assurance or guarantee. Outstanding healthcare industry professionals are first and foremost, excellent business persons. The healthcare business community sees value in physicians, but it is also highly cynical regarding their business skill potential.

Chase Capital Partners is one of the largest participants in the healthcare investment community. We have two physicians on staff. Both of us have M.B.A.s, and I have maintained some academic medical center involvement, including some patient care.

I'm sorry I don't have more time to chat with you, but I hope this has been helpful. I receive approximately five to ten inquiries per week from medical professionals, and I've concluded that this type of correspondence is more helpful and efficient than several weeks of "phone tag."

Best of Luck,
Mitchell J. Blutt, M.D.

- *Biotech Links*, which lists links to such organizations as the Biotechnology Industry Organization that have career pages with job listings (http://www.biotechresources.com/links.html).

Another approach, says Reddoch, is to search the classified sections of the on-line versions of newspapers from such biotech hotspot areas as Boston or the San Francisco Bay region. Conduct searches with keywords like "business" and "biology," for example, in the employment section of those cities' daily newspapers. Beckman and others also suggest getting in touch with university career centers for local openings and suggestions. Yet another approach is to post on-line resumes and surf job openings at on-line search firms, some of which are listed above.

In 1997, the *Wall Street Journal* developed a new "Careers" Web page (http://www.careers.wsj.com), with links to searchable job listings and other career information. The *Wall Street Journal* Web site also links to the Web site of the *National Business Employment Weekly* (http://www. nbew.com), and from there you can get to Weddle's Web Guide, which links to several on-line career centers with technical and business-oriented postings.

Others say that the best way to break into the business side of science is to get into technical sales and support services where one can gain administrative and communication skills by conducting seminars, field demonstrations, and employee training sessions. Executives say that the hiring of people with a technical background differs from company to company, so it pays to research the companies—via informational interviews and the Internet—that hire more technically oriented people.

And, says Denise Carr, a technical sales and marketing recruiter with a Ph.D. in chemistry and an M.B.A., both companies and jobseekers work with recruiters because many positions and jobhunters have highly specific requirements. Recruiters are listed in an annual called the *Directory of Executive Recruiters*, which can be found in large bookstores and libraries. But an easier way to learn of recruiters in your area, she says, might be through sales representatives that visit your lab.

9
CHAPTER

Law

Most scientists who are employed as lawyers practice in the specialty of intellectual property law. According to the American Bar Association (ABA)'s section on intellectual property law, there are primarily four areas in which to work: patent, copyrights, trademarks, and trade secrets. Former researchers are primarily employed in patent law, helping to develop and license patents for scientific inventions. Other areas that employ lawyers with science and engineering backgrounds include environmental law and medical-device product-liability law.

The boom in biotechnology in the past 20 years has been beneficial for life scientists-turned-patent attorneys, agents, or examiners. However, according to information on the Oppedahl & Larson Patent Law Web Server (http://www.patents.com), having several years of experience as a scientist or a doctoral degree in a technical or scientific area may not improve a person's job prospects in intellectual property law, except in the area of biotechnology. In fact, in some cases, a Ph.D., except in the life sciences, may be a slight detriment because of higher salary expectations, among other reasons.

The Server's section on Career Opportunities in intellectual property law makes the following general statement: "What really matters is your basic intelligence, ability to learn new things very quickly, and your strong academic or experience grounding in all areas—chemistry, industrial processes, software, electrical engineering, biology, physics, [and] mathematics." The Patent Law Web Server is developed by the intellectual property law firm of Oppedahl & Larson located in Frisco, CO.

CHARACTERISTICS OF A SWITCH TO A CAREER IN LAW

These attributes may not strike every reader the same way. Depending on your background and interests, you may view some of these as either attractive or unappealing.

- A Ph.D. in general may not improve your chances of landing a job.
- A Ph.D. in bioscience may be helpful in landing a job, compared to other disciplines.
- You might find that firms want you more for your technical than legal expertise.
- A law degree is not necessary right away or for all positions.
- There are multiple settings in which you can work.
- You get a chance to work with cutting-edge ideas.
- You can work with diverse types of professionals.
- The job market is competitive.

Scientist-lawyers can be employed in a variety of settings: corporations, law firms, universities, and government agencies. Private companies hire staff lawyers who litigate the protection of the intellectual property rights of the corporation, draft patent applications, and handle trademark and copyright cases, among other duties. Law firms also hire people with scientific and technological expertise as advisors to clients seeking science-related patents.

Not all scientists attached to law firms necessarily have a law degree, but they must have some understanding of patent law and the inner workings of the U.S. Patent and Trademark Office (USPTO). Universities involved in research and development also employ intellectual property lawyers. These attorneys, along with technology transfer experts, help shepherd an academic researcher's idea or invention through the commercialization process. See Chapter 7 on careers in technology transfer for more information on this area.

The different agencies of federal and state government also employ intellectual property lawyers. In general, attorneys employed by government agencies prepare patent applications and administer and negotiate patent rights that are associated with government contracts. According to the ABA, the patent office employs the most attorneys. Some patent examiners—those USPTO employees who judge the patentability of inventions, including scientific ones—have law degrees, but they aren't required to. Trademark examiners are required to have law degrees, however, but do not need scientific training.

A common way for a person to get into the area of patents is to take the patent bar exam, administered by the USPTO at various times throughout the year. This will allow someone with a strong technical background to practice before that office as a patent agent. In addition, a patent attorney can practice in the general courts as well as the USPTO. Most patent practitioners in the United States are patent attorneys. Many patent agents are people with a technical or scientific background who have not attended law school or who are currently attending law school. In fact, many patent lawyers suggest that it's smart to take the exam before graduating from law school. Many scientists interested in the law, however, start out as patent examiners, attending law school at night while working in the patent office during the day. See AAAS's NextWave Web site for more information on patent examination as a career (http://www.nextwave.org).

Read on for more about the individual experiences and advice from scientists at various points in their careers who are now practicing patent or environmental law.

One-on-One with Scientists-Turned-Lawyers

Charles Ryan, Vice President, Technology Management, Collaborative Group, Ltd., Stony Brook, NY

Ryan received his Ph.D. in oral biology and pathology in 1990 from the State University of New York, Stony Brook. His research focused on the metabolism of glucose and galactose in plaque bacteria. Immediately following graduate school, he began law school, graduating from Western New England College School of Law in Springfield, MA in 1993.

"I decided to go to law school after speaking with my Ph.D. advisor about alternative careers in science," recalls Ryan. "He had several patents and I knew several patent attorneys. After speaking with them, I decided to pursue a career in patent law. I was always interested in law and this decision provided me an opportunity to practice and study cutting-edge science at the same time. I also liked the idea of specializing."

Ryan practices intellectual property law, which includes patent, trademark, copyright, antitrust law, and licensing. At the law firm of Darby & Darby in New York, he handled legal matters for clients in the area of intellectual property, including litigating intellectual property cases, preparing and prosecuting patent applications, and assisting in licensing patented technology.

Most recently, he began work in early 1998 at the Collaborative Group, a holding company consisting of biotech companies and a contract research organization. He manages the entire intellectual property portfolio and oversees all licensing and contracts for the Group.

What general advice would you give a person thinking about embarking on a career in law?

These are the steps I would take to find a job in any nontraditional science career: Initially, research the profession in the library and on the Internet. Secondly, I would arrange informational interviews with people working in the field. Most people are willing to meet with you for 30 minutes over lunch to discuss their position. Ask several questions during the interview: What do they like most/least about their job? What is a typical work day like? How much travel is involved? Could I go to school at night?

Next, research companies looking for people with your background. Finally, send out your resume. It is very important to remember, a person only needs one job! Don't get discouraged by negative responses; they make the positive responses that much sweeter.

What practical advice would you give on how to prepare and market oneself for a career in law?

Many firms are looking for people with a Ph.D. to work as a patent agent. The biggest advantage to having a Ph.D. are the skills you developed getting your doctorate. Inventors, scientists, and other Ph.D.s are more likely to respect you. For some firms, you're a more attractive candidate than a non-Ph.D. On the other hand, the biggest disadvantage is that the firm will want you to work on technical questions and less legal questions. If you find you like the practice of law, you'll have to fight to get nontechnical legal work.

If you aren't certain whether you would enjoy a career in intellectual property law, you might consider pursuing a position as a technical advisor in a firm. Once you pass the patent bar exam, which is administered by the U.S. Patent and Trademark Office, you are registered to practice before that office. After working in the firm for one year, I would then recommend attending law school at night and working as a patent agent during the day.

Another common path towards a career as a patent attorney is to work as an examiner in the patent office during the day and go to law school at night. Of course, this alternative would require living in Washington, DC.

When applying for a position as a technical advisor, it is important that the applicant clearly identifies all his or her areas of science background and expertise. Moreover, I recommend applicants stress that they believe they would enjoy a career as a patent attorney because it would provide them with an opportunity to work with scientists and companies doing cutting-edge research, research that is not yet known to the public. The applicant should also stress research and communication skills.

Problem solving is also a skill developed while studying science. You want to stress your ability to solve complex problems using organized scientific reasoning and that you are well versed in using the library, the Internet, and databases such as Dialog and Medline to conduct background research for clients.

Louis S. Sorell, an Attorney with Baker & Botts in New York City

Sorell received his B.S. in chemical engineering from Cooper Union in 1978 and an M.S. in chemical engineering from Georgia Tech in 1981. He attended law school at night for four years while employed as a research chemical engineer at Texaco Inc. during the day. After working for three years as an in-house patent attorney for Texaco, he entered private law practice with Baker & Botts (formerly Brumbaugh, Graves, Donohue & Raymond) in 1989.

"I realized fairly early in my engineering career that research was not for me," recalls Sorell. "I very much enjoyed working with people and seeing the results of my work come to fruition. However, I found that research was often a very solitary type of work, where the payoff could be many years down the road. I sort of fell into law through sporadic contacts with the patent department at my company, although I did very little patent work before I was in law school."

Sorell's present position entails representing clients by obtaining patents through the USPTO or litigating patents in the federal courts. Any technical—science or engineering—discipline is suited for such work, he says.

What general advice would you give a person thinking about embarking on a career in law?

The most important skills needed for this type of work are the ability to analyze a problem and marshall the appropriate facts to solve it—a competency that many scientists are trained to hone—and the ability to write well. However, in my experience most scientists are poor writers and often get lost in the details without making sure that the most fundamental points are made. Beefing up writing skills through classes, even before law school, is a good idea.

What practical advice would you give on how to prepare and market oneself for a career in law?

A person considering such a career change has to consider

several issues. First, although one can become a patent agent (and represent clients in the Patent Office) without a law degree, a law degree is necessary to be able to practice the full range of activities in intellectual property law. Accordingly, anyone considering such a career move has to consider attending law school, with the attendant cost, both in terms of time and money. Second, a technical background is nothing special in intellectual property law. Thus, those who seek a career in this area have no particular advantage over other intellectual property lawyers, because we all have technical backgrounds. This is often an ego blow to the unknowing.

I do not think a lengthy resume does much good; a scientific career is different from practicing law. The best resume simply lists education and work experience in a succinct way.

Marta E. Delsignore, Associate with Baker & Botts in New York

Delsignore received her Ph.D. in physical chemistry from Rutgers University in 1982, after which she did two, one-year postdocs at the Polytechnic Institute of New York and the University of Southern California Institute for Toxicology, respectively. From there she moved into industry, working for Colgate Palmolive as a research chemist. A few years later she transferred into the patent group as a liaison between attorneys and R&D. In 1986, she started law school and eventually took the patent bar and became a patent agent for Colgate. In 1990, she graduated law school, and in the same year started at Baker & Botts (formerly Brumbaugh, Graves, Donohue & Raymond), where she works on patents for consumer and defense companies, as well as universities in the areas of chemistry, biochemistry, and mechanical engineering.

"I always had an interest in the law," says Delsignore. "But I pursued my interest in science. However, after I was working in industry for a while, I saw few advancement opportunities in research for women, and I was dissatisfied with the direction of my own research. When I became a patent attorney, it opened up a whole new set of opportunities for me, on many levels."

What general advice would you give a person thinking about embarking on a career in law?
    Pursuing a career in patent law can open up a lot of opportunities, if you're motivated. You get to be a virtual research director, evaluating other people's inventions and research. You really do get to use your technical background. The most valuable skills you obtain in scientific training are analytical skills: how to analyze

facts and pull them together to see the big picture, whether it is the potential of an invention or the weaknesses and strengths of a legal argument. People with scientific training tend to do well in patent law because of this.

What practical advice would you give a person on how to prepare for a career in law?
   The major drawback of hiring someone with scientific training is their lack of training in written and oral communication. Hone both of these, but know that the communication style is vastly different in practicing law as compared to science. When you're writing as an attorney, you're writing for an educated, but lay audience of judges, clients, and other lawyers. The most successful people are the ones that can communicate ideas effectively in a general, accessible way.
   Get a well-rounded education. For example, take as many additional courses as you can, such as English courses where writing is emphasized. Also develop your oral skills. While still in graduate school, take advantage of every opportunity that arises to speak in public. The more often you speak in front of people, the easier it becomes.
   As a lawyer, it's critical to be able to think and speak intelligently on your feet, especially when you're dealing with clients or find yourself in an adversarial situation.

Richard Meserve, Partner and Environmental Lawyer at Covington & Burling in Washington, DC

Meserve completed his work for a Ph.D. in applied physics at Stanford in 1972, after which he continued with a postdoc at Stanford for nine months. "While I was contemplating another postdoc, I observed that large numbers of my friends—many of them exceptional physicists—were floating from postdoc to postdoc, simply hovering over universities waiting for more permanent positions," he recalls.
   "I decided to take a more radical step and went to law school," says Meserve, deciding on Harvard University, where he eventually clerked after law school for Justice Harry A. Blackmun. "I expected to return to practice law in Boston after the Blackmun clerkship, but got a call from the president's science adviser indicating that he had a position for a lawyer." Meserve worked in the White House for several years. By then, he says, his family had put down roots in Washington, and was unwilling to leave the area. "With the election of Ronald Reagan in the early 1980s, I left the science adviser's office and joined Covington & Burling."

In explaining why he left physics for law, he says he decided to make that transition with the hope and expectation that he would use his scientific training in the practice of law. "That has been the case, but the precise nature of my work has changed over time from regulatory matters to environmentally related litigation," notes Meserve. "But the need to understand the technical intricacy of issues essential for my practice has not changed." Most of his projects now involve working with technical experts. This includes toxic tort cases that pertain to issues of exposure assessment and evaluation of dose-response.

What general advice would you give a person thinking about embarking on a career in law?

Each individual probably should strive to look somewhat unique in the marketplace. I believe that scientific training is helpful. However, first-class legal training—through law school, law reviews, and clerkships, for example—is probably more important in getting a good job as an environmental lawyer than particular environmentally related skills.

What practical advice would you give a person on how to prepare and market oneself for a career in law?

Each individual should find some aspect of his or her past experience that provides an advantage and build on that. I believe that technical training and experience in the physical and biological sciences is very useful in environmental work. Most people will learn some scientific knowledge in the course of environmental work, but the breadth of systematic graduate education study can be helpful.

Resources

Professional Societies

American Intellectual Property Law Association (AIPLA). AIPLA is a society for attorneys interested in all fields of intellectual property law. Contact:

American Intellectual Property Law Association
2001 Jefferson Davis Highway, Suite 203
Arlington, VA 22202
703-415-0780
Fax: 703-415-0786
http://www.aipla.org

American Bar Association Section of Intellectual Property Law. This sub-group of the main professional society for all attorneys practicing in the United States has information on the Web describing the entire field of intellectual property law, including employment opportunities and how to become an intellectual property lawyer. Contact:

American Bar Association
Section of Intellectual Property Law
750 N. Lake Shore Drive
Chicago, IL 60611
312-988-5000
info@abanet.org
http://www.abanet.org/intelprop/careers.html (the ABA Section
    of Intellectual Property Law, Careers in Intellectual Property Law)

American Bar Association Section of Science and Technology. This sub-group of the main professional society for all attorneys practicing in the United States has four divisions that deal with science, medicine, and technology: Computer Law, Electronic Commerce, Communications Law, and Life and Physical Sciences. For more information on the divisions and their materials, contact:

American Bar Association
Section of Science and Technology
750 N. Lake Shore Drive
Chicago, IL 60611
312-988-5000
sciencetech@abanet.org
http://www.abanet.org

Patent and Trademark Office Society (PTOS). PTOS is the professional society for USPTO employees. Contact:

Christopher Young, 1997 PTOS President
USPTO
PO Box 2089
Arlington, VA 22202
christopher.young@ustpo.gov
http://www.ptos.org

Association of University Technology Managers (AUTM)
49 East Ave.
Norwalk, CT 06851

203-845-9015
Fax: 203-847-1304
autm@ix.netcom.com
http://www.crpc.rice.edu/autm/

Education and Training

Whether you want to go into intellectual property, environmental, or another area of the law, there's a number of resources out there to help you get acquainted with the available training and formal degree programs.

Law Schools, Courses, and Workshops. To obtain information on how to become a registered patent agent and what technical and educational background is necessary to be eligible to take the patent bar exam contact:

Office of Enrollment and Discipline
U.S. Patent and Trademark Office
Washington, DC 20231
703-308-5316
Fax: 703-308-5276
http://www.uspto.gov

The American Intellectual Property Law Association Web page (http://www.aipla.org/) lists three searchable directories of law schools: the Yahoo Directory of Law Schools provided by Stanford University, the Directory of Law Schools provided by the John Marshall School of Law, and the Directory of Law School WWW Servers provided by Rutgers University.

The Council of Canadian Law Deans lists links and contact information for Canada's 20 law schools. Those specializing in intellectual property law are not specified. Contact:

Council of Canadian Law Deans
Sandra Rogers, Dean of the University of Ottawa Faculty of Law
57 Louis-Pasteur
Ottawa, Ontario
K1N 6N5, Canada
http://www.canadalawschools.org/council_e.html

Several private companies and university-based programs offer courses, workshops, written materials, and videos to help prepare for the patent bar exam. Oppedahl and Larson's Web site lists six such places. The ABA–AIPLA booklet *Careers in Intellectual Property Law*, published in 1995, lists four.

The Environmental Law Institute, an independent, nonpartisan, nonprofit organization sponsors information services and training courses and seminars for environmental law. Contact:

Environmental Law Institute
1616 P St., NW
Suite 200
Washington, DC 20036
202-939-3800
Fax: 202-939-3639
http://www.eli.org/

A Web search using the keywords "environment" and "law" also brings up several environmental law degree programs.

General Information. The ABA Section on Intellectual Property Law Web page (http://www.abanet.org/intelprop/careers.html) includes the following information on how to prepare to practice intellectual property law:

- admission to law school;
- choosing a law school;
- financing, competitions, and admission to the bar.

In addition to the information on the ABA and AIPLA Web pages, the societies' brochure *Careers in Intellectual Property Law* includes an appendix of resources with contact information for law schools that offer a significant number of intellectual property law courses, patent-bar-review programs, national intellectual property law organizations, and publications. You can obtain a copy of this booklet by contacting the ABA or AIPLA.

Also see Chapter 7 on careers in technology transfer for information from the AUTM on education and training programs in academic settings.

Jobhunting and Networking

Recently there's been a lot of discussion in the scientific community about the opportunities for researchers to become patent professionals, with some discussion about education and training programs, as well as jobhunting tips. For example, see AAAS's Next Wave's "New Niches" area on Scientists as Patent Professionals (http://www.nextwave.org/niches.html). The USPTO Web page (http://www.uspto.gov/) lists full descriptions of current employment announcements. The USPTO also periodically conducts patent examiner job fairs, usually in the Washington, DC area. The frequency of these fairs depends on the recruitment needs of the USPTO. According to the USPTO Office of Human Resources, there is no set schedule for the fairs, but people interested can contact the USPTO to get on a mailing list or find out when and where the next fair will be. Contact:

USPTO
2011 Crystal Drive, Room 707
Arlington, VA 22202
703-305-8231

The Web site of the ABA Section on Intellectual Property Law (http://www.abanet.org/intelprop/careers.html) includes a description of the general occupational settings that hire intellectual property lawyers: corporations, law firms, universities, and government agencies. Both ABA and AIPLA are starting to advertise positions in their newsletters. The ABA Section of Intellectual Property Law also plans to place resumes of jobseekers on their Web site sometime in the future.

According to Seth Nehrbass, a patent attorney at Garvey, Smith, Nehrbass & Doody, L.L.C. in New Orleans, and chairman of the law student committee of the ABA Section of Intellectual Property Law, one of the main places that any law firm advertises new positions is in the bar journals published by each state. These can be found in any law library.

The Oppedahl & Larson Patent Law Web Server provides detailed information and opinions, in their section on career opportunities in intellectual property law (http://www.patents.com/opportun.sht), on the following:

- whether a large number of years of experience and/or a Ph.D. in a scientific or technical field will improve job prospects;
- whether taking the patent bar exam is necessary to pursue a career in intellectual property law, including information on what firms expect of a job candidate.

The Patent Portal (http://www.law.vill.edu/~rgruner/patport.htm/), the Web site of Richard S. Gruner, a professor of law at the Whittier Law School in Costa Mesa, CA, includes links to several patent and intellectual law Internet newsgroups, news services, and listservs, as well as on-line journals. The Portal contains no separate job listings, but all of the firms with indexed Web addresses are likely employers for patent attorneys. In addition, Gruner suggests looking through the West and Martindale Hubble directories, which list patent attorneys and intellectual property law firms in a particular city. The Patent Portal includes links to both directories.

The ABA and AIPLA also maintain a list of firms specializing in intellectual law, and the USPTO has a directory of patent attorneys. AIPLA also keeps a list of headhunters who specialize in patent and intellectual property law.

Gruner maintains that the best starting point for someone investigating a career in patent law is to thoroughly tour the USPTO Web site, then to closely scrutinize the CNI Copyright and Intellectual Property Listserv Archive and the Usenet Intellectual Property Newsgroup, both of which have links in the News section of the Patent Portal. By perusing these, he says, scientists interested in patent law can look for interesting patent or intellectual property issues that relate to their former field of scientific, engineering, or managerial expertise.

"This will not only help them start to define a specialized practice area for the future, but it will give them something interesting to talk about with interviewers," says Gruner. Discussions on these newsgroups could also help a jobseeker identify some of the major players in certain areas of intellectual property law.

Also see Chapter 7 on careers in technology transfer for more information from the Association of University Technology Managers on jobhunting and networking links in academic and other settings. AIPLA's Web site doesn't have any direct links to job listings, but does publish some announcements in their publication called *The Bulletin*, which is only available to members.

The following list of Web sites may also prove useful for exploring issues, networking, and jobhunting in the area of intellectual property law:

- Intellectual Property and Technology Forum at the Boston College of Law: http://infoeagle.bc.edu/bc_org/avp/law/st_org/ipg/iptf
- Collection of Web sites of intellectual property law firms: http://www.yahoo.com/Business_and_Economy/Companies/Law/Intellectual_Property
- Collection of Web sites of intellectual property law consulting firms: http://www.yahoo.com/Business_and_Economy/Companies/Law/Intellectual_Property/Consulting
- Cornell University Patent Law Site: http://www.law.cornell.edu/topics/patent.html

- Electronic Frontier Foundation's on-line publication, "Intellectual Property Online: Patent, Trademark, Copyright Archive": http://www.eff.org/pub/intellectual_property
- Patent FAQs Web site that answers basic questions about patenting: http://www.sccsi.com/DaVinci/patentfaq.html

The Web site of the Environmental Law Institute lists employment opportunities within the institute. A search on the Web using keywords like "environment" and "law" brings up several environmental law firms that may hire scientists.

CHAPTER

Science Policy, Advocacy, and Regulation

☐ Science and Environmental Policy and Advocacy

Over the last half of this century, scientific, and more recently, environmental issues have become more and more important to politicians. In fact, according to the AAAS, there are now more than 35 American universities and 15 in other countries that offer graduate training in science and engineering public policy.

"I think there can be advantages to having scientifically trained people in policy positions," says Brett Stillman, a graduate student in pharmacology at Vanderbilt University who, in 1997, completed an internship with Research!America, a science advocacy organization based in Arlington, VA. "I've seen firsthand at Congressional subcommittee hearings, when scientists testify, they have a hard time communicating and connecting with members of Congress. There's a barrier that can be overcome by people in Washington who know about the scientific method and how new knowledge is incrementally acquired as well as how new policy is advocated."

People employed in science policy comprise a relatively small group and are almost exclusively based in Washington, DC and its immediate surroundings—the so-called Beltway. Policy experts are employed as analysts at an array of organizations, including federal agencies, professional societies, politicians' offices, advocacy groups, private think tanks, and international nongovernmental organizations.

CHARACTERISTICS OF A SWITCH TO A CAREER IN POLICY, ADVOCACY, AND REGULATORY AFFAIRS

These attributes may not strike every reader the same way. Depending on your background and interests, you may view some of these as either attractive or unappealing.

- It's a one-way switch.
- There's a relatively small job base, but good fellowship opportunities exist, except in regulatory affairs.
- You'll need to have an interest in and be comfortable dealing with issues, policy, and politics regarding how science is conducted.
- You'll also need a knowledge of how government functions, of regulations governing implementation of policy, and of other issue-oriented information.
- You must be comfortable communicating in a style and culture very different from academic science.
- You could make a tangible social contribution to better implementing science policy and educating lawmakers.
- You could work in a variety of settings and capacities, and with people from diverse professions and backgrounds.
- You get to work with the broad aspects of science.

Many of these people express a long-term interest in politics, specific issues, and how government works. They enter the world of science and environmental policy usually via internships and fellowships taken during their graduate education or while on a sabbatical from their regular jobs. Read on for the experiences and advice from several science and environmental policy experts employed in a variety of settings and at different stages in their careers.

One-on-One with Scientific and Environmental Policy Experts

Michal Freedhoff, Materials Research Society and Optical Society of America Congressional Fellow in the Office of Rep. Edward Markey

Freedhoff received her Ph.D. in 1995 in physical chemistry from the University of Rochester. After that she spent almost a year at the American Institute of Physics creating "Physics Success Stories," one-page glossy flyers that illustrate the societal and economic importance of federally funded research and are intended to be used by scientists on visits to their members of Congress.

"I switched to policy because, while I really enjoyed science and my research, I found myself more excited and energized by the work I was doing as a volunteer on committees of a grad student chapter of the Materials Research Society (MRS), and exploring policy-like issues for grad students such as education and employment," says Freedhoff. "I made the decision to try for the fellowships about one and a half years prior to the completion of my Ph.D., and moved to DC without a job, knowing that I would be able to find some way to enter the policy community even if I didn't win a fellowship. After my fellowship is over, I plan to stay in DC, hopefully on the Hill."

As a fellow, she focuses most of her time on nonproliferation issues, establishing a bipartisan task force on nonproliferation for Rep. Markey, inviting speakers such as Mikhail Gorbachev to speak to the group; and drafting legislation and writing op-eds and oversight letters to federal agencies. She has also worked on such issues as electricity restructuring and the environment.

Postscript: In May of 1998, Freedhoff became a science policy advisor for the House of Representatives Science Committee (Democratic staff), where she works on energy and nonproliferation technology issues.

What general advice would you give a person looking into a career in science policy?

Improve your ability to communicate science to the nonscientific public, either through teaching or writing. Get involved in politics at a local level—volunteer a half day a week at the office of your local Congressperson or Senator. You will probably be the only person in the office with a scientific background, so you may well end up being a valuable office resource. Work on political campaigns. Become involved in local chapters of technical societies. Organize and plan meetings, symposia, and events. Get involved in graduate student government or departmental committees. Volunteer to serve on committees for your professional society.

Subscribe to science policy email bulletins such as What's New, a bulletin put out by Robert L. Park at the American Physical Society (whatsnew@aps.org) and the American Institute of Physics (fyi@aip.org). Read the Washington, DC news and policy alert sections of technical society publications.

What practical advice would you give on how to prepare and market oneself for a career in science policy?

Talk to the professional societies' offices of public affairs. Occasionally they will have internships or volunteer openings for interested applicants. Contact the DC office of your alumni association; they may be able to help. If you have any industrial or National Lab experience, contact their DC offices. Take political science courses. Take a look at the many policy-oriented publications put out by the American Association for the Advancement of Science.

David M. Sander, American Society for Microbiology Congressional Science Fellow, 1996–1997, 1997–1998 in the Office of John E. Porter (R-IL), Chairman of the House Appropriations Subcommittee for Labor, Health, and Human Services and Education (http://www. tulane.edu/~dmsander/DMS/DMSHomePage.html)

Sander received his Ph.D. in molecular and cellular biology from Tulane University in 1996. His research primarily concentrated on retroviruses and their potential involvement in autoimmune disease. "Early on in graduate school, I recognized that while science needed a strong voice in society, we typically lacked one," says Sander. "I found this situation to be obvious at several levels. My fellow students were unorganized within the university; the science faculty was less organized and well spoken for than their humanities peers; and nationally, the science news covered by the media were generally plagued with inaccuracies in reporting, and political decisions often seemed to be made without any regard to the scientific evidence. I really began to wonder who was speaking for science. The answer, I soon discovered, was people who weren't trained as scientists.

"Having always had an interest in politics, I became involved in a number of organizations, and eventually found myself in a position of leadership for a number of them. By my second full year at Tulane, I was president of the Graduate Student Body and a member of Tulane's Board of Administrators. These experiences, and my continued growth as a scientist, led me to conclude that I should consider some alternate career options available to scientists.

"For me, politics has always been a passion, and the Congressional Science Fellowship seemed the perfect route to explore some of those alternate career possibilities." He works on such issues as research funding and healthcare policy. "As Fellows, we are expected to apply the scientific method to a variety of issues facing Congress," says Sander. "Most members are very receptive to our presence, as we come with no strings and are free, having been paid by our respective societies or AAAS directly."

Nearly any scientific discipline is suited to this line of work, notes Sander. He works as a legislative aide, monitoring legislation and policy in assigned issue areas, meeting with lobbyists and constituents, writing letters to constituents and government agencies, writing speeches and briefing Congressman Porter, going to seminars, and reading a great deal.

"I believe in public service," says Sander. "Fundamental to this belief is that the government has an obligation to tell the truth to its citizens, using the best resources that it can muster. In this regard, scientists bring something just a little bit different to the public policy debate than all the other experts."

What general advice would you give a person looking into a career in science policy?

Your communication skills must be superior. Much of this job is networking, writing, and speaking. If you lack ability in any one of these areas you will find yourself way behind in the game of politics. In addition to these skills, the unique abilities of a scientist are paramount to success as a legislative aide for science or as a lobbyist. The ability to distill large amounts of information in a short period of time, including the exclusion of "garbage," and then present it in an organized manner serves the science Ph.D. well in Washington.

It is also important that you have some understanding of the issues before arriving in Washington. Much of the necessary information regarding science policy can be obtained by reading the news sections of publications such as *Science, Nature,* or *The Scientist.* More practical experience might be gained from involvement in the local chapters of your national scientific societies or by volunteering to assist the public affairs branch of those societies in some manner. An above-average knowledge of how government functions is also necessary.

What practical advice would you give on how to prepare and market oneself for a career in science policy?

Applicants have a lot of competition and some prejudices to overcome. After all, scientists are all geeks, right? At least that's the stereotype that many people believe. To compensate, you must conform to most of the standards set by those already on Capitol Hill. An example: Resumes must only be one page and academic publications are meaningless. A history of political involvement is key.

Brett Stillman, Research!America Intern and Graduate Student in the Department of Pharmacology at Vanderbilt University, Nashville, TN

"I'm interested in science policy so that I can have a career that includes many of my lifetime interests," says Stillman. "This includes both science and politics. I want to be involved with a bigger picture, with decisions involving a broader level than designing and undertaking experiments in a laboratory."

He recently took a leave of absence from his graduate program to work in Washington as an intern at Research!America. "Although their main function is science advocacy, I was exposed to a broad spectrum of science policy activities in and around Washington by representing Research!America at meetings and conferences," says Stillman. "Overall, the internship was a test to see if I would like working in Washington, a way to get exposure to the Washington scene, and a step in building my resume when I look for a future policy job after graduate school. However, I still feel I will be exploring uncharted territory—most graduate students do not pursue this track."

> *What practical advice would you give on how to prepare and market oneself for a career in science policy?*
> Obtain as broad an education as possible in graduate school. Stress the well-roundedness in your experience. Cultivate the ability to speak and give seminars, write well, and use your organizational skills. Use the campus career center in areas that graduate departments do not usually help you with, such as networking skills, resume writing, and interviewing. If possible, try to intern for a couple of months or a summer during your graduate program to get some experience in science policy and advocacy.

David Applegate, Director of Government Affairs for the American Geological Institute (AGI), Alexandria, VA

Applegate has both a bachelor's degree and a Ph.D. in geology. During his doctoral work at MIT from 1989 to 1994, he became interested in the issues surrounding the siting of a high-level nuclear-waste-disposal site at Yucca Mountain, NV. "I came late to geology in college, having been a history major until a geology course at the end of my sophomore year turned my head, but I maintained an interest in matters politic," recalls Applegate. "For that reason, I was very intrigued by the Congressional Science Fellows program and applied as I was finishing my Ph.D. degree." After briefly postdocing at MIT, he received the American Geophysical Union's fellowship and came to Washington in 1994, placing with the Senate Committee on Energy and Natural Resources. The committee works on Yucca Mountain legislation, along with a wide range of other issues related to the geosciences.

After his fellowship year, he stayed on with the committee briefly, after which he took his current position as government affairs director at AGI, an umbrella organization for 31 geoscience societies.

"My program has a dual purpose: to provide information and concerns from the geoscience community to Congress and federal agencies and to keep our member societies informed of what those elected officials are up to and how their actions can affect geoscientists. My job principally entails a lot of writing, and these skills have perhaps more to do with being the son of an English teacher and having run a newspaper in college than with scientific writing skills, although scientific training helps one stick to the facts! I write a monthly column in *Geotimes*, articles for other publications, material posted to our Web site (www. agiweb.org), congressional testimony, official letters, email alerts and updates, reports, and proposals. I also talk to folks on the Hill and in the agencies to find out what is happening and to express geoscience concerns on issues or provide information, as well as give talks at universities and at society meetings."

The special skills required for this type of job, he notes, include the ability to write well and on deadline, good interpersonal skills, the ability to work on many projects at the same time, and a genuine interest in both science and public policy.

What general advice would you give a person looking into a career in science policy?

The most universal skills learned in scientific training are analytical ones, applicable to most any endeavor, but particularly to science policy where you will be confronted with issues for which you have little background, but must develop expertise on the fly. Research skills are important in that regard as well. Scientists are good at learning from one another, so they have the right impulses for going out and finding out who has the answers.

What practical advice would you give on how to prepare and market oneself for a career in science policy?

Hone skills of writing for a general audience, working to deadline, and being aware of your own biases. As to retooling, there are now many degree programs in science and environmental policy, so taking classes or getting a degree would work, particularly if one already has a strong science background. Volunteering for a political campaign, for local or state government, for environmental or other advocacy groups all provide good experience. There are many internship opportunities in Washington for those at the bachelor or master's level, as well as fellowships for postdocs.

Market yourself as a good scientist with an ability to communicate with nonscientists—someone with much to offer but a real sense of humility. You are not here to solve their problems or make their decisions. You are here to make sure that the policymakers' decisions are based on all the pertinent information presented in a clear and comprehensible fashion. A resume should not look like a CV with dozens of publications listed. Keep it short and sweet: acknowledge the publications, but also nonscientific activities and experiences that relate to your ability to work with a wide range of people and under pressure.

Rod Fujita, Senior Scientist, Environmental Defense Fund (EDF), Oakland, CA

"My experience in field ecology research led to an appreciation of the beauty and complexity of natural systems, and time spent on a coral reef in the Florida Keys threatened by oil drilling resulted in my resolve to protect ecosystems," says Fujita of his impetus to pursue a career in science-based environmental advocacy. He started work with EDF in 1988, after getting a Ph.D. in marine ecology from the Boston University marine program at the Marine Biological Laboratory in Woods Hole, MA. His first job was as an associate editor of Dr. Lynn Margulis's book, *Handbook of the Protoctista*. After that, he was awarded a NSF grant to study the rocky intertidal seaweeds of the Oregon coast at Oregon State University with Dr. Pat Wheeler, working at the Hatfield Marine Science Center in Newport, OR. From there, he did a postdoc studying the coral reefs of the Florida Keys, at the Harbor Branch Oceanographic Institution.

His job at EDF entails reviewing technical literature, developing environmental policy, advocating those policies, resolving disputes between stakeholders, lecturing, writing technical and popular articles, and speaking to the mass media.

Fujita says that in his position, "It's been important to have the research experience associated with a Ph.D., plus the publications. The ability to critically evaluate the scientific literature and to communicate scientific results and concepts to policymakers and the public is essential."

What general advice would you give a person thinking about embarking on a career in science advocacy?

Hone your communication and conflict-resolution skills, as well as your ability to translate complex science into understandable language. Become an expert in something, preferably in a recognized scientific discipline. Get experience with practical policies that work. An appreciation of economic realities and a willingness to deal with people as people with real interests, not nameless enemies of nature, also helps. Difficulties include severe criticism at times from those vested in the status quo, for example, polluting industries and exploiters of natural resources; having to go out on limbs (when science is uncertain, society still has to act); and having to deal with issues in which I'm not an expert. Benefits include a high level of fulfillment, making a difference, a high diversity of issues to learn about and deal with, and the satisfaction of helping people resolve conflicts.

The universal skills learned in scientific training upon which people could draw include an understanding of the limits of science, the nature of scientific research, a general sense of how ecosystems work, good writing and speaking skills (technical and nontechnical), and how to rigorously interpret data.

What practical advice would you give on how to prepare and market oneself for a career in science advocacy?

Get involved in some issue you care passionately about. Learn a real academic discipline and do real research to get a sense about the nature of science and uncertainty. Keep up with a variety of environmental issues and related social, cultural, and philosophical issues to get the big picture. Highlight academic achievements and practical experience in CVs and cover letters, showing that you know how to do real research and can communicate science well to the lay public. Show in the interview that you are nonideological and practical, with an open mind. Become an excellent fund-raiser.

As far as retooling for environmental advocacy, I'd say to get some experience in ecosystem restoration science and landscape ecology. I think these will be more marketable areas in the future.

Debra Lew, Senior Energy Advisor, International Institute for Energy Conservation, Bangkok, Thailand

Lew received her Ph.D. in high-temperature superconductivity from Stanford University in 1994. During her last year of graduate school, she did a volunteer internship at the Union of Concerned Scientists, where she wrote a report on the fuel cycles of biofuels and researched gasoline-vehicle and electric-vehicle emissions. From there she did a postdoc at Princeton's Energy and Environmental Studies Program working on large-scale windpower in China, followed by another postdoc at the National Renewable Energy Lab in Colorado designing wind and solar hybrid systems for villages and households in Chile and China. Since 1997 she has been investigating renewable-energy and energy-efficiency policy in Asia for the Bangkok office of the International Institute for Energy Conservation.

"I've gotten progressively farther afield from my technical background," says Lew. "I do zero technical work these days. Mainly I interface with government and utility policymakers in developing countries in Asia and try to promote sustainable energy use." This involves project management, oral presentations, writing reports for funders, policymakers and end-users, as well as setting up workshops and seminars. She also teaches local students about renewable energy and energy efficiency, and meets with industry people to learn their perspective about the barriers to energy efficiency.

"In this line of work, basic engineering, especially electrical and mechanical, skills are useful," she notes. "However, there are a lot of technically untrained people who do just fine in this field. A lot of it can be gleaned by a fast learner who has a technical mind. Generally speaking, the problems in energy policy are not technical, but rather institutional, infrastructural, financial, and educational."

What general advice would you give a person thinking about embarking on a career in science policy?

I think analytic skills are practically universally applicable. You can do just about anything with a sharp mind. The new skills that need to be acquired by scientists and engineers are often those people skills that aren't developed through graduate studies. Communication skills are essential, as people in the policy world spend most of their time writing and speaking (and they are crucial skills for landing jobs!).

Economics is a necessary evil that people should become comfortable with, because, let's face it, economics runs the world, and economics is what drives policy.

And of course, you must be driven by a desire to affect change.

What practical advice would you give on how to prepare and market oneself for a career in science policy?

The key to landing a job in policy is networking, building relationships, and being seen, whether through conferences, meetings, or publications. Another key is persistence. Many people think that letters and resumes get read. They usually don't. You should definitely try to meet with your prospective boss in person, or at least call. I've never known of anyone who has gotten a job by sending a resume to a human resource department. You have to contact the person who is actually hiring.

Another key is that you can make your own job opening! Often, posted job openings are already filled, at least in the mind of the person who is forced by organizational hiring policies to post all jobs before hiring. Your chances of hitting it off with the organization and making your own job opening are often higher than responding to posted jobs.

Another is timing. Organizations don't often go paging through old resumes to fill new positions. You have to check back with them every few months to find openings.

Also, if you are applying for a job in DC, you need to understand that by definition, DC posts involve politicking, schmoozing, and compromising. So, you have to learn or have a knack for dealing with this workstyle.

I think the best way to learn these skills is by doing. Experience counts for much more than classes. I would suggest volunteering as a great way to gain experience for your career, try out a new field to see if you like it, and give something back to the organization that is helping you transition to a new path. The other benefit of volunteering is that if it works out well, you will be first on their list when they hire for a new position.

One piece of advice that I got was to just start writing and publishing papers in the new field. This is pretty easy to do, because compared to science articles, policy publications vary widely from general interest to in-depth studies and can be published in many outlets. One colleague of mine started by submitting articles to the local newspaper.

Richard Pouyat, Legislative Assistant to Senator Daniel Patrick Moynihan (D-NY)

Pouyat received his Ph.D. in ecology from Rutgers University. "I took my advanced education one step at a time," says Pouyat. "I didn't consider getting a Ph.D. until I graduated and worked in the 'real' world for a few years. My original intent in going to college was to go into forestry. By my senior year, I realized I liked working with people, and the thought of working in the middle of the wilderness was not as appealing as it once was."

After receiving an M.S. degree in forest soils, he worked as a soil program coordinator for the Central Park Conservancy in New York City. "My first task was to develop a lab facility and program to assist the restoration of the park," recalls Pouyat. "After a year working in the park, I landed a job with the city's Department of Parks and Recreation. The next three years I coordinated a city-wide effort to map and assess the natural resources of the city. This was an exciting job that was only made possible because I had my M.S. degree. I developed 'people' skills, refined my communication skills and administrative skills on the job, although I did receive some formal training in supervision and management."

While working for the park system, Pouyat says that he realized he needed better training in ecology to better answer the land-management questions he had. So he returned to school to get his Ph.D. He worked on a forest ecology project, through the Institute of Ecosystem Studies in Millbrook, NY, the Forest Service, and Rutgers University.

"Upon finishing my Ph.D., I became a postdoc with the Forest Service, but continued as a visiting scientist in this capacity at the Institute, where I developed scientific skills: writing, making presentations, professional conduct, and interacting with students," notes Pouyat. "Up until the last year, I had a lot of experience working with natural resource managers, educators, and the public; however, I had very little exposure to the making of public policy."

To get this type of experience he applied for and later received a Congressional Science Fellowship in the spring of 1997 through the AAAS. Pouyat's fellowship was jointly sponsored by the Ecological Society of America, the American Institute of Biological Sciences, and the Society of Conservation Biology. As a legislative assistant he was responsible for all environment, agriculture, energy, and technology issues, which entails writing legislation and statements and briefing Senator Moynihan on issues; meeting with constituents, lobbyists, agency, and hill staff; working on press releases; representing the senator at meetings; and preparing for hearings. One of Pouyat's recent projects is developing acid-deposition legislation for Senator Moynihan.

Postscript: In early 1998, Pouyat returned to the Forest Service as a permanent research scientist. He is team leader of the Forest Service's role in the Baltimore Urban Long-Term Ecological Research Project.

What general advice would you give a person thinking about embarking on a career in science policy?
Science teaches us how to think critically—one can and should use this process in policy making. The best politicians, in my opinion, have the ability to think critically. Also, our most obvious skill is our experience with the scientific process.

Developing personal professional relationships is crucial. My decision to return to school for my Ph.D. was partly due to the suggestion of a scientist I was working with in New York City named Mark McDonnell, who at the time was an ecologist working at the Institute of Ecosystem Studies (IES). I would also add that it is important to find a suitable mentor when working for your Ph.D.—someone who is well known in their field, but also willing to work with students that may not desire to pursue an academic career. I was lucky enough to have Dr. McDonnell introduce me to Dr. Steward Pickett, who at the time had just accepted a position at IES. Dr. Pickett is a well-known plant ecologist who had no problem with my desire to work outside of academia.

Management training and developing supervisory skills are a must—inevitably you will be supervising someone once you get out of science. Between degrees, get work experience, particularly in positions working with the general public. Volunteering is a good way to do this.

What practical advice would you give on how to prepare and market oneself for a career in science policy?

Do your homework! Know as much as possible about the agency or politician you hope to work for. Be able to explain science or your research to the general public, using simple terms, metaphors, and analogies. That is, you should be able to explain your research and why it is important to a politician within 10 minutes. Practice with your friends, or better, your parents. Be excited about your research and why you think it is important to work with policymakers.

Patricia Hoben, Assistant Director for Education, The Bakken Museum and Library, Minneapolis, Minn.

Hoben received her Ph.D. in molecular biophysics and biochemistry in 1984 from Yale University, after which she was a postdoc at the University of California, San Francisco. In 1986 she moved to Washington, DC to take her first job in science policy at the Office of Technology Assessment, where she stayed for two years. Later, she held positions as a policy advisor and program director on biomedical research and science education issues in the DC area. She worked for the Assistant Secretary for Health at the U.S. Department of Health and Human Services, at the Howard Hughes Medical Institute, and at the National Institutes of Health.

About four years ago, Hoben moved to Minneapolis, where she directed a research program for the Minnesota Public Utilities Commission on stray voltage effects on dairy cows and a community-based project called RISE: Regional Initiatives in Science Education. RISE is an initiative of the National Research Council that assists schools and local communities on how to work together to implement the national science education standards. In late 1997, she joined The Bakken as assistant director, where she works full time on K–12 and public science education for the museum.

"I knew even as a postdoc that I wanted more diversity in my career," recalls Hoben. "I didn't want to surround myself only with scientists. I've always been more of a big-picture person. I enjoy all sorts of people and wanted to be around people with different perspectives on life. Also, I always enjoyed talking about science more than doing it, hence my interests in science policy and, eventually, science education."

What general advice would you give a person looking into a career in science policy?

First, it helps to realize that science policy is an ill-defined area.

Policymaking is interpreting laws and developing rules after obtaining public input. Keeping that in mind, I'd say honing your communication skills is very important. For scientists to be effective in the world of public policy, they have to be able to simplify scientific issues and concepts down to the big ideas they represent so that policymakers—agency heads, legislators, their staff, and others—will understand and be receptive.

You also have to learn to work as part of a team. Graduate school doesn't prepare people for that. As part of a team, you need to appreciate people who aren't trained as scientists and recognize them for what they can bring to a project.

What practical advice would you give a person on how to prepare for a career in science policy?

Get experience outside of your discipline. Take classes in other departments. Get writing experience with a peer group outside of science. Take creative writing and journalism courses. Learn how to make a nonscience presentation or speech; figure out what it is about you that makes you stand out and build on that.

The most successful people in policy are the ones that are the easiest to work with and for, so you'll need people and management skills. To get this kind of experience, volunteer to work at some kind of advocacy organization or at a local or state legislator's office—someplace in the real world—so you can see how things work before you jump in with both feet.

Linda Distlerath, Executive Director, Corporate Public Policy and Merck Research Laboratories-Public Affairs in Whitehouse Station, NJ

Distlerath received her Ph.D. in 1983 in toxicology and environmental health from the University of Cincinnati, after which she took a postdoctoral research position at the Center for Molecular Toxicology at Vanderbilt University. In 1984, she started work in the Merck Research Laboratories as a clinical research associate, where she helped plan and implement early-phase human clinical trials with new investigational drugs. "Clinical research provided an excellent introduction to pharmaceutical R&D, and also piqued my interest in understanding the larger business aspects that face Merck as a global, research-intensive company," she remembers. "But yet I wanted to maintain connections to the research environment at Merck."

In a move towards that general goal, she became the associate director for academic relations for the Merck Research Laboratories in 1988. In this post she directed programs that provided pre- and postdoctoral fellowships in the chemical and biological sciences at universities worldwide, undergraduate research grants in chemistry and biology, and support for external scientific meetings. From there she moved into a public policy-related position within corporate public affairs at Merck. In 1989 she became director of U.S. issues management, where she coordinated the evaluation of legislative, regulatory, or policy initiatives that could impede or enhance pharmaceutical R&D at Merck and throughout the industry. These issues included use of animals in research, biotechnology, AIDS drug development, and government funding of NIH. In her current role, she has overall responsibilities for public affairs for the Merck Research Laboratories and also heads the public policy function for Merck.

What general advice would you give a person thinking about embarking on a career in science policy?

Get involved in some aspect of public policy—monitor legislative and regulatory activities, visit your elected government official on issues important to your profession, or chair public communications or public policy committees for your scientific organizations—to gain experience and demonstrate your interest in stepping into the public policy arena. There are lots of excellent scientists and clinicians out there who think that dabbling in science policy sounds like fun, so you need to provide some evidence of effectiveness and passion for public policy or public affairs. Show that you are comfortable dealing with external nonscientific audiences outside the lab or clinic, that you are an effective and persuasive communicator, and that you can exert diplomacy, tact, and grace under pressure or in adverse environments. (Think about the person you see on C-SPAN undergoing a grilling by an agenda-driven member of Congress!)

Most importantly, develop your communication skills outside the scientific area. It's important in science policy to be able to translate scientific and technical information into lay language in a manner that conveys the key points with clarity, integrity, and enthusiasm. Volunteer to write for your scientific society's newsletter, or get involved in your society's policy or government relations committee to gain valuable experience in issue analysis and lobbying activities. Excellent public speaking and presentation skills are essential; seek speaking opportunities aimed at a variety of audiences and attend specialized training programs to enhance your presentation skills.

What practical advice would you give on how to prepare and market oneself for a career in science policy?

Additional graduate-level education or a science policy or congressional fellowship can provide those extra credentials outside the research science to facilitate a career in science policy. There are many good masters-level programs in public health, public policy, and science/health-oriented communications. Organizations like AAAS offer congressional fellowship opportunities. M.B.A.s and law degrees can be helpful as well. In my case, shortly after moving to my position in issues management in Corporate Public Affairs at Merck, I went to law school at night and obtained a J.D. from Rutgers Law School, Newark in 1994. This legal education provided fundamental knowledge of constitutional law, administrative law, intellectual property law, and other areas of law relevant to business and public policy, and helped sharpen my research, analytical, and advocacy skills.

Resources

Professional Societies

According to many science policy people, there are no societies specifically dedicated to career science policy specialists, although Sander notes that AAAS, the American Physical Society, the American Chemical Society, and the American Society for Microbiology have taken a leadership role in this area. Many of these have portions of their Web sites devoted to science policy fellowship activities.

Education and Training

Fellowships

White House Fellowships. Fellows from diverse backgrounds, including those with scientific and technical training, spend a year working with senior White House, Cabinet, and other executive branch officials. Assignments include speech writing and developing policy papers. Contact:

President's Commission of White House Fellowships
712 Jackson Place, NW
Washington, DC 20503
202-395-4522
http://www.whitehouse.gov

Congressional Research Service (CRS). The CRS provides Congress with research, analysis, and information services for issues at hand. It recruits graduate students, including those in science, technology, medicine, and environmental and natural resource areas, for entry-level policy analyst and reference librarian positions for the summer. Contact:

Congressional Research Service
Graduate Recruit Program
202-707-5776
http://www.loc.gov/crsinfo

American Association for the Advancement of Science (AAAS). AAAS sponsors six types of policy fellowships for Ph.D.s and some for people with an M.S. All applicants must be U.S. citizens.

- *AAAS Congressional Science and Engineering Fellows Program.* One year on Capitol Hill working with members of Congress or congressional committees on scientific and technical issues. Two fellows for 1998–1999.
- *AAAS Science, Engineering and Diplomacy Fellows Program.* One year at the State Department working in foreign policy or at the U.S. Agency for International Development (USAID) working on international development. One State Department and about 12 USAID fellows in 1998–1999.
- *AAAS Risk Assessment Science and Engineering Fellows Program.* One year with the Environmental Protection Agency (EPA) or U.S. Department of Agriculture (USDA). Five fellows at EPA and at least one at USDA for 1998–1999.
- *AAAS/Critical Technologies Institute Science and Engineering Fellows Program.* One- to two-year fellowships for candidates with a minimum of five years of industrial experience to midlevel and senior executives. Fellows spend one year at CTI, a Washington, DC-based, federally funded research-and-development center within RAND, a policy think tank working on issues related to research and development, technology transfer, and international competitiveness.
- *AAAS Defense Policy Fellowships for Scientists and Engineers.* One-year assignment to the office of the Under Secretary of Defense for Acquisition and Technology to work on defense policy and technology applications, among other topics.
- *AAAS/EPA Environmental Science and Engineering Fellows Program.* Ten-week summer placement with EPA working on assessing the significance of long-range environmental problems. Ten fellows for 1998–1999.

Contact information for all AAAS policy fellowships:

American Association for the Advancement of Science
Fellowship Programs
1200 New York Ave., NW
Washington, DC 20005

202-326-6600
202-289-4950
science_policy@aaas.org
http://www.aaas.org/spp/dspp/dspp.htm

AAAS also coordinates a congressional science policy program for over 20 scientific and professional societies in addition to its own program. Each society sponsors one or more postdoctoral or midcareer one-year fellowships. As with the AAAS program, fellows work on Capitol Hill in the offices of members of Congress or congressional committees on scientific and technical issues.

Contact information for the society-sponsored fellowships is on AAAS's Web page: http://www.aaas.org/spp/dspp/stg/conspon.htm. This page lists addresses and other contact information for sponsoring societies. Contact the individual societies for applications.

Professional Society Fellowships. Many other professional societies other than the AAAS-affiliated ones, such as the Society for Environmental Toxicology and Chemistry, also sponsor fellowships or are in the process of creating them. Contact the relevant societies in your disciplines to find out if they do or have plans to. For example, contact:

Society of Environmental Toxicology and Chemistry
1010 North 12th Ave.
Pensacola, FL 32501-3370
850-469-1500
Fax: 850-469-9778
setac@setac.org
http://www.setac.org

U.S. Public Health Service (PHS) Commissioned Officer Student Training and Extern Program. Students are placed in one of eight PHS agencies, including the Agency for Healthcare Policy and Research. Contact:

Junior Officer Program
Division of Commissioned Personnel
Attn: JRCOSTEP
5600 Fishers Lane, Room 4A-07
Rockville, MD 20857-0001
800-279-1605
301-594-2633
jrcostep@psc.dhhs.gov

Senior Officer Program
Division of Commissioned Personnel
Attn: SRCOSTEP
5600 Fishers Lane, Room 4A-07
Rockville, MD 20857-0001
301-594-2919
http://phs.os.dhhs.gov/phs/corps/student.html

Robert Wood Johnson Foundation Health Policy Fellowship. This one-year program administered by the Institute of Medicine is for midcareer health professionals working in academic settings or community-based healthcare organizations and institutions to gain an understanding of the health policy process. Contact:

Program Director
Robert Wood Johnson Foundation Health
  Policy Fellowships Program
Institute of Medicine
2101 Constitution Ave., NW
Washington, DC 20418
202-334-1506
Fax: 202-334-3862
hppf@nas.edu
http://www2.nas.edu/rwj

Research!America. This medical advocacy group sponsors biomedical research policy internships. Contact:

Research!America
908 King St., Suite 400 East
Alexandria, VA 22314-3067
703-739-2577
800-366-CURE
researcham@aol.com
http://www.researchamerica.org

National Science Foundation. The Science and Technology Studies and the Social Dimensions of Engineering, Science, and Technology programs support fellowships that allow scientists and engineers who wish to obtain further training in policy or ethics to undertake a research project under the supervision of a host scholar (and vice versa). Contact:

National Science Foundation
4201 Wilson Blvd.
Arlington, VA 22230
703-306-1234
http://www.nsf.gov

National Institutes of Health. Individual institutes and offices within institutes may offer fellowships, however, there is no central place to get information. NIH's department of human resources suggests a thorough search of opportunities listed on the NIH training and education Web site: http://www.training.nih.gov.

Other Opportunities. A Web site (http://www.wws.princeton.edu:80/ ~kammen/energy-jobs.html) maintained by Daniel Kammen, an assistant professor of public and international affairs in the Woodrow Wilson School of Public and International Affairs, and cochair of the science, technology, and public policy program at Princeton University has hotlinks to several federal organizations (including a guide to all the U.S. national laboratories), research institutes, advocacy groups, and nongovernmental organizations, some of which sponsor fellowships. Kammen also mentions that some companies like AT&T/Lucent Technologies Inc. and Bechtel Inc. also sponsor Congressional policy fellowships. His Web site contains links to these as well.

To contact other environmental organizations to see if they sponsor internships and/or jobs, check out the Amazing Environmental Organization Web Directory at: http://www.webdirectory.com.

Educational Programs. AAAS has recently posted its *Guide to Graduate Education in Science and Engineering and Public Policy* on the Web. It provides current information on such programs, including UC-Berkeley, Boston University, Cambridge University, Carnegie Mellon University, Clark University, Harvard University, MIT, Princeton University, and the University of Maryland. Kammen's Web site lists links to seven of these programs. The AAAS Web site also includes links to the schools' programs, frequently asked questions, and other helpful links to policy organizations and information sources. Contact:

AAAS *Guide to Graduate Education in Science
and Engineering and Public Policy*
Directorate for Science and Policy Programs, AAAS
1200 New York Ave., NW
Washington, DC 20005
202-289-4950
http://www.aaas.org/spp/dspp/sepp/index.htm

(*text continues on p. 232*)

Advice from Daniel M. Kammen, Assistant Professor of Public and International Affairs, Woodrow Wilson School of Public and International Affairs, and Cochair of the Science, Technology, and Public Policy Program, Princeton University

The following is excerpted from Dr. Kammen's Web site (http://www.wws.princeton.edu:80/~kammen/energy-jobs.html), with his permission:

I am often asked by young scholars from the social and physical sciences (and particularly by physicists) about the options, avenues, and support resources available to them as they expand their interests, or contemplate career shifts into the area broadly defined as the science and policy of "energy and the environment." Providing a complete, or even coherent, guide to the degree programs, fellowships, job opportunities, mentors available, and pitfalls is probably impossible, and I won't even make an attempt. Instead, I have collected here a highly personalized set of opinions and some pointers to resources that people newly interested in this field might want to consult.

One of the most common questions I am asked, and probably the least answerable is, "when should I try to move from mainstream physics (or substitute here chemistry, engineering, economics, etc. . . .) to energy and environmental research? Should I get a Ph.D. in a field of science, then get policy training, or should I get an interdisciplinary degree in the first place?" There are obviously a myriad of good answers, as well as stories of success, and of frustration.

My only consistent response is to study what you enjoy over what you think will afford you some idealized credential. Enthusiasm, dedication, and willingness to do the hard work to learn the literature and the state-of-the-art in other fields may be the best measure of when to "make the change." This is certainly harder than it sounds; some tremendously capable scientists have succumbed to the "prophet in a foreign land" mentality described in Ibsen's *Peer Gynt*. They often ended up disappointed, having done an insufficient amount of background training and research. Their work in the energy and environmental field is often only a brief foray, or worse, a dabbling.

One particularly prickly issue relating to the question of "when to enter the field" concerns the extent to which disciplinary or interdisciplinary training is crucial. Most people in the field today were trained in traditional disciplines: physics, economics, engineering, and so forth. Not surprisingly they tend to view disciplinary training as an important foundation and as a useful credential. Equally unsurprising, this view is far from universal. While there are a few truly interdisciplinary doctoral programs and centers, such as the Energy and Resources Group

(ERG) at the University of California, Berkeley, they are rare. Graduate education, however, is constantly evolving. Many universities have now formed, at least on paper, interdisciplinary research or teaching units, often organized around questions of environmental science, social science, and/or policy. The students who will shortly begin to emerge from these programs will have a very different training (and perspective?) from the previous generations.

In my case, I completed a B.A., M.A., and then a Ph.D., each in physics, focusing my dissertation on solid state physics, neural networks, information theory, and biological computing. I began my postdoctoral fellowship at Caltech not altogether sure which way I would go: continue my "physics" research on neural networks or branch into energy and environmental issues? Caltech in general, and my advisor in particular, were exceptionally flexible and supportive. I was funded by the Weizmann Fellowship that freed my advisor from direct salary responsibility for me, but left travel, equipment, and other expenses as well as the most expensive component of all: investment in training a young scholar. During my postdoctoral fellowship my work "migrated" from about an 80:20 physics:development mix to a reversal three years later. During that time, my advisor Christof Koch in the Computation and Neural Systems Group (Division of Biology) supported my increasing contacts with faculty in the Division of Humanities and Social Sciences, and my increasingly frequent trips to ERG and the International Energy Group at the Lawrence Berkeley Laboratory, and to Central America where I pursued field research. The Division of Biology also encouraged (and funded) me to teach a course on tropical development and conservation. My path was neither fully planned, nor particularly coherent. I simply kept working on what interested me. The most important feature, and really the only constant, in my case was the tremendous amount of advice and (generally) encouragement that I received from people already working on energy and environmental issues, as well as broadly curious and unselfish scholars such as Christof Koch.

Dr. Kammen gives the following general suggestions regarding career advice:

"Getting started" in energy and environmental work is not clear-cut in that there are few courses or conferences devoted to the topic. At the same time, most everyone working in this area will go out of their way to help you. That is not an invitation, however, to let others do your homework for you. If you are an undergraduate or early graduate student it is certainly not expected that you are familiar with the energy and environmental organizations or literature. But, you need to have done some advance reading and searching on the WWW. [A good start is the journals listed at the end of Kammen's Web site.] As a senior graduate student or recent Ph.D. you need to have done considerably more; by one account: "three-fourths of the people applying to our research group for postdoctoral positions are unable to articulate their interests beyond simple statements of interdisciplinarity." There is no excuse for not reading a sampling of papers by the people you plan to approach. This is not only useful intellectually, but it also shows that you are serious. It is remarkable how many people call up and say that they are interested in "energy and development," "the environment," or "appropriate technology," and have read next to nothing in the field. You would never do this (I hope!) in a traditional field.

Consistently I am told that a cover letter and resume are useful in advance of a phone call. Indicate in the cover letter (briefly!): (a) your accomplishments to date; (b) the types of research or activities you would like to undertake in the future; and (c) how you could contribute to the goals of the laboratory or organization you are contacting. Suggest in this letter that you will be following up with a phone call. The letter is useful both because it gives you the opening line of your phone conversation ("My name is Jill Johnson; I sent you a letter a couple of weeks ago") and it will have already forced you to figure out your fit with the organization you are contacting. If you get nervous and tongue-tied during the phone call, you can refer to the letter.

As for the timing involved in switching fields there is no formula and the only advice is simple (but surprising how often people don't consider it). If you are 6–12 months away from a Ph.D., stick it out. Switch later. If you have just finished the second year of a five-year process, maybe it makes sense to switch now. Many job openings are not posted; if they are posted, they may already have someone in mind. The best way to find an opening is often not through employment/human resources offices but through individual researchers in your area of interest. The key to finding these researchers is networking. Call professors who might have contacts; call authors of articles; call local nongovernmental organizations and ask them for advice on who to contact in finding a position. Get a list of possible people and call all of them and ask them for advice, etc. Someone along the line may have a position open or know of one or may come across one in the near future. Similarly, look into what conferences exist and attend them if at all possible. Many of the journals list meetings (*Environment*, the *EPRI Journal*, etc.). Once there, ask questions. Many people who are trying to make a transition into science policy start at a very high level of education and are expecting a high level position in this new field. Don't be discouraged by volunteer work or short-term internships or entry-level positions. Your advanced degrees may mean that you may be able to work your way up faster, but as you make this transition, you'll need a lot of training and can't necessarily expect to walk into your ideal position right away.

Jobhunting and Networking

What happens after people leave an internship or fellowship? Where do they look for jobs? Sander says that university-based policy positions are probably advertised in the *Chronicle of Higher Education*'s Academe This Week (http://chronicle.merit.edu) and that government agencies probably advertise individually on government Web sites, job hotlines, and agency human resources departments. Generally, permanent jobs are not attached to a Congressional office or committee, but will be administered through individual agencies like NSF, NIH, and DOE. He also says that about two-thirds of Congressional science fellows stay on in DC in some type of policy job, while the remainder go back into traditional research jobs, with about half of those remaining in academics.

Kammen's Web site has links to research institutes, industrial and consulting opportunities, and nongovernmental organizations that list jobs in energy and environmental policy. The site also has links to energy and environmental journals and newsletters that list jobs and internships.

The Amazing Environmental Organization Web Directory (http://www.webdirectory.com) also has a subsection on employment opportunities, some of which may pertain to policy.

☐ Science and Environmental Regulatory Policy

With more drugs going to market and mounting concern about the environment, there is a growing need for people with a technical background who also understand the laws that govern the manufacture and marketing of healthcare and environmental products and services. There is a complex web of regulations to which the healthcare and environmental industries must strictly adhere. This fuels the growing demand for people who can monitor, interpret, and help organizations comply with regulations, especially those set down by the Food and Drug Administration (FDA) and the Environmental Protection Agency (EPA).

According to the latest counts from the Regulatory Affairs Professionals Society (RAPS), which deals with the concerns of healthcare regulatory professionals, over one-third of their members work in the area of medical devices, about one-third in pharmaceuticals, and about one-quarter in biologics/biotechnology, with the remainder in in vitro diagnostics, cosmetics, veterinary, and food products. RAPS members are employed at large corporations, small businesses, and government agencies, in universities, and at nonprofit organizations. The backgrounds of regulatory affairs professionals are quite varied and include such disciplines as pharmacy, medicine, clinical laboratory science, nursing, law, engineering, and technical writing.

The EPA and other government agencies make regulations for monitoring and setting acceptable levels of substances released into the environment by industry and municipalities. Most scientists in regulatory affairs work at large industrial firms and for federal and state governments that must interpret and comply with these laws. Read on for the experiences and advice of several regulatory affairs professionals employed in a variety of settings and at different stages in their careers.

One-on-One with Regulatory Specialists

Alberto Grignolo, Vice President and General Manager, Worldwide Regulatory Affairs, Parexel International Corp., Boston

Grignolo received his Ph.D. in experimental psychology from the University of North Carolina, Chapel Hill and did a postdoc in neuropharmacology at Duke University Medical Center. "While doing my Ph.D., I became aware of the difficulties of securing government research grants and became interested in entering the drug industry," he states. "My credentials as a psychologist were not sufficient, so I felt that taking a postdoc in pharmacology would improve my chances. It did, but with a twist. I had expected to be hired into a pharmacology lab in a drug company; instead, I was offered a position in regulatory affairs, a discipline which was completely unknown to me. The money was good, training would be provided, so off I went!"

His present job is the senior position in the regulatory affairs division at Parexel. He is responsible for all regulatory and quality assurance activities and services, for both the company's internal colleagues and its clients. Grignolo describes his job as a combination of regulatory consulting (knowledge of how to deal with regulators and technical issues) and general management (hiring, motivating, strategic planning, and business management).

> *What general advice would you give a person thinking about embarking on a career in regulatory affairs?*
> Honing your ability to pay attention to detail—regulatory professionals are often asked to review documents with a fine-tooth

comb—is at the top of the list. Persistence, commitment, interest in doing an excellent job, and the ability to work in teams and contribute without taking over are also important. Certainly the RAPS certification program is a good mechanism to get retrained. Unfortunately, for the moment, the exam is not preceded by a formal curriculum, which would make it easier for people to take classes in an organized fashion. RAPS is working on this with a number of academic institutions.

The profession is interesting and accessible to people with college degrees; it provides opportunities for advancement, which can be leveraged through the person's positive attitude and willingness to work hard. People with hard-science degrees can become technical regulatory professionals, who are sorely needed. A chemist is a chemist, but a regulatory chemist who can manage the regulatory process is a chemist who is bringing the product closer to approval!

What practical advice would you give on how to prepare and market oneself for a career in regulatory affairs?

This is tough, because there is little history. Most employers look for experienced regulatory professionals and are unwilling to hire and train "green" people. We do hire and train such people because we recognize the labor shortage. We look for a sound scientific/technical background and, very importantly, a positive attitude towards learning, teamwork, communication, customer service, efficiency and effectiveness, and professional growth. A resume which reflects a good education and laboratory skills sits well with us.

Cindy Nolte, Associate Consultant at Medical Device Consultants Inc. (MDCI) in North Attleboro, MA

Nolte received her Ph.D. in biochemistry from Boston University in 1988. From 1989 to 1995 she worked as a bench scientist at a start-up medical-device company. "As part of my work I provided data and analysis for product QC and QA," she recalls. "When I left the company in 1996 I decided to explore switching fields to become a regulatory affairs professional. I was introduced to the president of MDCI through a family member who is a regulatory affairs consultant. MDCI happened to be in the process of preparing a submission containing microbiological-testing data. The company recognized that they could benefit from my scientific expertise so they offered me a job."

In her present position, she develops regulatory strategies for premarket applications, assists in the design of nonclinical testing protocols, and prepares regulatory submissions to government agencies. She also serves as a liaison between the manufacturer and FDA.

"Because of my scientific expertise, I have been given responsibility for projects which require scientific support, both in the design of the appropriate testing protocols and presentation of data," she says. "Special skills required to work in regulatory affairs also include such general attributes as attention to detail, organizational skills, technical writing, and communication."

What general advice would you give a person thinking about embarking on a career in regulatory affairs?
Build a network of contacts in the regulatory affairs profession. I suggest joining one or two networking groups—one with a scientific slant and the other medical products or regulatory affairs. The one I joined in my area was called Wednesday is Networking Day. I obtained practice in presenting myself and developed an extensive network of individuals with contacts in the regulatory affairs profession. Contact any mentor you have had in your present career and let them know what you are planning.

Another excellent way of making a switch is moving to a position within your present company. The company already knows you and what you are capable of. They would be more likely to take a chance with someone with whom they are familiar.

Join the Regulatory Affairs Professionals Society. I was part of a program they sponsored which was geared toward individuals looking to move into regulatory affairs.

Classes or a program in technical writing might help. However, the regulatory affairs profession is unique in that there have not been, up until now, many sources of professional training in the field. Most people have come to the field from another career and training has been on-the-job.

I have not had any experience with volunteering my time for a regulatory affairs project. Perhaps it would work if you approached a start-up company with limited resources who would be willing to use your services. Make sure your mentor in any such adventure was experienced. Your "free" time is a valuable commodity and you would want to make sure you got some real experience out of the project.

What practical advice would you give on how to prepare and market oneself for a career in regulatory affairs?
Regarding your resume, for each job you have held, list any exposure you have had in any aspect of the regulatory affairs profession. Group all exposure into a section entitled "Summary of Qualifications," directly following your stated job objective.

Regarding interviewing/negotiating skills, it may be difficult to obtain an interview for an advertised regulatory affairs position. These positions are usually to fill specific needs, and a resume from a career changer would most likely be discarded. It is best to attempt to obtain informational interviews with regulatory affairs professionals in companies you have targeted. Such interviews are not designed to obtain a position, but to learn about the profession and listen to the experiences of others who have entered the field. Learn as much as you can about the regulatory affairs profession and where your particular experience would best fit.

Rosina Robinson, Senior Staff Consultant at Medical Device Consultants Inc. in North Attleboro, MA

Robinson is a registered nurse by training. She also has a B.A. in psychology and a Master of Education in health promotion, which she received in 1990. "What led me to where I am is that I wanted to make a greater impact on patient care than the one-to-one relationship of clinical nursing," she explains. "The transition from clinical nursing to a position of customer trainer for a medical-device manufacturer came in 1978 and was attributable to a college elective called career and life planning. Once in industry, I had several promotions and finally a lateral move into the regulatory affairs arena. I started my most recent position in 1992, after a short return to clinical nursing and graduate school."

Robinson works with clients to obtain marketing clearance and approval for their medical devices. This includes strategy development, writing marketing applications, and representing the client with the FDA.

She says that the critical skills required in regulatory affairs include the ability to communicate clearly, interpersonal skills, organizational skills, and scientific knowledge such as in medicine, nursing, statistics, engineering, and pharmacy.

"Product-specific knowledge can be useful in getting that first position in the field," adds Robinson.

What general advice would you give a person thinking about embarking on a career in regulatory affairs?
    Talk to people who are currently in the field. Take the opportunity to attend some of the professional meetings like RAPS and the Food and Drug Law Institute to meet people. If you haven't had a research-methods course or biostatistics, take some. Take courses and attend meetings given by the professional organizations. There are a few college programs scattered throughout the country. If you're close to one, by all means this would be the place to start.

Read the trade sheets for the profession and the journals for the professional organizations. Volunteering is probably not the way to get experience. Regulatory affairs generally deals with many products in the development phase, where security would not lend itself to use of volunteers.

What practical advice would you give on how to prepare and market oneself for a career in regulatory affairs?
Because you can be trained in the details of the position, focus on your transferable skills and product-specific skills. It may, however, be necessary to plan for entry via a position in another department and move laterally when the opportunity arises like I did. Be open to the potential opportunities that may arise in the future.

Martha Carter, Vice President of Regulatory Affairs at GelTex Pharmaceuticals, Inc. in Waltham, MA

Carter received a B.A. in biology from Northeastern University in 1975, after which she worked in a pharmaceutical company as a medical affairs clinical research associate. Here she monitored Investigational New Drug studies. She attended graduate school at night but eventually came to the realization that her heart wasn't in laboratory research.

"An opening in regulatory affairs came up and it looked like it might be interesting," she recalls. "This was a lateral move for me, which is how many people get into regulatory affairs since there are not many training programs in the field yet."

Before moving to Genetics Institute in 1995 and GelTex in 1998, Carter worked as a regulatory affairs specialist for other biotech and pharmaceutical companies. At Genetics Institute and in her present position she liaises with such government agencies as the FDA that regulate the pharmaceutical industry to make sure that new drugs comply with U.S. and international laws.

She lists the necessary skills for a career in regulatory affairs: a good grasp of science at different levels, communication of science and "regulationese," the ability to read and digest complex material, and diplomacy and negotiation in building good relationships with the agencies.

What practical advice would you give on how to prepare and market oneself for a career in regulatory affairs?
This is difficult to answer. The dilemma is to get hands-on experience because there is no curriculum. Sometimes working in a related field, such as quality assurance, where there is a degree of

exposure to regulatory requirements, can be helpful. It's the pro-
verbial Catch-22. Because people are hired from the inside it's
difficult to come off the street and get a job. The profession is still
in its early days. Some companies have internships, but these are
entry level.

John Walker, Director of the Toxic Substances Control Act (TSCA) Interagency Testing Committee (ITC), EPA, Washington, DC

As Director of the ITC, Walker manages the activities of the committee,
which consists of senior executives and scientists from 16 federal organizations. The ITC is an independent advisory committee to the EPA
administrator created in 1976 under the TSCA. ITC members meet monthly
to identify and coordinate federal data needs for chemicals that can be
regulated under the TSCA, to consider these chemicals for information
reporting or testing needed to assess hazard or risk, to add recommended
chemicals to the TSCA Priority Testing List, and to recommend these
added chemicals for information reporting or testing to the EPA administrator. After these recommendations are published in the Federal
Register, the ITC establishes dialogue groups with producers, import-
ers, processors, and users of the recommended chemicals to discuss the
needed data. For additional information about the ITC, Walker suggests looking at the ITC's Web site at www.epa.gov/opptintr/itc.

Walker has been working in environmental toxicology and chemistry
in academic, industrial, and government settings for over 30 years.
After receiving his Ph.D. in aquatic toxicology from Ohio State University in 1971, he taught classes and conducted research at the University
of Maryland and served as chief scientist for numerous estuarine and
oceanographic cruises. In 1975 he started employment with Martin Marietta
Corp., where he established and operated a laboratory to study the
aquatic toxicity and degradation of proprietary chemicals. During that
time he also obtained a Masters in Public Health (M.P.H.) from the
Johns Hopkins University School of Medicine.

After completing his M.P.H., he was recruited by the FDA and EPA
as a senior scientist, where he established programs to score and rank
chemicals, evaluated toxicology protocols, and reviewed data developed in compliance with the Federal Food, Drug and Cosmetic Act and
TSCA. After 10 years at the EPA, including a 4-year term as EPA's
representative to the ITC, Walker was selected as its director.

"One of the best things I like about my job is providing valuable
products and services to government organizations," says Walker. "The
ITC is an organization that has tremendous potential to provide infor-

mation on commercial chemicals to anyone who needs it, especially the public under EPA's community-right-to-know initiative. The major reason I created ITC's Web site was to make all the information on commercial chemicals that ITC has obtained and generated since 1977 available to the public. One of the challenging features of my job is securing funding and meeting political challenges, but that's the scenario with most jobs that provide services to the public."

What general advice would you give a person thinking about embarking on a career in environmental regulatory affairs?

Key opportunities for me were attending schools where support, both financial and moral, was provided to pursue my education in biology, chemistry, and public health. My job requires a broad and interdisciplinary background—knowledge of biology, chemistry, public health, international chemical testing, and reporting regulations are all needed.

This is not a common career path for environmental scientists. Jobs are scarce. My experience working in the chemical industry and educational background provides me credibility in dealing with other scientists, legislators, and lawyers at large chemical trade associations, corporations, and the public.

I accepted jobs with the chemical industry because I was spending too much time writing research proposals and not enough time teaching. I was recruited by and accepted employment with the FDA and EPA because the jobs provided the opportunity (after many years of using methods to measure aquatic toxicity and degradation of industrial chemicals) to improve or develop better testing methods for environmental toxicity and biodegradation of substances.

What practical advice would you give on how to prepare and market oneself for a career in environmental regulatory affairs?

Take some courses in economics; I wish I had taken more. This will help on two levels: the need to justify budgets and the need to develop economically realistic environmental regulations.

If I were asked if environmental regulatory affairs was a good career choice for younger scientists, I'd say that you should take your first job in industry after graduate school or after a stint at basic research. Perhaps even line up an internship with industry during graduate school. This is because, eventually, if you do end up making or interpreting environmental regulations, you will either be working in industry or be in a government agency that deals very closely with industry. Your experience at a relevant industry will lend you credibility with the people with whom you work.

Honing communication skills is critical for dealing with a nonscientific audience. Most of the people I work with in industry regulatory affairs are lawyers, not scientists.

Join the Society of Environmental Toxicology and Chemistry. Professional-society connections can lead to job offers, give you a place to learn more about the profession, participate in government and policy committees to test your interest in regulatory affairs, and provide opportunities to make personal and professional acquaintances. Remember, success is partially who you know.

Resources

Professional Societies

Regulatory Affairs Professionals Society (RAPS). The main professional organization for regulatory affairs specialists in the biologics, drug, and medical device industries. Contact:

Regulatory Affairs Professionals Society
12300 Twinbrook Parkway
Suite 350
Rockville, MD
20852-1606
301-770-2920
Fax: 301-770-2924
raps@raps.org
http://www.raps.org

Drug Information Association (DIA). This is a technical-oriented organization with 16,000 members, including people in drug development, such as epidemiologists and statisticians. Contact:

Drug Information Association
321 Norristown Rd., Suite 225
Ambler, PA 19002-2755
215-628-2288
Fax: 215-641-1229
dia@diahome.org
http://www.diahome.org

Parenteral Drug Association (PDA). This is a manufacturing- and drug-regulation society for those involved in the pharmaceutical industry. Contact:

Parenteral Drug Association
7500 Old Georgetown Rd., Suite 620
Bethesda, MD 20814
301-986-0293
Fax: 301-986-0296
info@pda.org
http://www.pda.org

Society of Environmental Toxicology and Chemistry (SETAC). This professional society represents basic and applied scientists, as well as regulatory affairs specialists. Contact:

Society of Environmental Toxicology and Chemistry
1010 North 12th Ave.
Pensacola, FL 32501-3370
850-469-1500
Fax: 850-469-9778
setac@setac.org
http://www.setac.org

Education and Training

According to RAPS, not many formal education programs in healthcare regulatory affairs exist right now, but this is changing. Many are in the works. In fact, in the fall of 1997, RAPS held a forum to discuss the development of university-based regulatory affairs programs.

Educational Training Programs

San Diego State University. M.S. in interdisciplinary studies with an emphasis in regulatory affairs, a B.S. with an emphasis in regulatory affairs, and specialized certificate programs. Contact:

Stephen Dahms, Director, SDSU Biotechnology Research
   and Training Program, and Director, California State University
   System Program for Education and Research in Biotechnology
Center for Biopharmaceutical and Biodevice Development
San Diego State University
San Diego, CA 92182-4610
619-594-5578
sdahms@sciences.sdsu.edu

Temple University School of Pharmacy. M.S. degree in Quality Assurance/Regulatory Affairs. Most of the classes are held in the evenings and on weekends for the mostly full-time working students. Contact:

Thomas W. O'Connor, Associate Dean
Temple University School of Pharmacy
3307 North Broad St.
Philadelphia, PA 19140
215-707-4990
toconnor@astro.temple.edu
http://www.temple.edu/departments/pharmacy

SETAC maintains a directory of graduate programs entitled "Graduate Programs in Environmental Chemistry, Environmental Engineering, and Environmental Toxicology," which is available free from the society. It was updated in the summer of 1998. Classes in environmental regulatory affairs are part of many of these programs. SETAC also sponsors short courses that cover federal environmental regulations at their annual and regional meetings, as well as a training grant to attend these courses. Contact SETAC headquarters for more information on these programs.

Fellowships

The Food and Drug Law Institute. Four-day summer course in food and drug regulation for 40 to 60 attendees. Students must be enrolled in an ABA-accredited law school or science degree program that relates to food and drug science and must be participants of a summer internship sponsored by a government agency.

The institute targets regulatory affairs issues in its educational programs, books, and other materials. Contact for educational and course materials:

Food and Drug Law Institute
Julia K. Ogden, Director of Academic Programs
1000 Vermont Ave., NW, Suite 200
Washington, DC 20005-4903
202-371-1420
Fax: 202-371-0649
jko@fdli.org
http://www.fdli.org/

Regulatory Affairs Professionals Society. Conducts workshops and continuing education courses, and manages a certification program in regulatory affairs. Consult the society's Web page for recent information.

Drug Information Association (DIA). Conducts workshops, training courses, and internships. DIA also maintains a list of available internships in industry, some of which may relate to regulatory affairs. The association sponsors its own fellowship in Pharmacoepidemiology and Drug Regulatory Science. Consult the DIA Web page for recent information.

Parenteral Drug Association. Conducts workshops and training courses. Contact the society (see "Professional Societies" section for contact information) for a current calender.

Jobhunting and Networking

RAPS offers employment assistance, maintains a professional financial advice hotline, and posts advertisements for jobs in the back of the society magazine *Regulatory Affairs Focus*, which members automatically receive. Job listings are on the society's Web site. There's also a job board at the RAPS annual meeting and meetings throughout the year.

According to Linda Temple, RAPS's director of education, government agencies, private firms, and such consultancies as contract research organizations all hire regulatory affairs specialists. In addition to trade magazines like *Regulatory Affairs Focus* and the classified section of local newspapers, companies and other outlets advertise directly on the web on their own homepages. Government agencies like the FDA (http://www.fda.gov) will also list jobs on the Web. Temple notes that the FDA uses terms like "project manager," "consumer safety officer," and "medical or compliance officer/investigator/inspector," when describing openings that would be of interest to career-changers from science.

For positions that require more experience, there are specialized recruitment firms that specialize in regulatory affairs within a certain industry segment such as pharmaceuticals or medical devices.

The Food and Drug Law Institute maintains a job exchange on its Web site. Check the "Positions Available" section for job advertisements, which include jobs in regulatory affairs. The Drug Information Association also maintains an "employment opportunities in industry" section on its Web site, which includes regulatory affairs postings.

The Regulatory Affairs Information Homepage (http://www.medmarket.

com/tenants/rainfo/rainfo.htm) links with government agencies and industry for information on regulations pertaining to the pharmaceutical and medical-device industries, as well as information on the job market for regulations specialists.

Regarding environmental regulatory affairs, SETAC advertises these types of positions in its members newsletter *SETAC News*, as well as at its annual and regional meeting. The society also runs a placement service at its annual meeting.

APPENDIX 1: FOR FURTHER READING

Academic Environment: A Handbook for Evaluating Employment Opportunities in Science, Karl W. Lanks, Taylor & Francis, Washington, DC, 1996
—Contains chapter on "alternatives" to research careers in "high-profile research centers"

Alternative Careers in Science: Leaving the Ivory Tower, Cynthia Robbins-Roth (ed.), Academic Press, San Diego, CA, 1998
—Chapters on alternative careers, each written by careers changers

Careers for Chemists: A World Outside the Lab, Fred Owens, Roger Uhler, Corinne Marasco, American Chemical Society, Washington, DC, 1997
—Profiles over 60 chemists in 20 different allied science careers

Careers in Science and Engineering: A Student Guide to Grad School and Beyond, Committee on Science, Engineering, and Public Policy, National Academy Press, Washington, DC, 1996
—Contains many profiles of science career switchers

Career Renewal: Tools for Scientists and Technical Professionals, Stephen Rosen and Celia Paul, Academic Press, San Diego, CA, 1998
—Contains tips on making a career transition in the science and technology fields, including a few examples of switches into nontraditional areas

The Guide to Internet Job Searching, Margaret Riley, Frances Roehm, Steve Oserman, VGM Career Horizons, NTC Publishing, Lincolnwood, IL, 1996
—Contains lists of Web sites and newsgroups for locating job advertisements on the Internet, organized by job area, public vs. private sector, and location. Also includes international opportunities

Jump Start Your Career in Bioscience, Chandra B. Louise, Bookmasters, Inc., Ashland, OH, 1998
—Many descriptions of research and nonresearch positions for scientists at and away from the bench in government, industry, and academia

Marine Science Careers: A Sea Grant Guide to Ocean Opportunities, Tracey Crago, Steve Adams, University of Maine/University of New Hampshire Sea Grant College Program and the Woods Hole Oceanographic Institution Sea Grant Program, 1996
—Contains profiles of 38 people whose careers in the marine sciences range from traditional to nontraditional. Some examples in the latter category include underwater filmmaker, environmental communicator, ocean advocate, and naval architect. Available for $5.00 at:

Woods Hole Oceanographic Institution
WHOI Sea Grant Communications
193 Oyster Pond Road, CRL 209
Woods Hole, MA 02543-1525

A National Conversation on Doctoral Education: An Emerging Consensus. National Convocation on Science and Engineering Doctoral Education. June 15, 1996, National Academy of Science Committee on Science, Engineering, and Public Policy, Washington, DC
—Available at http://www2.nas.edu/convo/

Opportunities in Biotechnology Careers, Sheldon S. Brown, VGM Career Horizons, NTC Publishing, Lincolnwood, IL, 1994
—Chapter on nonscientific biotech careers

Outside the Ivory Tower: A Guide for Academics Considering Alternative Careers, Margaret Newhouse, Office of Career Services, Harvard University, Cambridge, MA, 1993
—Many career how-tos, like how to tailor CVs and cover letters; although not specifically aimed at people with training in science and technology there are some examples relevant for people with scientific training

A Ph.D. Is Not Enough: A Guide to Survival in Science, Peter J. Feibelman, Addison-Wesley, New York, 1993
—Advice for jobseekers, but mostly aimed at academic positions and most examples are from physical sciences.

Postdocs and Career Prospects: A Status Report, Commission on Professionals in Science and Technology, Washington, DC, 1997
—Single copies available at no charge from:

Commission on Professionals in Science and Technology
1200 New York Avenue, NW
Suite 390
Washington, DC 20005

Reshaping the Graduate Education of Scientists and Engineers, Committee on Science, Engineering, and Public Policy, National Academy Press, Washington, DC, 1995

Rethinking Science as a Career: Perceptions and Realities in the Physical Sciences, Sheila Tobias, Daryl Chubin, Kevin Aylesworth. Research Corp., Tucson, AZ, 1995

Science magazine, October 27, 1995 issue
—Career issue with many sections and articles devoted to the state of scientific careers

The Scientist as Consultant: Building New Career Opportunities, Carl J. Sindermann and Thomas K. Sawyer, Plenum Trade, New York, 1998
—Advice and how-tos for scientists looking to move into part-time or full-time consulting in a variety of fields

Society for Industrial and Applied Mathematics Report on Mathematics in Industry, SIAM, Philadelphia, PA, 1996.
—Survey on roles of mathematical scientists in nonacademic settings, including skills and attributes valued in nonacademic settings, educational programs, and job opportunities. Full report available at: http://www.siam.org/mii/miihome.htm

To Boldly Go: A Practical Career Guide for Scientists, Peter S. Fiske, American Geophysical Union, Washington, DC, 1996
—Contains chapter on geophysicists who have gone on to work in allied science-related careers, including policy, science writing, and business

Trends in the Early Careers of Life Scientists, Commission on Dimensions, Causes, and Implications of Recent Trends in the Careers of Life Scientists, National Academy Press, Washington, DC, 1998. Copies available from:

National Academy Press
2101 Constitution Avenue, NW
Washington, DC 20418
202-334-2138

The 1998 What Color Is Your Parachute?, Richard Nelson Bolles, Ten Speed Press, Berkeley, CA, 1998
—The quintessential jobhunting guidebook. It now contains a huge section on Web sites for jobseekers in many areas, including science and technology fields

APPENDIX 2: SOURCES ON THE WORLD WIDE WEB

The following is a list of sites with career advice and jobhunting tips, as well as listings for jobs, links to career-oriented sites, and resume-posting services. The sites, which were up-to-date at press time, are not exclusively for nontraditional science- and technology-related jobs, and might include more traditional positions, such as academic posts. Other sites, such as business-oriented ones, may also include nonscience positions.

General Jobhunting Sites (includes job listings in science and technology, and related fields)

Academe This Week, the *Chronicle of Higher Education*'s Web site
http://chronicle.merit.edu/.ads/.links.html

Academic Position Network
gopher://wcni.cis.umn.edu:11111/

America's Employers
http://www.americasemployers.com/

America's Job Bank, federal government job listings
http://www.ajb.dni.us./index.html

The Best Job Site
http://www.itec.sfsu.edu/jobs/

Contract Employment Weekly Online
http://www.ceweekly.com/index.html

Career placement and planning centers at various universities
http://www.rpi.edu/dept/cdc/carserv

Career City
http://www.careercity.com

Career Magazine
http://careermag.com/careermag/

Career Mosaic, recruiting site for high-technology companies and searchable
Usenet postings
http://www.careermosaic.com/

Career Path, classified job ads from U.S. newspapers, searchable by key
    words
http://www.careerpath.com/

CareerWeb
http://www.cweb.com/

College Grad Job Hunter
http://www.collegegrad.com/

Direct Marketing World
http://www.dmworld.com/

Employment Opportunities and Resume Postings
http://galaxy.einet.net/GJ/employment.html

E-span
http://www.espan.com/

Getting Past Go: A Survival Guide for New Graduates
http://www.mongen.com/getgo

Human Resources Electronic Advertising and Recruiting Tool
http://www.career.com/

Help Wanted USA
http://iccweb.com

Internet Job Locator, all major job-search engines on one page
http://www.joblocator.com/jobs/

Jobhunt
http://www.job-hunt.org

Jobs
http://www.inx.net/catalog/jobs.htm

JobCenter
http://www.jobcenter.com/

Jobnet.com
http://www.jobnet.com/

JobTRAK, employment service restricted to students or alumni
   of member universities
http://www.jobtrak.com/

JobWeb, maintained by the National Association of Colleges
   and Employers
http://www.jobweb.org/

MedSearch America
http://www.medsearch.com/

Monster Board
http://www.monster.com/

Online Career Center
http://www.occ.com/occ/

The Riley Guide
http://www.dbm.com/jobguide

Recruiters Online Network
http://www.recruitersonline.com/

Science- and Technology-Specific Sites
(includes job listings and jobhunting tips)

Academic Chemistry Employment Clearinghouse
http://hackberry.chem.niu.edu:70/1/ChemJob

American Chemical Society Job Bank
http://pubs.acs.org/plweb/indexp1.html

American Geophysical Union career guide and hotlinks
http://earth.agu.org/careerguide/links.html

American Mathematical Society and the Society for Industrial
and Applied Mathematics Careers Bulletin Board
http://www.ams.org/careers/mcbb.html

American Institute of Physics

Career Services Division
http://www.aip.org/careersvc/

AIP member societies, with employment links of their own
http://www.aip.org/aip/memsoc.html

American Society for Microbiology, information on jobs
and fellowships activities
http://www.asmusa.org

Association for Women in Science
http://www.awis.org

Best Bets in Science and Technology
http://www.lib.umich.edu/chdocs/employment/job-guide.science.html#5

BioMedNet, an Internet source for biological and medical researchers,
with job listings and career resources, including information on nontraditional careers. Includes on-line magazine HMSBeagle (http://
biomednet.com/hmsbeagle)
(http://biomednet.com)

Bio Online, an information and services site for biotechnology and
pharmaceutical research that has a noncommercial area for information and ongoing discussion about career issues
http://cns.bio.com/hr/forum/

BIOSCI, one-stop shopping for dozens of Usenet newsgroups and par-
allel email groups in the biological sciences on which career information is discussed
http://www.bio.net/

Career Planning Center for Beginning Scientists and Engineers, sponsored by the National Academy of Sciences, contains links to gradu-

ate student and postdoc organizations, professional societies, and university-based organizations and programs
http://www2.nas.edu/cpc/index.html

Cell and Molecular Biology Online
http://www.cellbio.com

Commission on Professionals in Science and Technology, data on science careers and links to professional societies
http://www.cpst.org

Contemporary Problems in Science Jobs, maintained by life scientist Arthur E. Sowers. Contains original essays on career advice—including nontraditional careers—and links to job listings
http://www.access.digex.net/~arthures/homepage.htm

Federation of American Societies of Experimental Biology Careers OnLine, job postings and resume-posting service
http://ns2.faseb.org/career/index.html

GrantsNet, a "one-stop shopping" site for information on grants and other forms of support for research and training in biomedical fields maintained by Howard Hughes Medical Institute and AAAS
http://www.grantsnet.org

National Academy of Sciences
http://www.nas.edu/

National Association of Graduate-Professional Students Job Bank and other career resources
http://www.nagps.org/NAGPS/

National Institutes of Health
http://www.nih.gov

National Science Foundation
http://www.nsf.gov

National Science Foundation Division of Science Resource Studies
http://www.nsf.gov/sbe/srs/stats.htm

Nature magazine
http://www.nature.com

Network of Emerging Scientists, an Internet forum devoted to the concerns of scientists and engineers at all stages of their careers. Includes ongoing discussions on career issues, as well as many links to job listings and articles on career issues, including nontraditional careers
http://pegasus.uthct.edu/nes/nes.html

NextWave, the AAAS's Internet resource for career advice and one of the first ongoing tools for discussing nontraditional science careers
http://www.nextwave.org

David Sander's Web site; Sander, an American Society for Microbiology Congressional Science Fellow, maintains a listing of top job sites for scientists
http://www.tulane.edu/~dmsander/garryfavwebjobs.html

Scientific Careers Transition Program, a program headed up by physicist Stephen Rosen that helps scientists change careers and find work
http://www.harbornet.com/biz/office/sct001.html

The Scientist, a biweekly newspaper for life scientists; career-oriented articles and classifieds section
http://www.the-scientist.com

Science Career Resources Online, information on careers, policy, and other issues; created by Dartmouth College
http://www.phds.org

Science magazine classifieds
http://science-mag.aaas.org/science

Survival Skills and Ethics Program, University of Pittsburgh
http://www.pitt.edu/~survival/homepg.html

The World of Chemistry
http://www.chemsite.com/

Women in Technology International
http://www.witi.com/Career/Opportunities/Jobs

Younger Chemists Committee Home Page
http://www.chem.hawaii.edu/ycc

Young Scientists Network
http://www.physics.uiuc.edu/ysn

Other

American Association of Domain Names, organizations and cross references
http://www.domains.org

Scholarly Societies Project, links to over 1,100 scholarly societies and their individual resources
http://www.lib.uwaterloo.ca/society/overview.html

Liszt, a directory of Internet newsgroups
http://www.liszt.com

INDEX